This book breaks new ground in offering an exposition of the theological message of the shorter Pauline letters. Karl P. Donfried expounds the theology of 1 and 2 Thessalonians, examining the cultural setting of these letters and the particular milieux in which their distinctive themes took shape. He shows that the notion of election is a key theme in the Thessalonian correspondence, while both letters have important things to say to people in our own day about Christ, about forgiveness, and about a sanctifying God who pours out his Spirit. I. Howard Marshall's study of Philippians brings out especially the understanding of the theological basis of the Christian life which underlies the letter, while his discussion of Philemon emphasises how the main theme of the letter is the relation between the gospel and Christian ethics; the implications of Paul's teaching on slavery are considered in a manner which goes much further than the surface of the text might imply.

This series provides a programmatic survey of the individual writings of the New Testament. It aims to remedy the deficiency of available published material, which has tended to concentrate on historical, textual, grammatical, and literary issues at the expense of the theology, or to lose distinctive emphases of individual writings in systematised studies of 'The Theology of Paul' and the like. New Testament specialists here write at greater length than is usually possible in the introductions to commentaries or as part of other New Testament theologies, and explore the theological themes and issues of their chosen books without being tied to a commentary format, or to a thematic structure drawn from elsewhere. When complete, the series will cover all the New Testament writings, and will thus provide an attractive, and timely, range of texts around which courses can be developed.

THE THEOLOGY OF THE SHORTER PAULINE LETTERS

KARL P. DONFRIED

Professor of Religion and Biblical Literature, Smith College

I. HOWARD MARSHALL

Professor of New Testament Exegesis, University of Aberdeen

CAMBRIDGE
UNIVERSITY PRESS

Published by the Press Syndicate of the University of Cambridge
The Pitt Building, Trumpington Street, Cambridge CB2 1RP
40 West 20th Street, New York, NY 10011–4211, USA
10 Stamford Road, Oakleigh, Melbourne 3166, Australia

© Cambridge University Press, 1993

First published 1993

Printed in Great Britain at the University Press, Cambridge

A catalogue record for this book is available from the British Library

Library of Congress cataloguing in publication data

Donfried, Karl P.
The theology of the shorter Pauline letters / Karl P. Donfried,
I. Howard Marshall.
p.   cm. – (New Testament theology)
ISBN 0 521 36491–4 (hardback). ISBN 0–521–36731–x (paperback)
1.Bible. N.T. Thessalonians Theology. 2. Bible. N.T.
Philippians Theology. 3. Bible. N.T. Philemon Theology.
I. Marshall, I. Howard. II. Title. III. Series.
BS2725.5.D65   1993
227′.806 – dc20   92–41218 CIP

ISBN 0 521 36491 4 hardback
ISBN 0 521 36731 x paperback

Contents

Editor's preface	*page*	ix
List of abbreviations		xi

THE THEOLOGY OF 1 THESSALONIANS
Karl P. Donfried   1

Note on the biblical translations		2
1	The setting of 1 Thessalonians	3
2	The theology of 1 Thessalonians	28
3	1 Thessalonians, the Pauline corpus and Acts	64
4	The significance of 1 Thessalonians for today	73

THE THEOLOGY OF 2 THESSALONIANS
Karl P. Donfried   81

5	The setting of 2 Thessalonians	83
6	The theology of 2 Thessalonians	90
7	2 Thessalonians and the New Testament	105
8	The significance of 2 Thessalonians for today	108

THE THEOLOGY OF PHILIPPIANS
I. Howard Marshall   115

Author's note		116
9	Exploring the building site	117
10	Laying the foundation	127
11	Building the walls	138
12	The shape of the Church	149

13 Philippians and its architect   162
14 A building that still stands   167

THE THEOLOGY OF PHILEMON
I. Howard Marshall   175

15 The gospel and slavery   177

Select bibliography   192
Indices (Thessalonians)
    Index of subjects   196
    Index of modern authors   198
    Index of texts   199
Indices (Philippians, Philemon)
    Index of subjects   204
    Index of modern authors   205
    Index of texts   206

Editor's preface

Although the New Testament is usually taught within Departments or Schools or Faculties of Theology/Divinity/Religion, theological study of the individual New Testament writings is often minimal or at best patchy. The reasons for this are not hard to discern.

For one thing, the traditional style of studying a New Testament document is by means of straight exegesis, often verse by verse. Theological concerns jostle with interesting historical, textual, grammatical and literary issues, often at the cost of the theological. Such exegesis is usually very time-consuming, so that only one or two key writings can be treated in any depth within a crowded three-year syllabus.

For another, there is a marked lack of suitable textbooks round which courses could be developed. Commentaries are likely to lose theological comment within a mass of other detail in the same way as exegetical lectures. The section on the theology of a document in the Introduction to a commentary is often very brief and may do little more than pick out elements within the writing under a sequence of headings drawn from systematic theology. Excursuses usually deal with only one or two selected topics. Likewise larger works on New Testament Theology usually treat Paul's letters as a whole and, having devoted the great bulk of their space to Jesus, Paul and John, can spare only a few pages for others.

In consequence, there is little incentive on the part of teacher or student to engage with a particular New Testament document, and students have to be content with a general overview, at best complemented by in-depth study of (parts of) two or three New Testament writings. A serious corollary to this is the degree to which students are thereby incapacitated in the task of integrating their New Testament study with the rest of their Theology or Religion courses, since often they are capable only of drawing on the general overview or on a sequence of particular verses treated atomistically. The growing importance of a literary-critical approach to individual documents simply highlights the present deficiencies even more. Having been given little experience in handling individual New Testament writings as such at a theological level, most students are very ill-prepared to develop a properly integrated literary and theological response to particular texts. Ordinands too need more help than they currently receive from textbooks, so that their preaching from particular passages may be better informed theologically.

There is need therefore for a series to bridge the gap between too brief an introduction and too full a commentary where theological discussion is lost among too many other concerns. It is our aim to provide such a series. That is, a series where New Testament specialists are able to write at a greater length on the theology of individual writings than is usually possible in the introductions to commentaries or as part of New Testament Theologies, and to explore the theological themes and issues of these writings without being tied to a commentary format or to a thematic structure provided from elsewhere. The volumes seek both to describe each document's theology, and to engage theologically with it, noting also its canonical context and any specific influence it may have had on the history of Christian faith and life. They are directed at those who already have one or two years of full-time New Testament and theological study behind them.

University of Durham   JAMES D. G. DUNN

Abbreviations

AnBib	*Analecta biblica*
ANRW	H. Temporini and W. Haase, *Aufstieg und Niedergang der Römischen Welt* (Berlin: Walter de Gruyter, 1972–)
BBR	*Bulletin for Biblical Research*
BETL	*Bibliotheca ephemeridum theologicarum Lovaniensium*
BJRL	*Bulletin of the John Rylands University Library of Manchester*
BNTC	*Black's New Testament Commentaries*
CBQ	*Catholic Biblical Quarterly*
EKKNT	*Evangelisch-katholischer Kommentar zum Neuen Testament*
EtB	*Études bibliques*
EThSt	*Erfurter theologische Studien*
ExpT	*Expository Times*
GCS	*Griechischen christlichen Schriftsteller der ersten drei Jahrhunderte*
HAW	*Handbuch der Altertumswissenschaft*
HNT	*Handbuch zum Neuen Testament*
HTKNT	*Herders theologischer Kommentar zum Neuen Testament*
HTR	*Harvard Theological Review*
HUTh	*Hermeneutische Untersuchungen zur Theologie*
IDB	*Interpreter's Dictionary of the Bible*
Int	*Interpretation*
JSNT	*Journal for the Study of the New Testament*
JSNTSup	*Journal for the Study of the New Testament, Supplement Series*

JTS	*Journal of Theological Studies*
Meyer*K*	*Kritisch-exegetischer Kommentar über das Neue Testament*
MM	J. H. Moulton and W. Milligan, *The Vocabulary of the Greek New Testament* (London: Hodder & Stoughton, 1914–30)
NCeB	*New Century Bible*
NICNT	*New International Commentary on the New Testament*
NIGTC	*New International Greek Testament Commentary*
NovT	*Novum Testamentum*
NTS	*New Testament Studies*
RTR	*Reformed Theological Review*
StNT	*Studien zum Neuen Testament*
TDNT	G. Kittel and G. Friedrich, eds, *Theological Dictionary of the New Testament*, trans. G. W. Bromiley (Grand Rapids: Eerdmans, 1964–76)
*TU*n.F	*Texte und Untersuchungen zur Geschichte der altchristlichen Literatur, neue Folge*
UBS	K. Aland *et al.*, *The Greek New Testament* (London: United Bible Societies, 1975³)
USQR	*Union Seminary Quarterly Review*
WBC	*World Biblical Commentary*
WUNT	*Wissenschaftliche Untersuchungen zum Neuen Testament*
ZNW	*Zeitschrift für die neutestamentliche Wissenschaft und die Kunde der älteren Kirche*

The theology of 1 Thessalonians

KARL P. DONFRIED

Note on the biblical translations

Most of the translations of texts from 1 and 2 Thessalonians are from the RSV. In some cases the NRSV has been used, and some translations are the author's.

CHAPTER I

The setting of 1 Thessalonians

THE RHETORICAL STRUCTURE

It is a major contention of this analysis that an awareness of the social situation in Thessalonica and a consideration of the structure of the letter itself will greatly assist the task of understanding the theology of 1 Thessalonians. The structure of a letter can be analysed by employing the methodologies commonly referred to as form and rhetorical criticism, analytical tools that can help determine Paul's intentions in writing this letter. The former, i.e., form-critical epistolography, explains how parts of letters are constructed; the latter, i.e., Graeco-Roman rhetorical criticism, allows us to see more vividly why the letter is constructed the way it is as well as giving us further insight into the lived situation of the letter.[1] Nevertheless, we need to be careful not to impose existing form-critical and rhetorical categories on 1 Thessalonians, especially when we are alert to the fact that this letter is a first attempt in Christian letter writing.

Theology, structure and social situation are closely interwoven in 1 Thessalonians and other Pauline letters. Thus rhetorical criticism can, by using its analytical tools, alert us not only to distinct emphases in a given letter but also to certain dimensions in the rhetorical situation, which give suggestions about the larger social situation that might otherwise have been overlooked. To recognise, for example, which of the

[1] For a further discussion see Frank Witt Hughes, *Early Christian Rhetoric and 2 Thessalonians*, JSNTSup 30 (Sheffield: JSOT Press, 1989), 19–50; and Stanley K. Stowers, *Letter Writing in Greco-Roman Antiquity* (Philadelphia: Westminster, 1986).

three types (*genera*) of rhetoric – deliberative, judicial or epideictic – a document is employing already gives important
clues to its social situation as well as its intention. Although
there may be overlap between these *genera*, the time reference
for deliberative rhetoric is the future, the appropriate time for
epideictic rhetoric is primarily the present, though often with
reference to both the past and the future, and the temporal
framework for judicial rhetoric is the past. To be precise in
identifying the different types of rhetoric, it is critical to note
the standard topics that are common to each. For epideictic
rhetoric these are primarily praise (e.g., 1 Thess. 2:1–12) and
blame (e.g., 1 Thess. 2:14–16) and in deliberative rhetoric
these standard topics are advantage and honour, viz., that
which is expedient and/or harmful to the intended recipients.
Thus the identification of these and other 'strategies of per-
suasion' will allow us to gain 'greater understanding of the
author, the audience, and the author's purpose in communi-
cating with the audience'.[2]

Understanding 1 Thessalonians as an epideictic letter allows
for some significant conclusions about both what Paul intended
and what he did not intend to communicate. On the one hand,
recognising 1 Thessalonians as belonging to the epideictic *genus*
of rhetoric – i.e., one emphasising praise and, to a lesser degree,
blame – allows us to see that the Thessalonian Christians have
become the object of Paul's praise. Hughes summarises the
matter well:

The heaping on of praise is something that Paul does, primarily
because it reinforces the good relationship between Paul and the
Thessalonians that had existed for some time – though the relationship was seriously troubled by Paul's non-presence in Thessaloniki
during the congregation's recent difficult time, characterized by the
deaths of beloved people in the congregation. Paul's persuasive
response to that bereaved congregation is to praise their faithfulness
and love, to explain in an affective manner the reasons for his
non-presence in Thessaloniki (2:17–3:10), to confirm teaching that

2 Frank Witt Hughes, 'The Social Situations Implied by Rhetoric' (an unpublished
  paper presented to the *Studiorum Novi Testamenti Societas* Seminar on New Testament
  Texts in their Cultural Environment, July 1991), 5.

he had already made (the first two proofs: 4:1–8 and 4:9–12), and to add teaching that he had not done before (such as the material in 4:13–5:3), which is not claimed to be prior teaching but rather revelation through a 'word of the Lord' (4:15). The fact that Paul did all those things, tying them together quite skillfully by the triad of virtues in 1:3, the listing of the *propositiones* in the *partitio* (3:11–13), and their careful and subtle recapitulation in the *peroratio* (5:4–11), seems to indicate that Paul either learned rhetoric in school or had quite a gift for rhetoric, sensing the appropriateness of the rules to his letter even without formally learning them.[3]

On the other hand, since 1 Thess. 2:1–12 does not contain any explicit and sustained charges against Paul it can be determined that this letter cannot be categorised as belonging to the judicial *genus* of rhetoric. In judicial rhetoric such charges would have to be taken up and defended in the *probatio* (proof). While 1 Thess. 2:1–12 may possibly suggest that some doubts about Paul's motivation had arisen among some in Thessalonica, certainly one cannot, as a result, conclude that Paul is arguing against opponents in this letter.

Although Graeco-Roman rhetorical theory does not focus significantly on letters, the actual practice of rhetoric did include letters. Therefore one can speak of a 'rhetorical letter' and, perhaps, add that in terms of epistolary genre 1 Thessalonians approximates, but is not identical with, ancient letters of consolation. In terms of rhetorical *genus* there is a clear connection with epideictic rhetoric. Not unimportant for this particular linkage is the fact that among the two most important categories of the epideictic *genus* of rhetoric is the funeral speech (*epitaphios*) and consolatory speech (*paramythetikos*). Paul's intention in writing 1 Thessalonians is to console a Christian community suffering the effects of persecution and death, to encourage the discouraged.

What follows is an abridgement and slight modification of the rhetorical structure of 1 Thessalonians proposed by Frank Witt Hughes.[4]

---

[3] Ibid., 13–14.
[4] Frank Witt Hughes, 'The Rhetoric of 1 Thessalonians', in *The Thessalonian Correspondence*, ed. Raymond F. Collins, *BETL* 87 (Leuven: University Press, 1990), 94–116.

I *Exordium* (introduction) (1:1–10)
    A epistolary prescript (1:1)
    B thanksgiving prayer (1:2–10)
II *Narratio* (narrative[5]) (2:1–3:10)
    A introduction to *narratio* (address) (2:1)
    B a description of Paul's first visit to the Thessalonians (2:1–16)
    C Paul's desire for a second visit (2:17–3:10)
III *Partitio* (Statement of propositions[6]) (stated as an intercessory prayer; 3:11–13)
    A first petition (transition from *narratio*): the topic of Paul's desired journey to the Thessalonians (3:11)
    B second petition: the topics of the three-part *probatio* introduced (3:12–13)
        1 first topic: 'increase in love' (3:12–13)
        2 second and third topics: 'being preserved at the Parousia' (3:13)
            a second topic; 'to establish your hearts blameless in holiness'
            b third topic: 'at the coming of our Lord Jesus Christ with all his saints'
IV *Probatio* (proof) (4:1–5:3)
    A first proof: 'how it is necessary to walk and to please God' (4:1–8)
    B second proof: 'concerning brotherly love' (4:9–12)
    C third proof: 'concerning those who have fallen asleep' (4:13–5:3)
V *Peroratio* (epilogue) (5:4–11)
    A transition from previous section (5:4)
    B honorific description of Thessalonians (5:5)
    C first consequence of description: wakefulness (5:6)
    D reasons for consequence: association of sleeping and drunkenness with night (5:7)

---

[5] Cicero in *De inventione* 1.27 defines the *narratio* in this way: 'The narrative is an exposition of events that have occurred or are supposed to have occurred.' Quintilian in *Institutio oratoria* 4.2.31 states that the *narratio* 'consists in the persuasive exposition of that which either has been done, or is supposed to have been done ...'

[6] In the *Rhetorica ad Herennium* 1.17 it is explained that this exposition or statement of propositions 'consists in setting forth briefly and completely, the points we intend to discuss'.

E second consequence of argument: preparation for action (5:8–10)

F third consequence of argument: console one another (5:11)

VI Exhortation[7] (5:12–22)

A introduction of exhortation (5:12)

B first exhortation: concerning church order (5:12)

C second exhortation: concerning church discipline (5:14–22)

VII Final prayers and greetings (epistolary conclusion) (5:23–8)

A intercessory prayer (5:23–4)

B a request for prayer (5:25)

C final greetings (5:26–7)

D final prayer(5:28)

The implications of these brief introductory remarks and of this rhetorical outline will be shown at several points as our study of the theology of 1 Thessalonians unfolds.

PLACE AND DATE OF WRITING

Place

Having been alerted to the rhetorical and epistolary classification of 1 Thessalonians, it is now appropriate to ask whether we have any knowledge as to the place of writing and Paul's own situation as he writes this letter.

To glean information about where and when 1 Thessalonians was written is not as uncomplicated as one might initially think. The clues found in 1 Thessalonians are few and do not always coincide with the information provided by Acts. Was this letter written in Athens, Corinth or elsewhere? According to Acts 17 Paul went to Athens from Beroea while Silas and Timothy remained in Beroea. The next reference to these Pauline co-workers is found in Acts 18:5, at which point Silas

---

[7] The descriptors of Categories VI and VII are left in English because they are not a usual *pars orationis* of the Graeco-Roman rhetorical handbook tradition. See further Hughes, *Early Christian Rhetoric*, 63–4.

and Timothy have arrived in Corinth from Macedonia. The point of tension between the Acts account and that found in 1 Thess. 3:1–3 is that Acts makes no reference to Timothy having been in Athens, which is the common way to understand the meaning of 1 Thess. 3:1–3: 'Therefore when we could bear it no longer, we were willing to be left behind in Athens alone, and we sent Timothy.'

One's perception of the accuracy of Acts plays an important role in relating these differing accounts. We hold that the theological framework in Acts is secondary but that there may well be some highly accurate kernels of information throughout Luke's second volume. Since we reject a radically critical or fundamentalist reading of Acts, it should be clear that we are not involved in any special pleading for its accuracy which would necessitate a forced reconciliation of the two accounts. But the apparent tension between the two descriptions does raise the questions of how one is to interpret Paul's assertions in 1 Thess. 3:1–3 and whether the accounts in 1 Thessalonians and Acts may be understood in a non-contradictory way.

The syntactical location of the phrase 'in Athens' is important for the understanding of Paul's argument in 1 Thess. 3:1ff. The reference to Athens is hardly meant to indicate either the place where 1 Thessalonians was written nor the place where the decision was made about sending Timothy to Thessalonica. The older view that Paul was writing in a city other than Athens is essentially correct. Otherwise would he not have written 'to be left *here* alone' instead of 'to be left in Athens alone'? Rather, Athens is the place where Paul 'decided to stay on *alone*'. The motif 'alone' is critical to the argument: being left alone in a strange environment without his circle of co-workers was certainly a hardship for Paul. This is the crucial point that Paul makes. As a result we would conclude that, according to both sources, Timothy was never in Athens and that it is an error to read 1 Thess. 3:1 in such a way. Similarly, to suggest that this letter is being written from Athens assumes a strained reading of this same text. Paul is writing 1 Thessalonians in the presence of Silvanus and Timothy who have returned from Thessalonica, a fact suggested by the opening sender formula (1:1) and, according to Acts 18:1, 5, the most likely place for this gathering is in Corinth. In 1 Thess. 3:7, Paul describes his own situation, presumably in Corinth, as one marked by 'distress and affliction'. Timothy's return to Corinth and his reunion with Paul with the good news of the faith and love of the Thessalonian Christians has brought 'comfort' and 'joy' to the Apostle's otherwise fragile situation. This mutuality, a feature so apparent from the rhetorical character of 1 Thessalonians, is expressively attested to here in 1 Thess. 3:6–10. As he intends to comfort and bring consolation to them by composing this letter, so here they have conveyed their comfort and consolation to him through his co-worker Timothy.

Date

When did Paul write 1 Thessalonians? To answer this question requires some discussion of the issues involved in determining the parameters of Pauline chronology. With regard to methodology, we acknowledge, with most scholars today, that there are essentially only two sources for our knowledge of the Pauline period: the letters of the Apostle himself and the events recorded by Luke in the Acts of the Apostles. Most New Testament scholars today give priority to the Pauline letters since Paul himself stands closest to the events he records. Further, it is increasingly recognised that Luke, in writing his second volume, reshapes many traditions to cohere with his overall theological purpose just as he does in the composition of the gospel of Luke. As a result, Acts becomes less useful as a source for exact chronological information since much of this information has been subjected to a larger theological programme. While Acts can still remain a valuable source of detailed and accurate information when separated from its programmatic framework it should never be given priority over the documents originating from Paul himself and should only be used when it does not contradict assertions made by the Apostle. Yet, however one views the data, *there can be no absolutely definite chronology of the Pauline period: all* attempts must be tentative and subject to correction and revision.

To answer our immediate question as to when 1 Thessalonians was written, we want to accentuate for our consideration just a few items among the broader chronological issues. In Gal. 1:21 the Apostle asserts: 'Then [*epeita*] I went into the regions of Syria and Cilicia.' Based on the parallel use in 1 Cor. 15:6 and 7, *epeita* in Gal. 1:21 is likely to refer to the immediately preceding event in v. 18, i.e., Jerusalem. The critical question with regard to this verse in Galatians is not so much the referent of *epeita* in Gal. 1:21, but, rather, how one is to understand the reference to Syria and Cilicia and the length of time spent there. Syria includes Christian centres in Damascus, the place of Paul's conversion, and Antioch, an area where, by Paul's own description, he had worked (Gal. 2:11) and a city extensively referred to in Acts (11:19ff; 13:1,14; 15:22ff; 18:22). In addition, Cilicia includes Tarsus, which, according to Acts 22:3, is Paul's native city. Is the intention of this reference to suggest that Paul spent some eleven to fourteen years *only* in Syria and Cilicia? Or, given the overall context of Paul's desire to distance himself from Jerusalem, does he merely wish to say that, 'then, after my fifteen-day stay in Jerusalem, I did not stay around that area but I began moving toward Syria and Cilicia' without in any way wishing to suggest that he worked only in that area? *How one interprets this reference to Syria and Cilicia will be crucial for the reconstruction of a chronology of the Pauline period.* For those scholars who understand the reference to Syria and Cilicia as not limiting Paul's activity to these regions, the Apostle may well have been involved in missionary work as far away as Philippi, Thessalonica, Athens and Corinth very early in his career. They would urge that the reference in Phil. 4:15 to 'the beginning of the gospel' refers literally to the beginning of Paul's independent missionary work in Philippi and that 1 Thess. 3:1ff refers to Paul's continuing work during this period in Thessalonica, Athens and Corinth. This interpretation allows for an 'uncrowding' of Paul's missionary work, for the maturing of his apostolic ministry and the development of his theology. Rather than an extended period of some eleven to fourteen years limited to Syria and Cilicia, this perspective allows for the beginnings of a European mission at a much earlier point in his apostolic career and does not reduce the remainder of his activity to such a severely limited time frame. If one accepts this reading of the evidence, then it is probable that 1 Thessalonians stems from his early period, at least several years prior to the conference visit in Jerusalem.

Let us turn to certain chronological information provided by Luke, particularly the Gallio inscription and the edict of Claudius. In Acts 18:12 reference is made to Paul's visit to Corinth: 'But when Gallio was proconsul of Achaia, the Jews made a united attack upon Paul and brought him before the tribunal ...' Although the precise details, implications and context of the events described are disputed, there is little doubt that Paul made one of his visits to Corinth at the time that Gallio was proconsul of the province of Achaia. In light of the epigraphical evidence now in hand most scholars place Gallio's term of office in the years AD 51/52, although AD 52/53 is also possible. While at first glance Acts 18:12 appears straightforward, caution must be exercised. Was Paul's visit to Corinth in the vicinity of AD 51/52 his first visit, or does Acts 18:12 actually refer to a subsequent one? Acts 18 may well conflate two or more Pauline visits to that city into one account. Among the several factors pointing in this direction is the fact that in Acts 18:8 Crispus is the ruler of the synagogue and in 18:17 Sosthenes is the ruler of the synagogue! If Acts 18 is conflating at least two visits of Paul to Corinth, the Apostle may well have been in the city at a much earlier date.

Another piece of information relating to secular history mentioned in Acts that may be useful in reconstructing Pauline chronology is the reference to the edict of Claudius in Acts 18:2. It is likely that Suetonius in *Claudius* 25.4 is referring to this edict: '*Iudaios impulsore Chresto adsidue tumultuantes Roma expulit*' ('Since the Jews continually make disturbances at the instigation of Chrestus [Claudius] expelled them from Rome'). Since Suetonius does not date this edict, one cannot be certain whether it is referring to one issued by Claudius in AD 41 or

whether it is referring to disturbances later in his reign. If the
Claudius edict is dated in AD 41, then one would have strong
evidence for the dating of Paul's first visit to the city at some
point after the arrival of Aquila and Priscilla from Italy. If the
more usual dating of this edict in the year AD 49 is to be
accepted, this would not necessarily speak against an earlier
visit of Paul to Corinth, for it is difficult to know how thoroughgoing the conflation in Acts 18 is. For example, a case could be
made that Acts 18:1 had its original continuation in verse 5 and
that verses 2–4 are a retrojection made from a later period. To
place Paul's first arrival in Corinth as early as AD 41 is possible;
yet some flexibility is in order since one does not know how
long it took Aquila and Priscilla to travel to Corinth, or if they
went there directly. It is possible, therefore, that Paul's original
visit to Corinth took place sometime between AD 41 and AD 44.
As a result we would date 1 Thessalonians in the general period
of Paul's first visit in Corinth, i.e., AD 41–4.

THE GENERAL BACKGROUND

Essential for the interpretation of the Thessalonian correspondence is the reconstruction of the religious and political history
of Thessalonica at the time of the earliest Christian community. What was Thessalonica like when Paul first visited and
established a Christian community there and what impact does
this information have for understanding 1 Thessalonians?

Even though the cults in Thessalonica were closely associated with one another, it will be necessary for didactic reasons
to distinguish between the 'religious' and the 'political' cults.

The religious cults of Thessalonica

During the first half of the twentieth century archaeologists
discovered two temples in Thessaloniki, some 250–300 metres
west/northwest of the agora, one a temple of Serapis (*serapeum*)
and the other a small temple of the Roman period located
under the narthex of the first. This rich evidence makes it clear
that the rites of the Nile were performed diligently in this

serapeum by a board of some fourteen priests who were referred to as the 'priests of the gods'. It is likely that other cults of the city also practised their secret rites in this temple complex.

Among the more influential religious cults of the city is the cult of Dionysus, which is epigraphically attested to have begun in 187 BC. For the adherents of these Dionysiac mysteries the hope of a joyous afterlife is central and appears to be symbolised by the phallus; initiation 'consisted in revealing just this symbol'. Originally linked to the theme of fertility for an agricultural people, it was common for phalli to be erected on tombs suggesting the use of the phallus as a 'life-giving power, like the eggs and seeds which were laid down in the tomb ...'[8] But these sexual symbols of the cult were not mere representations of the hope of a joyous afterlife; they were also sensually provocative. The fact that the god Dionysus was the god of wine and joy often gave allowance for a strong emphasis on noisy revelry of all sorts. Already in an anticipatory way we might ask whether this emphasis on the phallus and sensuality offer a possible background for the exhortations in 1 Thess. 4:3–8 in general and for the interpretation of the term *skeuos* (vessel, 4:4) in particular.

In the Homeric Hymn to Dionysus[9] we read how the infant Dionysus was cuddled and nursed by the nymphs of Nysa, who eventually take on the role of the divine women so central to Dionysiac mysteries. Homer refers to these female attendants as 'nurses'. These women, these nurses, represent archetypal femininity so that 'all beauty, sweetness, and charm must combine their rays into the sun of motherliness that warms and nurtures the most delicate life for all eternity'.[10] Plainly the nurse is linked to the loved one by a delicate bond. Is there any relationship between this language and imagery and the words of the Apostle in 1 Thess. 2:7–8: 'So, being affectionately desirous [*homeiromai*] of you, we were ready to share with you

8 Martin P. Nilsson, *The Dionysiac Mysteries of the Hellenistic Age* (Lund: Gleerup, 1957), 44–5.

9 Number 26; we have used the edition by Apostolos N. Athanassakis, *The Homeric Hymns* (Baltimore: The Johns Hopkins Press, 1976).

10 Walter F. Otto, *Dionysus: Myth and Cult* (Bloomington: Indiana University Press, 1965), 178.

not only the gospel of God but also our own selves, because you have become very dear to us'? *Homeiromai* is a *hapex legomenon* (i.e., appears only once) in the New Testament. Why does Paul use it here? Hesychius, the first century AD lexicographer, equates the term with *epitheumeō*, and Heidland defines it as 'to feel oneself drawn to something, with strong intensification of the feeling'.[11] The possibility that the Dionysiac background, together with similar references in the mysteries of Samothrace, might illuminate the verses just cited, as well as explain the reference to the term 'nurse' in 1 Thess. 2:7, deserves further reflection.

Having just made reference to the mysteries of Samothrace it should be added that evidence for intercourse between Thessalonica and the island just before and during the Pauline period is unambiguous and Paul himself stayed overnight in Samothrace (Acts 16:11). Although there are many Samothracian motifs that would not be unimportant to a larger study – viz., the implied hope for a blessed afterlife, the theme of the *hieros gamos* (sacred marriage), the male genitals as symbol of fertility – we limit our comments to the frieze of the dancing maidens where each of these maidens and the musicians carry a *polos*, headgear reserved for divinity. As Phyllis Lehmann points out, as 'participants in ritual actions, they become assimilated to divinity by wearing a garb that otherwise is restricted to the gods'.[12] This concern with special headgear is widespread: Thessalonica produced a series of coins with the helmeted head of Roma on the obverse and on the reverse the inscription THESSALONIKEION. Another series depicts Cabirus wearing a laurel crown. Also, Macedonia was famous for its crowns made from roses, crowns which were used in the commemoratory sacrifice of the cult of Dionysus. So when Paul urges his hearers to put on for 'a helmet the hope of salvation' (1 Thess. 5:8), he himself may well have been influenced by Isa. 59:17, but the use of the term 'crown/helmet' might have prompted some very different associations for his audience.

[11] H. W. Heidland in *Theological Dictionary of the New Testament*, ed. Gerhard Friedrich, vol. 5 (Grand Rapids: Eerdmans, 1967), 176,.

[12] Phyllis Williams Lehmann and Denys Spittle, *Samothrace: the Temenos*, Bollingen Series, vol. 60 no. 5 (Princeton: Princeton University Press, 1982), 221.

Of the other divinities worshipped at Thessalonica we know that Zeus played an important role; additionally there are references to Asclepius, Aphrodite, Demeter and others. But since the information is so sparse, we will move on to what may have been the most important religious cult of Thessalonica at the time Paul founded a Christian congregation in this city, the *cult of Cabirus*, whose god promoted fertility and protected sailors. This cult is often referred to in the plural as the cult of the Cabiri; this is a correct way to refer to the cult in general but not in Thessalonica, since there was only one Cabirus in this cult, a fact attested to in both the literary and numismatic evidence. The most complete literary reference to the cult of Cabirus in Thessalonica is that given by Clement of Alexandria.[13] Here we learn that two brothers killed the third, wrapped his head in a purple cloth, placed a crown on it and buried it at the foot of Mt Olympus; henceforth the third brother became the focal point of the cult. To explain the origin of the name Cabirus, Clement recounts a myth in which this pair of murderers took the phallus of Dionysus in a small box to Tyrrhenus. This myth attests not only to the antiquity of the name Cabirus but also to the centrality of the phallic symbolism in it. Aside from these fragmentary and enigmatic references we know nothing further about the practices of this cult; this is especially unfortunate given its significance in Pauline Thessalonica.

The civic cults of Thessalonica

In Acts 17 we learn that the Jews together with some persons from the *agora* (marketplace) in Thessalonica attacked the home of Paul's sponsor, Jason. In verses 6 and 7 it is reported that 'when they could not find them, they dragged Jason and some of the brethren before the city authorities, crying, "These men who have turned the world upside down have come here also, and Jason has received them; and they are all acting against the decrees of Caesar [*ton dogmaton Kaisaros*], saying

---

[13] *Protrepticus*, ed. Otto Stählin, *GCS* (Berlin: Akademie-Verlag, 1972), 2.19.1–4.

that there is another king, Jesus."'' What are these *dogmata Kaisaros* which Paul and his associates violated? One cannot help but be favourably impressed with the reliability of certain details in Acts when, for example, such a unique term as 'city authorities' (*tous politarchas*), used in Acts only with regard to Thessalonian authorities (17:8), has been archaeologically verified.

In an important study E. A. Judge cites a number of imperial decrees which might have been referred to as 'decrees of Caesar' in Thessalonica.[14] Based on these Judge offers a probable explanation for the accuracy of the reference to the 'decrees of Caesar' in Acts 17. In all likelihood the politarchs in Thessalonica were responsible for administering an oath of loyalty and for dealing with its violations. In view of this situation we need to ask whether there were elements in the proclamation of Paul and his co-workers in Thessalonica that might have been perceived as so politically inflammatory as to provoke the crisis described in Acts and whether the unusually strong civic cult in the city would have created an environment particularly hostile to early Christian proclamation and language.

It is difficult, if not impossible, to reconstruct the original Pauline message proclaimed in the city; all we can hope for are glimmers of it in the written correspondence. If in fact 1 Thessalonians contains traces of Paul's original preaching, then we certainly do find elements that could be understood or misunderstood in a distinctly political sense. In 2:12 God, according to the Apostle, calls the Thessalonian Christians 'into his own kingdom'; in 5:3 there is a frontal attack on the *pax et securitas* programme of the early principate; and in the verses just preceding this attack one finds three heavily loaded political terms: *parousia*, *apantēsis* and *kyrios*. Milligan notes that *parousia* is related to 'the "visit" of the king, or some other official'.[15] Dibelius also urges that when used as court language *parousia* refers to the arrival of Caesar, a king or an

---

[14] E. A. Judge, 'The Decrees of Caesar at Thessalonica', *RTR* 30 (1971), 4.
[15] George Milligan, *St Paul's Epistles to the Thessalonians* (New York: Macmillan, 1908), 145–8.

official.[16] Best has shown that *apantēsis* refers to the citizens meeting a dignitary who is about to visit the city. The term *kyrios*, especially when used in the same context as the two preceding terms, also has a definite political sense. As Deissmann has shown, the people in the eastern Mediterranean applied the term *kyrios* to the Roman emperors from Augustus on, although the first verifiable inscription of the *kyrios*-title in Greece dates to the time of Nero.[17] All of this, coupled with the use of *euangelion* (gospel) and its possible association with the eastern ruler cult, suggests that Paul and his associates could easily be understood as violating the 'decrees of Caesar' in the most blatant manner.

We now turn to an examination of the civic cult of Thessalonica. When Macedonia became a Roman province in 146 BC, Thessalonica was made the capital and thus the centre of Roman administration. The city supported the victorious Antony and Octavian prior to the famous battle of Philippi in 42 BC, an event which ushered in a prosperous new era for Thessalonica. After Brutus' defeat, Thessalonica was able to celebrate its new status as a 'free' city with immunity from tribute and to establish games in honour of the victors. The Thessalonians' fortunes were determined heavily by Roman interests from the middle of the second to the middle of the first century BC, and in view of this situation it was necessary for the Thessalonians to develop ways to honour their Roman benefactors so that their benefaction and favours would continue.[18] The extensive coinage of Thessalonica underscores its prosperity, which was certainly due to its status as a free city and its location as a main station on the famous Via Egnatia, which ran through the city on an east/west axis.

As Roman benefaction gained an importance for the citizens of Thessalonica, increasingly the Roman benefactors were included as objects of honour alongside the gods. During the

---

[16] Martin Dibelius, *An die Thessalonicher I II An die Phillipper*, HNT 11/3 (Tübingen: Mohr/Siebeck, 1937), 14–15.

[17] Adolf Deissmann, *Light from the Ancient East* (New York: Doran, 1922), 351–8.

[18] On this entire subject see the work of Holland Lee Hendrix, 'Thessalonicans Honor Romans' (Cambridge, Mass.: Th.D. dissertation, Harvard University, 1984), 253.

first century BC the goddess Roma is joined to the Roman benefactors and it is evident that the Thessalonians acclaimed her divine status. As the priesthood of the gods became increasingly associated with these Roman benefactors and honours to the gods, Roma and the Roman benefactors became increasingly interrelated in the practice of the city.

Another advance occurs in the interpenetration of the civic with the religious: a temple of Caesar was built in the reign of Augustus. Associated with this temple was a priest and superintendent of public games of the Roman emperor. Numismatic evidence is most helpful as an aid in understanding this development. From this it is clear that Thessalonica acknowledged Julius as a god. Coins minted in Thessalonica about 27 BC were the first to portray the heads of Romans. Hendrix notes that although 'the title "son of god" (*theou huios*) does not appear with Octavian/Augustus on any of the coins, the juxtaposition of the Divine Julius with his son may reflect Thessalonican awareness of the Imperator's status as *divi filius* and is indicative perhaps of local importance to it'.[19] It is also significant in this overall process that at this time the head of Augustus displaces the head of Zeus on the coins of the city. Recognising the divine sanction for these developments, a new temple of Caesar was built and a priest of the Emperor Augustus, 'son of god', was appointed and given priority over the other priesthoods. Prominent attention to this priesthood is called for precisely because that 'particular strand of royal theology which is most apparent in Thessalonica's honorific activity is the attention paid to the legitimation of Augustus' rule and his successors'.[20]

THE SPECIFIC BACKGROUND

During Paul's brief original visit to Thessalonica, which we have placed in the early forties of the first century AD, he aroused such hostility (Acts 17:1–9; 1 Thess. 2:13–16) that he was forced to leave hurriedly. During both Paul's presence and his absence it may have been put about by some that he and his

19   Ibid., 170.
20   Ibid., 311.

message were dangerous and fraudulent; such a critique could be equally forceful from either a Jewish or a Roman perspective.[21] Following his abrupt departure the persecution of his followers intensified and some deaths resulted.

As we have already suggested, and as we have yet to develop in more detail, Paul writes this letter to the Thessalonian Christians in order to console them and to encourage them to stand firm during continued persecution. Thus we understand 1 Thessalonians as being similar to a 'paracletic' letter, as a *consolatio*, i.e., as a letter intended to comfort and encourage. But in order to carry out effectively this purpose the Apostle will also remind them that the message he proclaimed while present with them had its origin with God and, because of that, continues to be valid in the present, and, as is typical for epideictic rhetoric, he will accentuate through praise the good relationship that existed between Paul and the Thessalonians from the very beginning.

Royal theology and the suffering of the Thessalonian Christians

Is Paul referring to a specific set of circumstances with his several references to affliction and suffering in 1 Thessalonians? In 1:6 he reminds the Thessalonians that they 'received the word in much affliction [*thlipsei pollē*]'; in 2:14 he refers to their suffering (*epathete*); in 3:3 he sends Timothy to them so 'that no one be moved by these afflictions [*thlipsesin*]'. This theme is well summarised in 3:4: 'For when we were with you, we told you beforehand that we were to suffer affliction [*thlibesthai*]; just as it has come to pass, and as you know.' What did Paul have in mind when he made his warning to the congregation during his visit and what exactly had come to pass?

Not unrelated to this question are the Satan/tempter references. In 1 Thess. 2:18 Paul indicates that Satan repeatedly hindered him from visiting the Thessalonian congregation. Is this, perhaps, an indication that the political opposition to him

---

[21] We understand *symphyletēs* in 1 Thess. 2:14 in a local rather than in a racial sense. Thus, the reference by no means excludes those Jews who instigated the persecutions in Thessalonica.

remained so strong that it was impossible for Paul to reenter the city? Is F. F. Bruce not on the right track when he suggests that 'Paul might well discern Satanic opposition behind the politarchs' decision'?[22] This also relates to the 'tempter' reference in 3:5: 'For this reason, when I could bear it no longer, I sent that I might know your faith, for fear that somehow the tempter [*ho peirazōn*] had tempted you and that our labour would be in vain.' It is fully possible that the Apostle is concerned that the political opposition and pressure on the young Christians might be so strong that they would be tempted to abandon their faith in Christ. That the climate of such a concern is a realistic possibility should be evident in light of our review of the civic cult in Thessalonica.

In the midst of this situation of affliction and suffering, produced in all likelihood by political opposition, 1 Thessalonians assures the congregation that God has chosen them (1:4), language which may well be related to the persecution/affliction theme of the letter, and emphatically stresses the twin themes of hope and *parousia*. How does this emphasis fit into the overall perspective of the situation and what specifically caused Paul to place such emphasis on these themes?

It is noteworthy that 1 Thessalonians opens in 1:3 and closes in 5:8 with the triadic formulation 'faith, love and hope' which forms an *inclusio* within the rhetorical structure of the letter. However, when Timothy reports back to Paul about the condition of the Thessalonian church he brings only the good news of their 'faith and love' (3:6). The element of hope is absent. This section of the letter ends with Paul praying that he might see them soon face to face so that he might 'supply what is lacking [*ta husterēmata*]' in their faith (3:10). Given the strong emphasis on hope (*elpis*) and *parousia* in the *partitio* (statement of the case) and the *probatio* (proof) of the letter,[23] it is likely that what is lacking in the faith of the Thessalonians is the

22 F. F. Bruce, *The Acts of the Apostles* (Grand Rapids: Eerdmanns, 1951), 327. See also his *NICNT* commentary (Grand Rapids: Eerdmanns, 1988), 325–6.

23 Note the presence of the term 'hope' in such strategic locations as 1:10, 2:19 and 3:13, locations which mark the closing of the first three chapters, and, similarly, of *parousia* in 2:19, 3:13, 4:15 and 5:23.

dimension of hope. This observation is underscored by what Dahl has referred to as the 'superfluous rehearsals and reminders',[24] viz., the many 'you know'-type references, examples of which can be found in 1:5; 2:1, 2, 5, 9, 10 and 11; 3:3b–4; 4:1, 2, 6, 10 and 11 and 5:1. These 'superfluous rehearsals and reminders' come to an abrupt halt in 4:13, the beginning of the third proof, which deals with those persons who have died prior to the *parousia*. The verb *agnoeō* (to be ignorant), a word not found elsewhere in the Thessalonian correspondence, is used by Paul as a rhetorical device (*praeteritio*) to signal that an unfamiliar disclosure is to follow. To indicate that this new information has come to an end, the Apostle uses another rehearsal formula in 5:1: 'But as to the times and the seasons, brethren, you have no need to have anything written to you.' Thus, 4:13–18 is a section of critical importance for 1 Thessalonians; within the eschatological framework of Paul's initial proclamation, a new issue has arisen: what is the status of those who have died in Christ prior to the *parousia*? Negatively, Paul argues that the Thessalonian Christians should not be like the remainder of the Gentile population, who have no hope. Paul's positive response to this issue is to refer to the faith they hold in common: 'we believe that Jesus died and rose again'. By the use of an apocalyptic 'word of the Lord' (4:15), the Apostle can establish that when the Lord comes 'the dead in Christ will rise first; then we who are alive' (4:16–17).

It is important to ask why this issue concerning the 'dead in Christ' (*hoi nekroi en Christō*, 4:16) is so central to the letter, and, further, we must ask whether it is possible to identify those who have fallen asleep (*tous koimethentas*, 4:14). F. F. Bruce makes a bold suggestion: 'perhaps those who "fell asleep" so soon (I Th. iv. 13) were victims of this persecution [the one referred to in Acts 17]'.[25] Bruce's suggestion is an unorthodox one in view of the fact that few scholars discuss the matter of death by per-

---

[24] Nils Dahl in reflections presented to the Society of Biblical Literature Paul Seminar in 1972, p. 2. See also Karl P. Donfried, 'The Cults of Thessalonica and the Thessalonian Correspondence', *NTS* 31 (1985), 348.

[25] Bruce, *Acts*, 327–8. See also the revised and enlarged third edition of this 1951 commentary (Grand Rapids: Eerdmanns, 1990), 372.

secution this early in Christian history. Yet there are a number of items which could give positive support to Bruce's suggestion. The use of *koimaō* in Acts 7:60 is remarkable: 'And as they were stoning Stephen, he prayed, "Lord Jesus, receive my spirit." And he knelt down and cried with a loud voice, "Lord, do not hold this sin against them." And when he had said this, he fell asleep [*ekoimethe*].' In this text the verb *koimaō* refers explicitly to one who has suffered death through persecution. In 1 Thess. 2:14–16, which we have argued elsewhere to be authentic,[26] Paul makes a very clear parallel between the situation of the Thessalonian church and that of the churches in Judea; they 'became imitators of the churches of God in Christ Jesus which are in Judea' and they 'suffered the same things' (*ta auta epathete*) from their countrymen and that clearly involves the dimension of death (2:14–15). And, finally, the Thessalonian congregation became an example to all the believers in Macedonia and in Achaia precisely because they 'received the word in much affliction' (1 Thess. 1:6–8). Further they became 'imitators' of Paul, Silvanus and Timothy (1 Thess. 1:6) in suffering, a theme which Paul articulates in 2:2: 'but though we had already suffered and had been shamefully treated in Philippi, as you know, we had courage in our God to declare to you the gospel of God in the face of great opposition [*en pollō agōni*]'. Paul uses this same term, *agōn*, only once again, in a very similar context, in Phil. 1:30.

The question, of course, that arises in light of these suggestions centres on their persuasiveness: is it probable that the afflictions and *ad hoc* persecutions in Thessalonica could lead to *occasional* deaths? Can it be that Paul's vision 'for the eschatological community that presents a utopian alternative to the prevailing eschatological ideology of Rome'[27] has the potential for creating such a harsh reaction? One need only refer to the Paphlagonian oath of loyalty to the Caesarian house in 3 BC which compels Romans and non-Romans alike to report cases

[26] Karl P. Donfried, 'Paul and Judaism: 1 Thessalonians 2:13–16 as a Test Case', *Int* 38 (1984), 242–53.

[27] Helmut Koester, 'From Paul's Eschatology to the Apocalyptic Schemata of 2 Thessalonians', in *The Thessalonian Correspondence*, 458.

of disloyalty and to hunt down physically the offenders.[28] The seriousness by which this is meant to be taken – even to the point of death for those who are disloyal – is self-evident. If this possible parallel has any relevance for the political situation in Thessalonica at the time of Paul, then certainly the Apostle's 'political preaching' and his perceived attack on the *pax et securitas* emphasis of the early principate was not likely to lead the citizens to give Paul a warm or extended welcome.

THE STRATEGY OF PAUL'S RESPONSE TO THE THESSALONIAN CHRISTIANS

What can we say, at least in a preliminary manner, about the method and strategy of Paul's response to the Thessalonian situation as we have described it? To begin with, it is remarkable to note the significant emphasis Paul places on the theme of 'the word' and 'the gospel' in this brief letter, a frequency which is probably unparalleled in his other letters when calculated proportionate to their length. *Logos* (word), when referring specifically to the word of God, appears in 1:5, 6 and 8; 2:13 and 4:15 and 18. *Euangelion* (gospel) appears in 1:5; 2:2, 4, 8 and 9 and 3:2. When one observes the heavy concentration of occurrences of these terms in 1 Thess. 2:1–9 it may not be amiss to conclude that Paul's response is intended both as a commendation of the gospel and as praise for his own apostolic work in transmitting this gospel.

Previously we have made reference to the recurring 'you know' expressions in the letter. Why does Paul make such frequent use of this phrase? At issue in Thessalonica is the continued validity of that gospel which he had preached from the outset. Some may be questioning its applicability to the new situation of persecution and discouragement. As a result Paul must advocate the gospel in two ways. First, he must remind the Thessalonian Christians that it is a message originating from God; therefore its performative character is recalled in 1 Thess. 1:4–7 and 2:13. Second, and more par-

---

[28] Judge, 'Decrees of Caesar', 6.

ticularly, he must bring to recollection certain specific elements of his preaching and emphasise anew their appropriateness lest they be regarded as unrelated to the situation in Thessalonica. Thus, all of these 'you know'-type phrases in the letter are not simply to be regarded as 'superfluous rehearsals' but as key components in Paul's advocacy of the gospel he preached and presented to the Thessalonians during his initial visit. This emphasis on the gospel is intimately linked with the repeated rehearsal that this gospel has continued applicability.

There is another factor which needs to be considered in this context. It appears as if Paul's description of his message as truly a word of God, on the one hand, and the repetition and the new application of his previous proclamation and teaching, on the other hand, pave the way for the unprecedented and decisive information and consolation which he is about to give in 4:13–18. At the heart of the pronouncement stands a 'word of the Lord' (*en logō kuriou*). This new information attempts to console the Thessalonian Christians at a most neuralgic point: some of them have died and now some are about to jettison a critical dimension of their faith, viz., hope. Paul's word of consolation would be worthless if he had not first attempted to demonstrate the validity of the word of God that he had preached previously. Only then can this word of the Lord, presented here as new information, viz., information not shared during his visit in Thessalonica, be considered a convincing intervention to the problem of death caused by persecution.

A major rhetorical strategy in 1 Thessalonians is the topic of praise. Paul's own apostolic ministry, the faithfulness and love of the Christians in Thessalonica, and the nature of the good relationship between them all become the subject of praise in this earliest extant Christian letter. The turmoil being experienced by these Christians and Paul's non-presence during this period of difficulty make necessary such an affective response precisely because a situation of unrest threatened to weaken the caring relationship that had been established between the Apostle and the Thessalonian church. Paul had to leave Thessalonica hurriedly after a brief stay because of opposition originally mounted by the Jews but which had quickly spread to the non-Jewish population. As a result Paul travels to Athens but the Thessalonian Christians must remain and continue to experience the painful consequences of this attack. They experience persecution, perhaps, in the case of a few, even death. It is not inconceivable that some, inside and outside the community, may have placed at least some blame on Paul for their difficult predicament. A persuasive response becomes imperative.

Dio Chrysostom speaks negatively about certain philosophers who 'merely utter a phrase or two, and then, after railing at you rather than teaching you, ... make a hurried exit, anxious lest before they have finished you may raise an outcry and send them packing'.[29] Especially because some may have viewed Paul in a somewhat similar manner, it is urgent for him to speak of his anguish and deep affection for them during his absence. Not to be confused with those wandering philosophers who did not become involved in the struggle (*agōn*) of life, Paul reminds them that he and his co-workers preached the gospel of God to them 'in the face of great opposition' (*en pollō agōni*; 1 Thess 2:2), a reference placed very deliberately at the beginning of the Apostle's synopsis of their relationship to one another. Perhaps, because of a possible implicit or an explicit criticism that Paul deceived them by not telling them about the possibility of continued affliction, the Apostle must distance himself from possible thoughts of flattery and greed and must elsewhere in the letter repeatedly include himself as a participant in suffering and affliction – a suffering and affliction which he shared with them when present and now continues to share in Corinth. Certainly 1 Thess. 3:7, 'in all our distress and affliction' refers to Paul's situation at the time he is writing 1 Thessalonians in Corinth. To demonstrate that his preaching was not a 'cloak for greed' (1 Thess. 2:5) the Apostle recounts, by utilising the rhetorical topic of praise, how hard Silvanus, Timothy and he worked and how 'righteous and blameless' (1 Thess. 2:9–12)

---

[29] Dio Chrysostom, *Oration* 32, 11.

was their behaviour toward the Christian community in Thessalonica.

Thus it can be said that Paul's narrative review of his relationship with the Thessalonian congregation in 1 Thessalonians 2 is in response both to the severity of their afflictions and to his own absence, an absence which could be interpreted as issuing from neglect or lack of concern. Among the several reasons the letter is written is to clarify any possible misunderstanding with regard to his affection and care for the Thessalonian Christians and, further, to suggest that their life in Christ is worth the affliction they are experiencing in order that they may receive the full gift of salvation for which they have been destined (1 Thess. 5:9).

In terms of the substantive issue raised in the central third proof, 1 Thess. 4:13–18, Paul attempts to assure the community that those who have died will not be forgotten and that those who are alive at the *parousia* will not have precedence. As we will have opportunity to explore further, the use of a prophetic 'word of the Lord' and of apocalyptic language serve to support his conclusion. Given Paul's intention of wanting to *relativise*, not eradicate, the distinction of being dead or alive at the *parousia*, it is important to recognise that the theme of the *parousia* dominates 1 Thess. 4:13–5:11, and, beyond that, the entire letter. The relationship between the problem of being dead or alive at the *parousia* and the centrality of the *parousia* is summarised by the Apostle himself in 1 Thess. 5:9–11: 'For God has not destined us for wrath, but to obtain salvation through our Lord Jesus Christ, who died for us so that whether we wake or sleep we might live with him. Therefore encourage (*parakaleite*) one another and build one another up, just as you are doing.'

1 Thessalonians has thus much in common with a *logos paramythetikos*, a word of consolation and encouragement to a Christian church suffering the effects of persecution. *Paramytheisthai* is used only in 1 Thess. 2:12 and 5:14 within the Pauline corpus. In fact the advice given in 5:14, 'encourage [*paramytheisthe*] the fainthearted', is not far from the mark in describing the intention of the letter as one of encouragement

to the discouraged. They are discouraged precisely because 'hope' has become disengaged from their faith. The preservation of 1 Thessalonians in the canon is a testimony to its effectiveness in correcting, through encouragement, this environment of hopelessness among some in the church of Thessalonica. Paul's intention in writing 1 Thessalonians shows a resemblance to Second Isaiah's announced intention in 40:1 'Comfort [*parakaleite*], comfort [*parakaleite*] my people, says your God.'

CHAPTER 2

The theology of 1 Thessalonians

We have had opportunity to review a number of external factors that may have contributed to the writing of 1 Thessalonians, as well as to observe some strategies and goals of the Apostle as he responds to the dilemmas occasioned by these circumstances. Now it is necessary to turn directly to the theological content of Paul's attempt to encourage and console the Christians of Thessalonica.

ELECTION BY THE LIVING AND TRUE GOD

God is the one who is present among his elect and suffering people and who is leading them to their promised salvation. This thematic emphasis in 1 Thessalonians is intended as a response to the situations created by persecution and martyrdom as well as to the challenge of living the Christian life as God's elect in the midst of a pagan culture.

The motif of election is a key theological component of this letter. The concept is expressed or referred to in the following texts: *ekklēsia* in 1:1; *eklogēn* in 1:4; *kalountas* in 2:12; *ekalesen* in 4:7 and *kalōn* in 5:24. In all cases except the second these expressions are linked to the verb *kaleō* (I call). In the case of *eklogēn* it is related to the verb *eklegō* (I choose). In attempting to determine Paul's intent in using this concept of 'calling' or 'election', the most telling use of the motif is found in 1:4 – *eklogēn*. For our purpose Bruce's more literal translation of *eklogē* is to be preferred: 'knowing as we do [the genuineness of] your election, brothers so dear to God'.[1] But what does Paul mean when he speaks of their 'election' or 'selection'?

[1] F. F. Bruce, *1 & 2 Thessalonians*, WBC 45 (Waco, Texas: Word, 1982), 10.

There are seven occurrences of the noun *eklogē* in the New Testament; Paul, in addition to this reference, uses it elsewhere four times (Rom. 9:11; 11:5, 7, 28), and it always has the meaning of divine choice. It is closely related to *bahir* in the Old Testament, which consistently refers to divine choice or selection (1 Ch. 16:13; Ps. 89:3; 105:6, 43; 106:5, 23; Is. 42:1; 43:20; 45:4; 65:9, 15, 22). In comparing this noun to the terms derived from *kaleō* in 1 Thessalonians, it can be said that *eklogē*, meaning God's choice, election or selection, is the prior term, and that *kaleō* marks the act of realising and actualising this prior divine choice. Paul reminds the Thessalonian Christians that God has chosen them and that as a result of that selection they must now live out the consequences of that choice and accept the privileges and responsibilities of the call into the kingdom of God.

At the heart of the Apostle's proclamation, then, is a God who is described as 'a living and true God' who raised his Son, Jesus, from the dead, and the claim that this action will deliver the Thessalonian believers from the 'wrath' to come.[2] The intention of God goes beyond protecting the Christians from wrath; it involves salvation. Thus Paul can say in 5:9: 'For God has not destined us for wrath, but to obtain salvation through our Lord Jesus Christ'. The description of the current situation as one of waiting 'for his Son from heaven' underscores a pattern of 'already – not yet'. Already now, in the present, God acts decisively in the revelation, death and resurrection of his Son, but the imminent consummation, the approaching deliverance of 'the wrath to come' and the fulfilment of the promise of salvation is yet to occur.

The Thessalonians have heard and responded to the call of *this* God, as had Paul and his co-workers before them. Their

---

[2] In 1 Thessalonians Paul uses the term 'God' (*theos*) thirty-six times; in addition, God is described as 'Father' five times. The term 'Lord' (*kurios*) is found some twenty-four times. In one-half of these cases it refers explicitly to Jesus (e.g. 'Lord Jesus Christ') and it is probable that Jesus is also the referent in the other twelve cases. Thus, there is no unambiguous reference to God as 'Lord'. When a distinction is intended, it is frequently one between 'God our Father' and the 'Lord Jesus Christ' (e.g. 1:1, 1:3, 3:11, 13).

response is in the form of having 'faith [*pistis*] in him' (1:8), in turning to him (1:9) and in having courage in him (2:2). They are now members of the 'called out' community, the church (*ekklēsia*), which is always a church '*in* God the Father and the Lord Jesus Christ' (1:1) and they are now in fellowship with all the churches *of God*, including those in Macedonia, Achaia and Judea (2:14). Because of God's continual presence (3:9; 4:8, 17), Paul gives thanks (1:2, 2:13, 3:9), prays for and remembers (1:2–3) the Thessalonian congregation without ceasing. As a result of these marvellous actions by God on behalf of the Thessalonians and because this living and true God is constantly present, the Apostle can urge the Thessalonians to 'rejoice always, pray constantly, give thanks in all circumstances' (5:16–18).

For Paul, the God who elected and destined the believers for salvation also possesses a 'will' (*thelēma*) which is to guide the Christians during this time of waiting. Not only is rejoicing, praying and giving thanks an expression of 'the will of God' (5:18), but also abstaining from 'unchastity' (4:3). To do the will of God is to please God (2:4, 4:1) and one dimension of that is 'to lead a life worthy of God, who calls you into his own kingdom and glory' (2:12). Pleasing God is doing the 'will of God, your sanctification' (*hagiasmos*; 4:3). For Paul the Thessalonians already know what it means 'to lead a life worthy of God' because they have 'been taught by God' (*theodidaktoi*; 4:9). Paul's ethical advice, given at several points in 1 Thessalonians, is thus a reminder of that which they already have been taught by God, the God who gives 'his Holy Spirit to you' (4:8). God's choice of the Thessalonian Christians, then, announced by Paul through the gospel and responded to in faith, is to be realised and actualised, despite all external adversities, through a lifestyle informed by love and established in hope. Thus Paul can transform the non-Christian use of the term *ekklēsia*, into a theologically descriptive title for this audience, viz., those who are called out. They indeed are the 'called out' from among the citizens of Thessalonica (1:1) and are 'called into' the kingdom.

CHRISTOLOGY, ESCHATOLOGY AND THE PROMISE OF
SALVATION

Paul's use and transformation of the early Christian tradition

Since the heart of the gospel is about God's action in Jesus Christ, it is not unimportant to ask what Paul actually communicates about Jesus in 1 Thessalonians and what the sources of that information are. In addition to referring to him simply as Jesus in 1:10 and 4:14 and Son in 1:10, one finds a variety of christological titles used in several combinations in this brief letter: 'Lord', 'Lord Jesus', 'Christ', 'Christ Jesus' and 'Lord Jesus Christ'. Prior to reviewing these titles in greater detail it would be well to concentrate on three pre-Pauline *christological* traditions which Paul has employed in this earliest extant Christian letter: 1:9–10, 4:14 and 5:9–10. Before examining these pre-Pauline traditions, some more general comments need to be made concerning the relationship of these early traditions to the composition of this letter.

The coherence between portions of 1 Thessalonians and the theology of the Hellenistic church is remarkable. In many of its formulations and in its use of traditional materials this letter appears to be more pre-Pauline than 'Pauline'. Repeatedly Paul incorporates traditions circulating in the Hellenistic church, many of which had in turn been appropriated by that church from a variety of sources, including Hellenistic Judaism and, through it, popular Hellenistic philosophy. These traditional elements include: the triadic formula 'faith, hope and love', the fragments of missionary preaching located in 1:9–10, the language of the popular philosophers and Hellenistic cults in 2:1–12, the anti-Jewish *topoi* of 2:14–16, the paraenetic elements in 4:1–12 and chapter 5 and certain phrases in 4:13–18. These *topoi* suggest that Paul is to be placed within the milieu of the Hellenistic church's missionary movement, the very context in which he received much of his missionary training.

The Pauline contribution to those traditions, which he inherited from Antioch and elsewhere, are found exactly at

those points where the Apostle is shaping these earlier traditions in light of the gospel and his own apocalyptic hermeneutic to meet a difficulty which has developed in the Thessalonian church, viz., that some have died before the *parousia*. To
deal with this dilemma Paul, as can now be recognised in
1:9–10 and in 4:13–18, expands and applies the proclamation
of the Hellenistic church. To explain and unfold what it means
to wait for Jesus, not only in light of the fact that they have
turned to the true and living God from the idols but also
because they have just recently experienced some unantici-
pated deaths, becomes a major goal in 4:13–18. That gospel
which came in 'full conviction' (1:5) and in 'the Holy Spirit'
(1:5) and is alive and 'at work' (2:13) in the believers must now
be dynamically applied to and articulated in an unforeseen
situation. We have here one of the first extant instances where
Paul the apocalypticist, in light of his emphasis on the impending triumph of God, attempts to draw out the implications of
the gospel for a situation hitherto not addressed. In so doing he
develops a pattern which is then utilised in his other letters as
well. It is precisely at such points of specification and concreti-
sation that one sees the complex relationship between the
gospel, which has its origin with God, the interpretation and
amplification of that gospel by the pre-Pauline church, and,
now, Paul's attempt to interpret and apply *both* to a unique
circumstance in the life of the Thessalonian church.

Let us now examine somewhat more closely the early Christian traditions about Jesus that Paul receives and makes use of
in 1 Thessalonians.

1 Thess. 1:9–10

1 Thess. 1:9–10 can be structured in the following way:

1 'you turned to God from idols, to serve a living and true
  God,
2 and to wait for his Son from heaven,
3 whom he raised from the dead,
4 Jesus who delivers us from the wrath to come.'

The phrase 'his Son' (*ton huion autou*) describes Jesus as the
coming Saviour from heaven and is not found elsewhere in Paul

with this eschatological nuance despite the wide range of meaning which Paul can attribute to the title 'Son' in other contexts. This, together with the absence of any reference to the death of Jesus and the fact that Paul uses the verb *sozō* rather than *hruomai* for the meaning 'to deliver' in eschatological contexts referring to the final return of Jesus, makes it once again probable that Paul is using here an earlier fragment belonging to the Hellenistic church, which itself incorporated this material from the missionary literature of Jewish Hellenism and modified it (e.g., 'whom he raised from the dead, Jesus') in the light of the Christ event and its own missionary needs.

1 Thess. 4:14

By using a well-known rhetorical device (*praeteritio*) in 4:13 ('we would not have you ignorant'), the Apostle and his associates indicate they wish to convey some new information. It is here in chapter 4 that Paul wishes to specify more exactly the content of 1 Thess. 1:9–10 in view of the unexpected deaths in the Thessalonian congregation. It is possible that some drew an erroneous conclusion from this earlier statement, viz., that there would be no deaths before the *parousia*, a view which had been contradicted by the Thessalonian persecution. Paul's refutation of this perspective begins with a contrast similar to that found at the end of chapter 1, where a contrast is made between the Christians and those 'who have no hope'.

The formula 'we believe that Jesus died and rose again' (*Iēsous apethanen kai anestē*) is undoubtedly a pre-Pauline formula since Paul consistently uses the verb *egeirō* rather than *anistēmi*. This phrase repeats the content of 1:10, but does so more precisely: essentially, however, no new information is added. This pre-Pauline formula, 'Jesus died and rose', serves as the foundation of the new information which is to follow, viz., that the death and resurrection of Jesus is the basis for the belief that Christians will be united with Christ at his *parousia*.[3] The essential core of the new information is that 'God will

---

[3] As we will observe below, the pre-Pauline phrase 'who died for us' in 1 Thess. 5:10 is a similar Pauline amplification of 1 Thess. 1:9–10.

bring with him those who have fallen asleep'. (4:14) and this is confirmed with a word from the Lord (4:15). According to this word, when the Lord descends from heaven on the last day, 'the dead in Christ will rise first; then we who are alive, who are left, shall be caught up together with them in the clouds to meet the Lord in the air' (4:16–17).

Lüdemann is correct in defining Paul's hope in this letter as a *parousia*-hope, and not primarily a resurrection-hope.[4] Further, he is to be followed when he urges that the introduction of the disclosure about the resurrection of the prematurely deceased Christians does not decisively alter Paul's earlier view that the union of Christians with Christ will be at the *parousia*. This new information functions to preserve the eschatological hope of the early Paul and it does not introduce a new doctrine of resurrection-hope. That follows only in 1 Corinthians.

There is a noticeable consistency between Paul's assertions in 1 Thess. 4:13–18 and in 1 Cor. 15, even though 1 Corinthians moves beyond his previous assertions. The problem in Corinth is not death due to unexpected persecution but arises from reflections about the mystery of death itself in a Hellenistic context. Thus in 1 Cor. 15:50 it is stated that 'flesh and blood cannot inherit the kingdom of God'. Because of Paul's imminent expectation of the *parousia* in 1 Thessalonians and the unique predicament of the Thessalonian Christians, there is found neither any detailed reflection on the enigma of death itself nor any response to the challenges presented by Hellenistic dualism.

This pattern of consistency with previous assertions as well as the expansion and the more precise articulation of such assertions in view of a different, contingent situation is a characteristic of Pauline thought which can be observed at many points in his letters. An example of this, relevant to our discussion of 1 Thess. 4 and 1 Cor. 15, is Paul's use of christology. In both letters it is christology that shapes the anthropological dimension. In 1 Thessalonians, on the one hand, it is the connection

---

[4] Gerd Lüdemann, 'The Hope of the Early Paul: from the Foundation-Preaching at Thessalonika to 1 Cor. 15:51–57', *Perspectives in Religious Studies* 7 (1980), 196–7.

with Jesus' resurrection and the fact that the believer is *en Christō* which leads to Paul's assurance of the believer's union with Jesus at the *parousia*. To be *en Christō* represents the fundamental act of inclusion into God's new eschatological event which will soon be completed at the *parousia*. In 1 Cor. 15, on the other hand, where Paul has to come to terms with the problem of death itself as well as the challenges posed by Hellenistic dualism, resurrection is not simply the method by which the dead believers are transferred to their meeting with the heavenly Lord as in 1 Thessalonians; rather, resurrection involves the transformation of all bodies, the survivors as well as the dead, on the last day.

1 Thess. 5:9–10

We have already suggested the phrase 'our Lord Jesus Christ who died for us' is a pre-Pauline formula and that it too was used to further specify and amplify 1 Thess. 1:9–10 in light of the crisis confronting the Thessalonian Christians. In this text the historical death of Jesus, specifically referred to in 2:14–15, is now interpreted soteriologically by means of the phrase 'for us' (*hyper hēmōn*). This is the first time in the extant Christian literature that the death of Jesus is interpreted in this way, viz., soteriologically.

The phrase under examination has remarkable similarities with Rom. 5:6, 8:3 and 14:15 and 1 Cor. 15:3, and Wengst has concluded that all are dependent on a pre-Pauline *Sterbensformel* (death formula).[5] The formula in its original form probably read 'Christ died for our sins' and in 1 Thess. 5:10 the Apostle undoubtedly modified this tradition (as he did similarly in Rom. 5:6, 8:3 and 14:15) so that it would apply to the unique situation in Thessalonica concerning the unexpected deaths of some. For that reason it reads, quite uniquely: 'our Lord Jesus Christ who died for us so that whether we wake or sleep we might live with him'. Paul takes up this formula and adapts it so that it serves to comfort the Thessalonians in their distress. The emphasis is shifted from 'our sins' to the Christian's incor-

[5] Klaus Wengst, *Christologische Formeln und Lieder des Urchristentums*, StNT 7 (Gütersloh: Gerd Mohn, 1972), 32–3.

poration with Christ: thus '*our* Lord Jesus Christ who died *for us*
so that whether *we* wake or sleep *we* might live *with him*'. In
each of these emphasised words a unique linkage between the
believers and their Lord is accentuated. Here, then, Jesus'
death is interpreted soteriologically in the sense of giving life,
which is the result of serving 'a living and true God' (1:9). The
living God, through his Son, gives life at all times, now and in
the future. Thus hope, such a prominent theme in 1 Thessalonians, is rooted in this life-giving God who gives salvation, viz.,
life now and eternally for those who are *en Christō* through the
death of Jesus.

By way of summary, what can we say about Paul's use of the
three traditional formulae present in 1 Thess 1:9–10, 4:14 and
5:9–10? 1 Thess. 1:9–10 may well represent part of the proclamation that Paul delivered during his original visit to Thessalonica. This message must now be amplified and concretised in
light of the unexpected deaths of some who are *en Christō* within
the community of believers. He does this in two steps. By taking
up the traditional phrase 'we believe that Jesus died and rose
again' in 4:14 and explaining it further, he can reach the
conclusion that the dead are not excluded from salvation at the
parousia because 'God will bring with him those who have
fallen asleep'. This is then summarised and broadened in 5:9–10
through an innovative interpretation of a pre-Pauline soteriological formula so that it will become evident that *all* who are
en Christō, whether dead or alive, live in communion and
fellowship with him.

Paul and the teachings of Jesus

Paul's obvious use and transformation of the early Christian
tradition leads to an urgent question: to what extent did Paul,
in this his first letter, have access to and make use of the
teachings of Jesus? In 1 Thessalonians there are two passages
that may be relevant in answering this question: 2:11–12 with
its use of the term 'kingdom', a concept central to teaching of
the historical Jesus, and 4:15 with its reference to a 'word of the
Lord'.

1 Thess. 2:11–12

Paul writes: 'we exhorted each one of you and encouraged you and charged you to lead a life worthy of God, who calls you into his own kingdom and glory'. Paul also uses 'kingdom/ kingdom of God' language in Gal. 5:21, 1 Cor. 4:20, 1 Cor. 6:9–10, 1 Cor. 15:24, 1 Cor. 15:50 and Rom. 14:17. 'Kingdom of God' also occurs in 2 Thess. 1:5. Whether or not 2 Thessalonians is Pauline in the strict sense will be taken up later in this volume. In most of these passages, with the exception of 1 Cor. 15:24 and 1 Thess. 2:11–12, the phrase 'kingdom of God' is used. In the 1 Thessalonians passage one finds only the reference 'kingdom', and this may be because Paul has just referred to God and may wish to avoid redundancy.

Prior to these verses Paul has praised the conduct of his co-workers as well as himself, a conduct that results from the gospel that he preached to them. This same gospel also invites the Thessalonian Christians 'to lead a life worthy of God, who calls you into his own kingdom and glory'. In the verse that follows, 2:13, Paul praises their positive response to the message he proclaimed among them. Thus, the invitation 'to lead a life worthy of God' is couched in a context of double praise. In addition, they are reminded that the God who has elected them has elected them for 'his own kingdom and glory'. It is not unimportant to note that the verb 'to call' (*kalein*) is in the present tense, thus emphasising the present and continuing nature of the event in which they now participate and which will be brought to fulfilment in the future.

In all probability Paul used the word 'kingdom' during his missionary activity in Thessalonica, urging and counselling the new Christians that since God has called and continues to call them they are expected to live a life that is constantly transformed by the gospel. In 5:5 Paul reminds them that already now 'you are all sons of light and sons of the day'; as a consequence, 'let us be sober, and put on the breastplate of faith and love, and for a helmet the hope of salvation' (5:8). By repeating the triadic formula 'faith, love and hope' in 5:8 (note 1 Thess. 1:3) Paul reveals again his understanding of the Christian life as eschatological, as 'already, not yet'. Already now, partially and proleptically, through Christ and his gospel, God's rule and glory have broken into this transient world and are at work in the Thessalonian Christians because they have 'turned to God from idols, to serve a living and true God, and to wait for his Son from heaven' (1:9–10). The newness of their life in Christ has already begun and will be completed on the last day. As a result he can declare that 'God has ... destined us ... to obtain salvation through our Lord Jesus Christ' (5:9).

The use of the adverb *axiōs* (literally, worthily) in 1 Thess. 2:12, fairly infrequent in the Pauline corpus, may suggest that Paul is dependent on an early Christian baptismal tradition, a suggestion strengthened when one notes the similar use of this adverb in Phil. 1:27, Eph. 4:1 and Col. 1:10. Such a baptismal context may lie behind the kingdom references in 1 Cor. 4:20–1 and 1 Thess. 2:11–12. If this is indeed the case, then Paul can hardly be consciously referring to a saying of Jesus when he refers to the 'kingdom of God'. Our own study of all the kingdom references in Paul parallels the conclusions reached by F. Neirynck when he maintains that elsewhere 'in the Pauline letters there is no certain trace of a conscious use of the sayings of Jesus. Possible allusions to gospel sayings can be noted on the basis of similarity of form and context but a direct use of a gospel saying in the form it has been preserved in the synoptic gospels is hardly provable'.[6] Neirynck continues that 'Paul's knowledge of a pre-synoptic gospel, of the Q-source or pre-Q collections has not yet been demonstrated'[7] since the paucity and anonymity of such possible allusions make it doubtful whether Paul was specifically referring to them as sayings of Jesus.

A similar conclusion is reached by Nikolaus Walter: Paul quotes no sayings of Jesus but he is familiar with the Jesus tradition.[8] He observes that in the extant Pauline letters the Jesus tradition is used primarily in paraenetic contexts and in

---

[6] F. Neirynck, 'Paul and the Sayings of Jesus' in *L'Apôtre Paul*, ed. A. Vanhoye, *BETL* 73 (Leuven: University Press, 1986), 320.

[7] Ibid., 320.

[8] 'Paulus und die urchristliche Tradition', *NTS* 31 (1985), 498–522.

those sections in which Paul either defends or reviews his apostolic ministry. Walter cites 1 Cor. 4:11–13 and 9:14; we would add 1 Thess. 2:1–12. It is also noteworthy that when Paul cites the Jesus tradition it is usually without detailed reflection and that that tradition can be used with enormous freedom, viz., he can refer to it and yet not be bound by it (e.g., 1 Cor. 9:1–18).

The Jesus–Paul debate is an enormously intricate one and we do not wish to minimise its complexity by making these tentative comments and suggestions. It is likely, however, that the kingdom of God references in the Pauline corpus support those scholars who would wish to show that a fundamental unity and continuity between Jesus and Paul can be detected with regard to some central themes which are common to both. But that does not necessitate the view that Paul is directly dependent on the teachings of Jesus as reflected in the synoptic tradition. Rather, these words and themes seem to be transmitted through baptismal/paraenetic and other liturgical formulae and traditions of the earliest church.

1 Thess. 4:15

The phrase 'the word of the Lord' in v. 15 introduces new information to the Thessalonian Christians. The first problem that needs to be resolved is whether the contents of this 'word of the Lord' are limited to v. 15, vs. 15–16 or 15–17. The second problem is the origin of this material. Options include that it is a lost saying of Jesus (*agraphon*), that Paul has freely adopted a saying of the historical Jesus, that the Apostle has modified a word proclaimed by the risen Lord in the post-resurrectional period, and that we have here a prophetic announcement from the risen Lord through the prophet Paul.

Our assessment of Paul is that of an ecstatic prophet thoroughly shaped and influenced by the milieu of Jewish mystical-apocalypticism. Factors supporting this perspective of the Apostle include a charismatic understanding of apostleship dependent on a vision of the risen Christ (Gal. 1:11–17), his attestation of mystical ascensions to the heavenly worlds (2 Cor. 12:1–10) and his frequent use of Jewish mystical vocabulary, such as *symmorphous*, to describe the transformation experienced by the ones who are in Christ. Based on such an evaluation of Paul we would understand this 'word of the Lord' as one transmitted by the heavenly Lord to the prophet Paul. We are dealing, then, with a prophetic expression, and not one stemming from the historical Jesus.

According to the recent argument of Helmut Merklein[9] it is likely that the prophetic utterance is to be limited to v. 15b: 'We who are alive, who are left until the coming of the Lord, shall not precede those who have fallen asleep'. Verses 16–17 are further elaborations of the prophetic declaration using a variety of traditional apocalyptic motifs. By means of an instructive comparison of 1 Thess. 4:13–18 with 1 Cor. 15:50–8, Merklein has discovered a number of parallels between these two chapters that give further support to limiting the prophetic word to v. 15b as well as allowing us better to comprehend it and its interpretation. With regard to 1 Thessalonians we note the following unfolding of the pattern: in 4:14a dimensions of the gospel, already familiar to the recipients, are expressed; in 4:14b an introductory and transitional thesis is presented that must be confirmed and expanded by the yet to be announced prophetic word and its further elaboration; in 4:15b a hitherto unknown eschatological mystery is disclosed, although such prophetic revelation does not stand in contradiction in the gospel to which it is always subordinate; in 4:16–17 the interpretation of the prophetic word seeks to clarify matters not immediately evident from the gospel itself as a result of issues prompted by local, contingent situations and is not intended as a further dogmatic expansion of the gospel; in 4:18, the concluding part of this prophetic discourse, the basic intention of *consolatio* is unmistakable: 'Therefore comfort one another with these words'.

This analysis of 1 Thess. 4:15–17, then, reveals that embedded in v. 15b is a prophetic word transmitted by the heavenly Lord to the prophet Paul, with vs. 16–17 providing a

[9] 'Der Theologe als Prophet: zur Funktion prophetischen Redens im theologischen Diskurs', *NTS* 38 (1992), 402–29.

further interpretation of this eschatological mystery. We have no evidence that this is a word from the historical Jesus and Merklein's study goes far to eliminate this as a serious option. Therefore we must conclude that 1 Thessalonians provides no basis for supposing that Paul is *directly* dependent on the teachings of Jesus as they are discovered in the synoptic tradition. Rather, the words and themes reminiscent of the teaching of Jesus appear to be transmitted to Paul through a variety of baptismal/paraenetic, liturgical and miscellaneous ecclesial traditions.

Christological titles and their function

Christological titles – i.e., the processes by which the earliest Christians came to understand and interpret Jesus as they did – are dynamic, not static, and to a large extent they are determined by the generating power of the situation to which they are addressed. Certainly Paul inherits these titles from the tradition that preceded him, but he employs and shapes them to communicate his thoughts to the various contingent circumstances for which he writes. Thus the context in which these titles are found can disclose much about the theological intentions which are being expressed by them. Since the definition of christological titles evolves, one must be watchful not to impose more developed meanings upon earlier ones. Such caution must be heeded especially with regard to this earliest extant Christian writing. One must examine the exact context in which these titles appear in 1 Thessalonians and the significance Paul intends to connote by their use.

Lord Jesus Christ
The christological title 'Lord Jesus Christ' is the most comprehensive that Paul uses and all others – 'Lord', 'Lord Jesus', 'Jesus', 'Son', 'Christ' and 'Christ Jesus' – can be related to it.[10] It is found five times in 1 Thessalonians: in 1:1 and 3; and in 5:9,

---

[10] For this reason our discussion of the titles 'Christ' and 'Christ Jesus' will be incorporated with 'Lord' and its variants. The term 'Son' has been reviewed in our discussion of the pre-Pauline traditions.

23 and 28. We now turn to these five passages for a more detailed examination.

1:1, '*To the church of the Thessalonians in God the Father and the Lord Jesus Christ.*' There are many assemblies of the Thessalonians (*ekklēsiai Thessalonikeōn*), political and religious, but only one that gathers 'in God the Father and the Lord Jesus Christ'. This assembly, this church, is rooted in the God who is identified as Father, and in Jesus Christ who is confessed as Lord. Accordingly, these references in 1:1 serve not only as identifiers over against pagan Thessalonica, viz., that this *ekklēsia* (an appellation that had not yet existed in the vocabulary of Christians) is Christian, but also as a liturgical reminder that they are the elect of God through this Jesus whom they call Lord and are now, because of this event, in a new, living relationship with God. This solidarity between the believer and the Lord is reinforced by the references to the dead *en Christō* in 4:16. Given the total context of the *en* references in 1 Thessalonians,[11] Deissmann can be followed when he suggests that already here, at the beginning of this letter, Paul is suggesting that Christians are united 'within the pneumatic body of Christ'.[12] Thus we are inclined to see an incorporative force in the *en*, and not simply an instrumental one which understands the preposition as merely indicating that the Christian community was brought into existence by God the Father and the Lord Jesus Christ. Paul, indeed, given the overall goals of this letter, wishes to remind these Thessalonian Christians that they are participants in Christ's risen life and are members of his church. While recognising that the frequency of incorporative language is more characteristic of the later letters, we cannot overlook that these and other incorporative phrases are already present in 1 Thessalonians as, for example, the reference to living 'with him' (*syn auto*), whether awake or asleep, in 5:10.

[11] See 1 Thess. 2:14, 3:8, 4:16, 5:12.
[12] G. Adolf Deissmann, *Die neutestamentliche Formel 'in Christo Jesu'* (Marburg: N. G. Elwert, 1892).

1:3, '. . . *remembering before God the Father your work of faith and labour of love and steadfastness of hope in our Lord Jesus Christ.*' The Apostle lifts before the God who is present among the believers the quintessential gifts which he has given to his people whom he has chosen, and he especially reminds his audience that their steadfastness of hope is therefore always a hope grounded in the gift 'of our Lord Jesus Christ'. The Greek text reads, literally, 'of our Lord Jesus Christ', and it is best to take this as an objective genitive after 'hope', which is a key theme in this communication. Those 'in Christ' have placed their hope in him, a hope that will be realised at his *parousia*. Precisely because their hope is grounded in and will be fulfilled in Christ they need 'not grieve as others do who have no hope' (4:13).

5:9, '*For God has not destined us for wrath, but to obtain salvation through our Lord Jesus Christ, who died for us . . .*' Even though the context is eschatological and one that looks forward to the *parousia*, the prepositional phrase 'through our Lord Jesus Christ' looks back to the death of Jesus as the foundation of the promised eschatological hope of salvation. Although the phrase 'who died for us' is likely pre-Pauline, Paul has received this tradition and made it his own.

5:23, '*May the God of peace himself sanctify you wholly; and may your spirit and soul and body be kept sound and blameless at the coming of our Lord Jesus Christ.*' As in 1:3 and in certain other references to the term 'Lord' or 'Lord Jesus', the full reference here to 'our Lord Jesus Christ' refers to the *parousia*, a major theme in this first Pauline letter.

5:28, '*The grace of our Lord Jesus Christ be with you.*' This farewell greeting relates back not only to the prayer formula of 5:23 but also to the opening epistolary greeting in 1:1. As a result of this communication, the Thessalonians' understanding of 'grace' will have been immeasurably deepened and enhanced, particularly by enriched understanding of hope and the relationship of both the living and the dead to the *parousia*.

These five reverences to 'Lord Jesus Christ' are indeed extensive in their range of meaning. They are anchored in the promised eschatological hope of Jesus' *parousia*, a hope anchored in his death and a hope in which the Thessalonian Christians already participate. As one would expect, this christological title overlaps with those we will next examine, 'Lord' and 'Lord Jesus'.

Lord and Lord Jesus

Paul uses the christological titles 'Lord' and 'Lord Jesus' primarily with regard to five areas of concern: suffering, eschatology, being in the Lord, ethics/exhortation and the gospel as the word of the Lord. Let us review briefly these five contexts in which 'Lord' and 'Lord Jesus' function as one way to gain access to the theological themes present in 1 Thessalonians.

Suffering   Although the use of the titles 'Lord' and 'Lord Jesus' in connection with suffering is minimal, occurring only in 1:6 and 2:15, these are indeed powerful references. The Apostle reminds the Thessalonians that their situation of suffering is not unique: Paul, their Lord and the churches in Judea have had to deal with rejection. It is in this sense that they 'became imitators of us and of the Lord, for you received the word in much affliction [*thlipsis*], with joy inspired by the Holy Spirit'. Not only have Paul and the Lord served as such an example (*typos*; 1:7) but the Thessalonians themselves have become examples to the believers in Macedonia and Achaia. 1 Thess. 2:15 ('killed both the Lord Jesus ...') functions in a similar context of suffering and imitation. Thus the references to the suffering of the Lord himself, of Paul and of other Christian congregations serve as a fundamental encouragement for the Thessalonian Christians, who find themselves in a difficult situation. Some are certainly pondering whether continued fidelity to the gospel that Paul preached is worth the risk.

Eschatology   All of the christological references in this category (2:19; 3:13; 4:15, 16, 17; 5:2) refer explicitly to the *parousia*. A similar reference to the *parousia* was also encountered in 5:9–10 with regard to the title the 'Lord Jesus Christ'. There the 'Lord Jesus Christ' is described as the one who died for our salvation and who will appear again at the final consummation of history, and there it is emphasised that whether we are awake or asleep this coming Lord is present both now and at the future judgment. Such strong accent on the *parousia* will shape the christology of 1 Thessalonians.

Paul's application of this theme to the Thessalonian situation allows us to recognise why he does not discuss in this, his earliest, letter such concepts as body, flesh or death or, for that matter, life, sin, freedom and law, not to mention the absence of words having the root *dik;*(righteousness/justification)[13] or *staur-* (cross/crucify). What the Apostle does discuss, and with much frequency, is *parousia* and the relationship of *parousia* to sanctification (*hagiasmos*, 4:3, 4, 7 and *hagiazein*, 5:23). For those who have been elected by God, sanctification is the process of being made holy that will result in salvation rather than wrath (5:8–9). This is why he emphasises the necessity for being 'blameless' (3:13, 5:23). Thus Paul uses the concept sanctification synonymously with the term 'to serve God' and then further applies this to the concrete situation in Thessalonica in 4:1–8 through his discussion of 'licentiousness' (*porneia*, 4:3) and 'transgression' (*pleonexia*, 4:6). Earlier we noted that the response to God's election of these Christians was not only 'to wait' but also 'to serve a living and true God' (1:9). In other words, there is a very keen relationship between eschatology and ethics in 1 Thessalonians; in fact, it seems clear that the intimate relationship between eschatology and ethics is at the heart of Paul's consolation and encouragement.

Being in the Lord   The christological phrase 'in the Lord' is used three times in 1 Thessalonians: 3:8; 4:1 and 5:12. The reference

---

[13] Except *dikaios* in 2:10, to be discussed below.

in 3:8, 'for now we live, if you stand fast in the Lord', appears to have more in common with such incorporative phrases as 'in Christ' (2:14; 4:16; 5:18) and 'in the Holy Spirit' (1:5) than with the primarily instrumental/representational usages in 4:1 and 5:12. These latter references occur in a more specifically ethical context and we will discuss them in the section that follows. In 3:8 the phrase 'in the Lord' has more the sense of incorporation into a Spirit-led existence and participation in a community guided by the Lord.

The terms 'in the Lord' (as used in 3:8), 'in Christ' and 'in the Holy Spirit' are derived from a pre-Pauline baptismal tradition in which the emphasis on salvation is accentuated. Yet for Paul these concepts are embedded in his manner of seeing and interpreting things apocalyptically and their meanings can only be derived from that perspective. We have already encountered the use of 'in Christ' in 1 Thess. 4:16. There it affirms that the communion with Christ inaugurated at baptism will not conclude with death but will continue right up to the final meeting with the Lord at the *parousia*. Here, too, Paul takes the original soteriological-ontological sense of 'in Christ' and links it specifically to the eschatological hope that he is attempting to communicate to the downcast Thessalonian Christians.

This new state of being 'in Christ' becomes the basis for Paul's ecclesiology, as we will discuss in greater detail further on. *Ekklēsia* means to be constituted in Christ (1:1) in anticipation of the *parousia*. In this sense Paul's use of 'in Christ' in 2:14 ('For you brethren became imitators of the churches of God in Christ Jesus which are in Judea') can carry a broader ecclesiological meaning. In this latter reference the imitation of Christ in terms of suffering in persecution is emphasised and in 3:8 the motif of holding firm to the end (to 'stand fast in the Lord') is accentuated. What allows one to be 'in Christ' or 'in the Lord' and to remain 'in Christ', or 'in the Lord', particularly during adverse conditions, is the working of God's Spirit. Spirit, in the sense of God's Spirit, occurs in 1 Thess. 1:5 and 6, 4:8 and 5:19. It is not only a sign of God's election and a source of one's soteriological and ontological placement 'in Christ', but also, and especially, a wellspring of joy in the midst of suffering. Since the Spirit continues to be given to them in the present (note the use of the present participle *didonta* in 4:8), it serves as the advocate and sustainer of the Christian congregation from its beginning, in and through persecution, right up to the *parousia*. Therefore Paul warns in 5:19 that the Spirit dare not be quenched.

In various ways, then, we can observe how Paul's *parousia*-hope allows the Apostle both to actualise and to transform the christological tradition he receives in ways that are appropriate to the crisis in Thessalonica.

Ethics/Exhortation   The coming Lord is present now not only as comforter but also as the Lord who exercises sovereign authority and who expects fidelity from all who bear his name. Thus the term 'Lord' or 'Lord Jesus' is used several times in a context of ethical exhortation (3:11, 12; 4:1, 2, 6; 5:27). Paul uses the phrase 'in [*en*] the Lord Jesus' at 4:1 and 5:12. In both 4:1 ('Finally, brethren, we beseech you and exhort you [*parakaloumen*] in the Lord Jesus, that as you learned from us how you ought to live and to please God, just as you are doing, you do so more and more') and 5:12 ('to respect those who labour among you and are over you in the Lord and admonish you ...') 'in the Lord' functions primarily instrumentally (i.e., as authoritative representative) and within a wider context of ethical exhortation. Having said this, it is important, nevertheless, to emphasise that one should not exclude the locative, incorporative dimension from 4:1 and 5:12 in the same way that one should not overlook the ethical context in the incorporative use of 3:8. In general, one may suggest cautiously that the instrumental/representational sense of 'in the Lord' (as in 4:1 and 5:12) may imply more the situation 'in which Jesus demands the obedience of his people ...' whereas the incorporative sense of 'in Christ' (as in 4:16) or 'in the Lord' (as in 3:8) places the emphasis more on the new community

achieved by the death of Jesus.[14] For 1 Thessalonians such a
distinction is likely.

At 4:2 Paul employs the phrase 'through [*dia*] the Lord
Jesus' (also at 5:9 with the full title 'Lord Jesus Christ'). Does
this use of *dia* differ significantly from the instrumental/
representational use of *en* discussed above? To find a satisfac-
tory interpretation for the phrase 'through [*dia*] the Lord Jesus'
in 4:2 ('For you know what instructions we gave you through
[*dia*] the Lord Jesus') is not made easy by the lack of consensus
in the literature. Yet the simplest interpretation may also be
the most likely, especially when one recalls that *dia* used with a
genitive of person often refers to the initiator of an action.
Therefore a probable meaning of this verse is that Paul gave
these instructions not by his authority but by the authority of
the Lord Jesus – i.e., they originate with the Lord Jesus. This
usage, then, is virtually identical to the instrumental/represen-
tational use of 'in the Lord'. What instructions does the Apostle
have in mind?

Earlier we attempted to indicate the importance of the
religious cults of Thessalonica for an understanding of the
social environment in which the Pauline congregation finds
itself. Even a general knowledge of the cults in Thessalonica
allows us to understand with more precision such references as
1 Thess. 1:9, 'you turned to God from idols', or 1 Thess. 4:5,
'not in the passion of lust like heathen who do not know God'. 1
Thess. 4:1–9 is filled with what we might refer to as 'high
density' ethical language and is also likely to be better understood against this broader background. The most frequent use
of *peripateō* (to walk) in Paul is to be found in the Corinthian
letters (1 Cor. 3:3, 7:17, 2 Cor. 4:2, 5:7, 10:2, 12:18). The
specific reference 'to please God' (*areskein theō*) is found only in
Rom. 8:8. The reference to 'instructions' (*parangelias*) is found
only here in the Pauline letters, and the verbal form, besides in
the Thessalonian letters themselves, only in 1 Cor. 7:10 and
11:1. The only other reference to 'the will of God' (*thelēma tou*

---

[14] I. Howard Marshall, *1 and 2 Thessalonians*, *NCeB* (Grand Rapids: Eerdmans, 1983),
    104. See further our discussion about this distinction on page 59 and in '2 Thessalo-
    nians', pages 97–98.

theou) in a specific ethical context of 'doing the will of God' is in Rom. 12:2. To 'disregard' (*athetōn*) God who gives you the Holy Spirit has no exact parallel anywhere in the writings of Paul, with the possible exception of Gal. 2:21, where he talks about setting aside the grace of God. Further, Paul does not often use the full title 'the Holy Spirit' except for the most solemn occasions such as in Rom. 5:5; 9:1; 14:17 and 15:13, 16 and 19, or when he uses the term in a catalogue (2 Cor. 6:4) or in a benediction (2 Cor. 13:14). Finally, the reference to 'unchastity' (*porneia*) is again found only in the Corinthian correspondence (1 Cor. 5:1; 6:13, 18; 2 Cor. 12:21), except for its use in the catalogue of vices in Gal. 5:19. All of this suggests that Paul is, in fact, dealing with a situation of grave immorality, not too dissimilar to the cultic temptations found in Corinth. Thus, Paul's severe warnings in this section, using the weightiest authorities he possibly can, is intended to distinguish the behaviour of the Thessalonians as Christians from that of their former pagan life which continues to find ritual expression in the various cults of the city.

Given this background and context, can we suggest a meaning for the word *to skeuos* (literally, vessel) in 1 Thess. 4:4? Taking into consideration the ambiguity of the reference and the intensity of the scholarly discussion, as well as the cultic backgrounds just discussed, it is difficult to agree with John Eadie's conclusion: 'One may dismiss at once the more special meanings assigned to it, as *membrum virile*.'[15] This seems difficult to sustain, since both Antistius Vetus[16] and Aelianus[17] use the term *skeuos* as referring to the *membrum virile* and, given the strong phallic symbolism in the cults of Dionysus, Cabirus and Samothrace, such a reference is hardly surprising. The additional verb *ktaomai* which Paul uses would suggest the phrase means something like 'to gain control over the *skeuos*'.

---

[15] John Eadie, *Commentary on the Greek Text of the Epistles of Paul to the Thessalonians* (New York: Macmillan, 1877), 127.

[16] First century AD in *Anthologia graeca* 16, 243, 4; Walter Bauer, *A Greek-English Lexicon of the New Testament and Other Early Christian Literature* (ed. W. F. Arndt, F. W. Gingrich and F. W. Danker) (Chicago: University of Chicago Press, 1979), 754.

[17] AD 170–235 *De natura animalium* 17, 11; Arndt-Gingrich, 754.

The specific meaning of this term would surely not be lost on the Thessalonian audience nor its wider meaning of 'gaining control over the body with regard to sexual matters'. The reference to *pragmati* (matter) in 4:6 would certainly refer back to this intended meaning.

Finally, one should not overlook the obvious parallels between the following texts and the mystery cults: 1 Thess. 5:5–7 with its reference to darkness and drunkenness and 1 Thess. 5:19–22, where Paul explicitly urges his hearers not 'to quench' the Spirit but 'to test' it. Quite clearly the Apostle does not wish the gift of the Spirit to be confused with the excesses of the Dionysiac mysteries; for Paul the Spirit does not lead to 'Bacchic frenzies' but to joy precisely in the context of suffering.

Word of the Lord   For the sake of completeness in this survey of christological titles in 1 Thessalonians, we need to mention two other references to 'Lord': 1:8 and 4:15. Both are used in the context of 'the word of the Lord'. Since both of these usages are examined elsewhere in our analysis of 1 Thessalonians, we refer the reader to those sections.[18]

Before reviewing the remaining christological titles, let us briefly summarise our observations concerning the several variations of the title 'Lord' in 1 Thessalonians. In all cases they are anchored in the historical person Jesus, his life, suffering, death and resurrection. He is present in the midst of the Thessalonian church as the living Lord whose words and exhortations are authoritative until the consummation of all things and the complete implementation of salvation at the time of his *parousia*. In its most *general* sense, the title Lord does appear to express a mystical presence of Christ in the church, through whose activity the church exists.

Jesus Christ, Christ Jesus and Son
We have already had opportunity to note the references to Jesus in the pre-Pauline traditions cited in 1:10 and 4:14. There is, however, a second reference to Jesus in 4:14 and one which

---

[18] See pp. 51–53 and pp. 39–41.

presents certain problems for translation: *kai ho theos tous koimē-thentas dia tou Iēsou axei syn autō.* The issue is whether *dia tou Iēsou* goes with *koimēthentes* which precedes this phrase or with *axei* which follows it. If we understand the structure of the sentence in the latter sense, the translation would read: 'For since we believe that Jesus died and rose again, even so, through Jesus, God will bring with him those who have died.' But, if the *dia tou Iēsou* is to be taken with the second half, as this translation suggests, then there is an element of redundancy in the *syn autō* phrase. Pobee, however, is to be followed in reading *hoi koimē-thentes dia tou Christou,* that is, seeing *dia tou Iēsou* connected with *hoi koimēthentes.*[19] He understands the *dia* as expressing atten-dant circumstance, viz., those who have died on account of faith in Jesus. In this case one would make the following translation: 'For since we believe that Jesus died and rose again, even so, God will bring with him those who have died on account of Jesus.' Pobee's conclusion with regard to this phrase is that it 'refers to the Christians who died in their zeal for Jesus as was demonstrated by their patient endurance of persecution, before the *parousia* of Christ. The attendant circumstances of the death were the persecutions raging in the church of Thessa-lonica'.[20] This is possible and it fits nicely with our overall conclusions concerning the Thessalonian crisis. As attractive as this proposal is, however, one should, finally, not discount the possibility that *dia* may simply refer to those who were 'in relationship with' Christ at the time of their death.

THE CHURCH AS A RESPONSE TO THE GOSPEL

The Spirit-filled gospel

In 1:8 Paul writes: 'For not only has the word of the Lord sounded forth from you in Macedonia and Achaia, but your

[19] John S. Pobee, *Persecution and Martyrdom in the Theology of Paul,* JSNTSup 6 (Sheffield: JSOT Press, 1985), 113–14. Other exegetes joining *dia tou Iēsou* to *tous koimēthentes* include Ephraim, Chrysostom, Calvin, Lightfoot, von Dobschütz, Dibe-lius and Frame. This is not to suggest, however, that their understanding of *dia tou Iēsou* is identical.
[20] Ibid., 113–14.

faith in God has gone forth everywhere, so that we need not say anything.' Here the phrase 'the word of the Lord' simply means the gospel (see 2:9), which Paul can also describe as 'the word of God' in 2:13. Since he had referred to the Thessalonians' imitation of himself and the Lord in suffering just a few verses before (1:6), he may well continue using the term 'Lord' not only as a reference to the risen One to whom the church is responsible now and on the last day but also as a reminder that he whom they declare as Lord is also the One who was despised and suffered at the hands of human beings. Despite the difficulty of their situation, the gospel, especially because it is the word of the suffering and risen Lord, has burst forth from Thessalonica in such a powerful way that the Thessalonians have become an example (*typos*, 1:7) to all the believers in Macedonia and Achaia. Perhaps Paul is wishing to suggest that they were not only a model in suffering but also, precisely because of their willingness to suffer, an example, an actualisation, even if imperfectly, of that hope which is present in their midst now, although its consummation still lies in the future.

Even though we have mentioned this fact previously, it needs to be repeated in this context: given the brevity of 1 Thessalonians, it is at first surprising to realise that the term 'gospel' (*euangēlion*) is used six times (1:5; 2:2, 4, 8, 9; 3:2) and its synonym, 'word' (*logos*), three times (1:6, 8; 2:13). This is a rather large number when compared with, for example, appearances of these terms in Romans.[21] In 1 Thessalonians Paul makes the following assertions about the gospel as word of God:

1 that the gospel was proclaimed in Thessalonica, not only in word, but also in power and in the Holy Spirit and in full conviction (1:5), i.e., it is a performative word and it is actively at work (*energeitai*) in and among the believers (2:13); as a generating centre it is foundational for the existence of the church.

2 that the Thessalonian Christians received the word in the midst of affliction (1:6). In so doing they became imitators of

---

[21] *Euangelion* occurs nine times in Romans (1:1, 9, 16; 2:16; 10:16; 11:28; 15:16, 19; 16:25) and *logos*, specifically as 'word of God', appears only once (9:6).

Paul and his associates, as well as of the Lord. In addition, by receiving the word in the midst of affliction they received it with joy inspired by the Holy Spirit (1:6); this in itself is a sign of hope even if the Thessalonian Christians had not fully recognised it as such. Paul also acknowledges this existential situation when he asserts in 2:2 that he declared to them 'the gospel of God in the face of great opposition'.

3 that the word has proceeded out of Thessalonica to all the believers in Macedonia and in Achaia. As a result, whether intentionally or not, the Thessalonian church became a missionary base for the gospel (1:8).

4 that this gospel has been entrusted to Paul in a special way by God (2:4).

5 that this gospel is something which is 'shared' by Paul with the Thessalonians and it is proclaimed without burden to them because Paul 'worked night and day' (2:8–9). In other words, he did not make demands on his new converts, even though he was an apostle.

6 that Timothy is God's servant in (*en*) the gospel of Christ. It is Paul's hope as well as Timothy's that when the Christian community in Thessalonica is more thoroughly rooted in the gospel the result will be a firmer establishment, encouragement and stabilisation of their faith in the midst of their current afflictions.

The gospel of faith, love and hope

In 1 Thessalonians Paul describes the central content of the gospel in terms of election. As a further specification of this gospel of election, Paul uses the triadic formulation 'faith, love and hope' in 1 Thess. 1:3 and 5:8. While reviewing each element of this triadic formula separately, we need to remember their intimate coinherence within this letter and the other Pauline letters as well. The discussion that follows, then, will allow us the opportunity to place 1 Thessalonians within the broader context of the entire Pauline corpus, a theme that will be developed more fully in chapter 3.

Faith

Paul uses this term as one who grew up as a Pharisee and he is using it to a congregation in Thessalonica partially composed of Hellenistic Jews and 'God-fearers'. The New Testament and the Greek Old Testament express the understanding of faith principally with two terms (*pistis, pisteuein*), which are related to the primary Old Testament verb 'to be true' or 'be trustworthy' (Hebrew *'āman*). Although the Old Testament concept is considerably broader than this term and its cognates, yet *'āman* remains the most profound expression to describe faith in the Old Testament.

In the apostle Paul one finds the broadest and most profound articulation of the Old Testament understanding of faith in early Christianity. Faith has as its object God (1 Thess. 1:8) and results in a turning away from idols so as 'to serve a living and true God' (1 Thess. 1:9). The Old Testament theme of faithfulness is dominant. Since God has called the Thessalonians they are no longer to be involved in idolatry and must avoid the continuous temptation to apostasy. Further, for the Christian Paul, God's salvific manifestation towards those whom he has called (1 Thess. 1:4) is through the death and resurrection of Jesus Christ (1 Thess. 4:14). This act of God in Christ is proclaimed (Rom. 10:17: 'So faith comes from what is heard, and what is heard comes by the preaching of Christ'; also 1 Thess. 1:8, 2:2) and is received by faith (1 Thess. 1:8, Rom. 3:25); this faith rests in the calling and power of God (1 Thess. 1:4, 1 Cor. 2:5), who has acted in human history. Those who have received the good news of God's act in Christ, namely, the gospel, are called 'believers' (1 Thess. 1:7). There is only one gospel (1 Cor. 15:11) and its goal is salvation (1 Thess. 5:9, 1 Cor. 1:21); its security does not rest in political propaganda (1 Thess. 5:3) but in complete trust of God.

For Paul the concept of faith is a dynamic one. Thus, he can refer to the 'activity of faith' (1 Thess. 1:23), an activity that manifests itself in love (Gal. 5:6 'faith working through love'; also 1 Thess. 1:3; 3:6; 4:9, 10; 5:8). Faith involves 'progress' (Phil. 1:25); it is not something static, captured once for all, but involves striving (Phil. 1:27); it increases (2 Cor. 10:15) and it is an energy at work in believers (1 Thess. 2:13). Particularly this last reference emphasises that the origin, continued activity and future consummation of faith rest solely in God's initiative; they do not arise from the desires of the human heart. Since faith is not a static possession, Paul urges that faith be established (1 Thess. 3:2) and made firm (1 Cor. 16:13, 2 Cor. 1:24), for it is possible not only to have deficiencies in faith (1 Thess. 3:10, Rom. 14:1) but also to believe in vain (1 Cor. 15:2, Rom. 11:20). Essential for Paul's understanding of faith is the conviction that God assigns to each the measure of faith he wishes (Rom. 12:3, 6; 1 Cor. 12:9). To the Thessalonian church it was given with such generosity that Paul can proudly assert that 'not only has the word of the Lord sounded forth from you in Macedonia and Achaia, but your faith in God has gone forth everywhere, so that we need not say anything' (1 Thess. 1:8). Yet no matter what that measure of faith is, the obedience of faith is expected from all (1 Thess. 4:1–8; Rom. 1:5, 16:16).

Paul refers to faith in the context of the triadic formula 'faith, hope and love' (1 Thess. 1:3, 5:8, 1 Cor. 13:13). On the one hand, faith must be active in love; without love faith is empty. On the other hand, faith must be constituted in hope, as hope is grounded in faith, so that faith recognises that the first fruits of God's promises manifested in the death and resurrection of Christ, which is part of the content of faith (1 Thess. 4:14: 'we believe that Jesus died and rose again'), will be fulfilled on the last day (1 Thess. 5:9; Gal. 5:5; Rom. 6:8, 15:13). The specific hope of faith is rooted in the resurrection of Christ as an anticipation of the fulfilment of the last day (1 Thess. 4:13–18; 1 Cor. 15:14, 17; 2 Cor. 4:14). Yet this faith that is received in baptism (note the baptismal context of 1 Thess. 5:1–11 and Gal. 3:27–28) and allows one entrance into the church (1 Thess. 1:1) is a faith that has as its model the suffering and death of Jesus (1 Thess. 1:6, 2:15). Therefore during this earthly sojourn faith may well be called forth to a cruciform existence (1 Thess. 3:1–5, Rom. 8:18, Phil. 1:29). Further, this new act of God in Christ received by faith involves new existence not only for the believer but for the church itself (1 Thess. 4:5, 9–12; 4:13; 5:5; in Romans, it is expanded to include the promise of a new existence for the world, Rom. 8:18–25).

Love
In order to understand Paul's perspective on love, it is important to remember that not only in 1 Thess. 1:3 and 5:8, but also in 1 Cor. 13:13 and Gal. 5:5–6, love is linked with faith and hope. Love is a possibility only because God has elected those who are 'in Christ' (1 Thess. 1:4: 'For we know, brethren beloved by God, that he has chosen you') and because the believer has responded to God's salvific act in the death and resurrection of Christ with faith (Rom. 5:8: 'But God shows his love for us in that while we were yet sinners Christ died for us'; see Gal. 2:20). Love is given to the believer by God as a gift – they have been 'God-taught' as a result of the performative word at work in the believers (1 Thess. 4:9) – to be exercised in the present (1 Thess. 4:10) as a sign of the future consummation of that new creation that God has begun in Christ, the fulfilment of which is expected in hope. This relationship of love to hope is also emphasised in Rom. 5:5: hope 'does not disappoint us, because God's love has been poured into our hearts through the Holy Spirit which has been given us'.

Love is the primary term describing the result of faith both for the believer and the community in Christ. Because Christ has died, the Holy Spirit has given the believer (1 Thess. 1:6) the gift of love and joy. Paul can write to the Corinthians that the 'love of Christ controls us' (2 Cor. 2:4). Paul is emphatic that love does not originate in the human heart. It is not a human possibility, it is a divine gift. It is Christ who now lives in the believer (1 Thess. 2:13, Gal. 2:20); therefore the believer must actualise this love of Christ even 'more and more' (1 Thess. 4:10). Faith works through love (Gal. 5:6) and it must increase and abound (1 Thess. 4:12). Love must be concerned not with self-elevation and boasting, but with the needs of the body of Christ, its weak members as well as its leadership (1 Thess. 5:12–15).

Hope

The broadest use of the word for hope (*elpis*) and the most developed concept of hope in the New Testament is found in the Pauline letters. Already in 1 Thessalonians hope is referred to four times (1:3, 2:19, 4:13, 5:8), twice in the triadic formula of 'faith, love, and hope' (1:3, 5:8). Paul, who is so affectionately bonded to this community of Christians (2:19: 'For what is our hope or joy or crown of boasting before our Lord Jesus at his coming? Is it not you?'), warns them not to 'grieve as others do who have no hope' (4:13; see also the deutero-Pauline text in Eph. 2:12) and then proceeds to relate, as we have already noted, their confession that Jesus died and rose to the problem of those among them who had just recently died.

The fact that hope appears as part of the triadic formula not only in 1 Thessalonians but also in 1 Cor. 13:13, and, somewhat more loosely, in Gal. 5:5–6, suggests that it belongs to that process of new life in Christ that begins with faith and is fulfilled at the consummated salvation event of the last day.[22] Thus hope emanates from faith and it reflects the guarantee (*arrabōn*, 2 Cor. 5:5) that what God has begun in Christ will be brought to consummation on the last day. The 'good courage' (2 Cor. 5:6) nurtured by hope as a gift of the Spirit allows the believer to actualise faith through love (Gal. 5:6). The problem with the Thessalonians is that hope had become uncoupled from faith; it is this component which is 'lacking' in their faith (1 Thess. 3:1–10, especially 10). Basic for Paul is the understanding that hope provides the essential linkage between the already/not-yet of the salvation event in Christ: hope assures the believers, provided they remain faithful to the kindness of Christ (Rom. 11:22, 1 Cor. 15:2), that what has begun in baptism will be completed when they meet the Lord on the last day (1 Thess. 4:13–18).

The Apostle's perspective with regard to hope in 1 Thessalonians is foundational for what is said in his later correspondence. For the later Paul, writing over against different situations

[22] See further Karl P. Donfried, *The Dynamic Word* (San Francisco: Harper & Row, 1981), 50–64.

and polemical challenges, the differentiation between justification (a term not used in 1 Thessalonians) and salvation is fundamental to his understanding of hope: justification marks the beginning of the new life in Christ and sustains it to the end; salvation is the consummation of the gifts already experienced as a foretaste in baptism and in the living of the new life in Christ. This is precisely the point in Rom. 5:1–3, a most crucial text. What the Christian has obtained in this life is *access*, not completed entrance, to God's grace, and the Apostle rejoices in the 'hope of sharing the glory of God' at the future consummation. This confidence is already expressed in 1 Thess. 5:9: 'For God has not destined us for wrath, but to obtain salvation through our Lord Jesus Christ'. A sign that the believer has access to this grace now is that 'you yourselves have been God-taught to love one another' (1 Thess. 4:9), a theme which is reiterated in Rom. 5:5: 'God's love has been poured into our hearts through the Holy Spirit which has been given to us'. Thus Paul can assert that the ones in Christ who have 'the first fruits of the Spirit groan inwardly as we wait for adoption as sons, the redemption of our bodies.[23] For in this hope we were saved' (Rom. 8:23–4). Rom. 8:18–25 is also an important text, for it shows, as all the authentic Pauline references to salvation do, that salvation has a future orientation and is not yet consummated (see, for example, Rom. 5:9–10 and Phil. 3:7–14). As Paul develops the theme of hope in the letters which follow 1 Thessalonians he demonstrates that God's revelation in Jesus Christ affects not only individuals, but creation itself which God has subjected in hope 'because the creation itself will be set free from its bondage to decay and obtain the glorious liberty of the children of God' (Rom. 8:19–21).

The gospel as the foundation of the church

Some interesting surprises await the careful reader of 1 Thess. 1:1 'Paul, Silvanus and Timothy, to the church of the Thessalonians in God the Father and the Lord Jesus Christ: Grace to

---

[23] Compare here 1 Thess. 5:23.

you and peace.' First, the *nomen gentilicum*[24] is used in address-ing the church[25] rather than its geographical location as, for example, in 1 Cor. 1:2, 'To the church of God which is at Corinth.' Second, the congregation's relationship to God is described in the dative (*en theō patri*), perhaps to underscore their separation from false gods (1:9) and to emphasise their new relationship to God through Jesus. Otherwise Paul does not use this unusual phrase 'in God';[26] there is, however, a remarkably similar reference in Acts 17:27–8. In a context about seeking and finding God, it is written: 'Yet he is not far from each one of us, for "In him [*en autō*] we live and move and have our being."' In speaking to the Thessalonian Christians about being 'in God' and 'in Christ', the Apostle wishes to accentuate their new relationship with Christ as a result of the proclamation of the gospel.

In 1 Thessalonians the followers of Jesus are described as a 'church' (*ekklēsia*), as a 'called out' community, for the first time. They are the elect because the church is called out by God through the Spirit-filled gospel; as a result God gives 'his Holy Spirit to you' (plural) (4:8). This is why Paul can state that this 'called out' community is '*in* God the Father and *in* the Lord Jesus Christ' (1:1). This new state of affairs is possible because 'Christ died for us' (5:9–10) and because of their faith (1:8, 2:13). Most often Paul refers to this new relationship *in* God and *in* Christ simply as *en Christō* (2:14, 3:8, 4:16, 5:12). As we stated above, we see in the use of *en Christō* an *incorporative* meaning and not simply as instrumental one. In other words, this phrase means not only that the Christian community was brought into existence by God the Father and the Lord Jesus Christ through the preached word, but that there also exists a mystical and spiritual union with the Father and the Son made real through participation in the church as the eschatological 'called out' community which waits for the last day.

---

[24] The name proper to a particular Roman *gens* (people).

[25] Several possible reasons have been suggested in the commentaries. Not to be overlooked is the inscription ΘΕΣΣΑΛΟΝΙΚΕΩΝ (of the Thessalonians) found on both the Augustus and Cabrius coins. Is Paul consciously attempting to differentiate the Christian community from both the civic and religious cults in Thessalonica?

[26] Note the different uses of the phrase in Rom. 2:17 and 5:11.

The context for Christian living and learning is provided for in this 'called out' community. In it those who are God-taught (4:9) receive God's sustaining and nurturing will and sanctification as they wait to inherit the kingdom (2:12). Although awaiting the future consummation, these believers are cognisant that this sanctified life must be lived out in the present; as members of this new, eschatological community of the end-time they must become exemplary in their love for one another. They are to build up one another as well as to engage in manual work because of the outsiders (4:9–12). There must not only be a respect for the opinion of those outside the community, but there must be a healthy distance from them. Those outside of the 'called out' community are described in a variety of ways: as idolaters (1:9–10), as those who oppose the gospel (2:14, 16), as those who do not know God (4:5) and as those who are without hope and, as a result, grieve for those who have died (4:13).

The church of the Thessalonians is in relationship to the Father, to the Son and to the Holy Spirit (1:1–5), to other churches (1:8, 2:14) and to the Apostle who first declared to them the gospel of God. Paul not only gives thanks for this community (1:2, 2:13, 3:9) but also prays for, consoles, exhorts, remembers and agonises over them (1:2–13, 3:1). The intensity of the relationship between the founder and the believers is due to the fact that through their baptism they belong to one and the same eschatological family. Family structures, although transformed in Christ, are basic to the internal structure of the community and the community's relationship to the Apostle. Because this is the case Paul can employ traditional kinship patterns in his association with the Thessalonian family; he is in solidarity with them as brother, father, nurse, orphan, or beloved.

Although family structures lie at the heart of this new family in Christ, can anything further be said about the structures of authority within this Thessalonian fellowship in Christ? Even though Paul does not accentuate the 'demands' (1:7) that Silvanus, Timothy and he might have made of the Thessalonians, and even though he uses the phrase 'apostles of Christ'

(1:7) in the plural, which certainly is not intended to emphasise his individual apostolic authority, there can be little doubt
about Paul's authoritative relationship to this congregation
with whom he has such an affectionate relationship. Paul has
been 'approved by God' and 'entrusted with the gospel' (2:4);
he can be gentle, consoling and encouraging, yet he can also
admonish and adjure (*enorkizō*) 'by the Lord' (5:27).

As Paul has encouraged, exhorted and cared for the Thessalonian Christians, so they must care for one another. Specifically, they must continue to 'encourage [*parakaleite*] and build
one another up [*oikodomeite*], just as you are doing' (5:11).
'Building up' will become a key metaphor for Paul's understanding of the church in 1 Corinthians (8:1; 10:23; 14:3–5, 12,
17, 26 and elsewhere). To 'build up' the church is for the
believers to encourage one another to grow in sanctification,
i.e., to produce spiritual maturity and stability, a theme that
runs throughout this final part of the letter. But such a task
requires leadership and guidance and it is to this subject that
Paul turns in 5:12–13: 'But we beseech you, brethren, to
respect those who labour among you and are over you [*proistamenous*] in the Lord and admonish you, and to esteem them
very highly in love because of their work.'

From these verses it is apparent that there was leadership in
this Thessalonian church, whatever form it may have taken,
and that it is a leadership 'in the Lord'. It is a position not for
self-aggrandisement or power, but one of service in the Lord
who had suffered on behalf of all. This becomes the model for
the kind of influence they are to exercise. These persons
'labour' on behalf of the others, they are 'over you' and they
are 'those who ... admonish you'. Harnack argued that these
persons who 'toil, govern and admonish' are specifically 'office
bearers of the congregation' who presumably had an 'appoint-
ment'.[27] Although this is an overstatement of the evidence, that
the *proistamenoi* are more than helpers is strongly suggested
by the inclusion of the function of 'warning' or 'exhorting'

---

[27] A. von Harnack, 'ΚΟΠΟΣ', *ZNW* 27 (1928), 1–10. See further the positive evaluation of Harnack's position given by E. Earle Ellis, *Prophecy and Hermeneutic* (Tübingen: Mohr, 1978), 5–7.

(*nouthetountas*) among their responsibilities. Horsley's examination of an inscription from Ephesus (ca. 162–4) that uses the
term *proistēmi* suggests 'the ease with which Graeco-Roman
urban dwellers accepted the compatibility of the two notions of
benevolent actions and structured authority'.[28] Also not irrele-
vant to his discussion is the reference to this same verb in 1
Tim. 3:4–5, where the role of the *episkopos* (bishop) is being
reviewed: 'he must manage his own household well, keeping
his children submissive and respectful in every way, for if a
man does not know how to manage [*prostēnai*] his own household, how can he care for God's church?' Given the kinship
and familial dimensions of Paul's relationship to the Thessalonian congregation, this role of leadership within that family
should come as no surprise. Paul served as both benefactor and
authoritative leader to this new family in Christ and it is
essential that these functions continue in his absence. As these
responsibilities are carried out by the leaders in their midst the
Thessalonian Christians are to esteem them 'very highly in
love' (5:12).

CONCLUSIONS

During the early forties, the Thessalonian Christians had
experienced suffering and death, probably as a result of an *ad
hoc* persecution that resulted from the perceived threat posed
by this community to the existing religious/civic cults of the
city. By his emphasis on election the Apostle assures these
Christians that they have been chosen and loved by the God
whose Son suffered, died, was raised and will come again in
glory. It is this God who is present in their midst, encouraging,
strengthening and calling them to fidelity. This declaration,
with its emphasis on hope in the *parousia* of Jesus, will allow
them to endure with assurance the daily tribulations that
confront them. Through his application of various early Christian traditions and by his transmission of a prophetic word,
Paul affirms that the proclamation of the death and resurrec-

[28] G. H. R. Horsley, *New Documents Illustrating Early Christianity* (New South Wales:
Macquarie University Press, 1987), vol. 4, 74–82.

tion of Jesus is a pledge that those who have died in Christ will not be forgotten at the *parousia*; they will, in fact, rise first. The christological titles used in this letter illumine and interpret the issue of suffering and hopelessness in light of the *parousia* of Jesus. In addition, these titles point to the theme of a new, called-out community in Christ as well as to the ethical implications and expectations of such a new, corporate existence in the midst of a hostile and pagan world. The Spirit-filled gospel of faith, love and hope is the foundation of the church: in faith it calls the church into being, in love it permits the fellowship of believers to serve as a proleptic kingdom community and in hope it is assured of victory despite all the contrary signs that daily threaten to disable it. Our examination of the theology of 1 Thessalonians thus confirms what was suggested in a preliminary manner by our rhetorical analysis: the goal and intention of this letter is to console and encourage a desolate and discouraged people.

CHAPTER 3

1 Thessalonians, the Pauline corpus and Acts

THE EARLY AND THE LATE PAUL

General perspectives

In several of our previous discussions we have compared, on occasion, selected themes in 1 Thessalonians with other writings in the New Testament and particularly with some of the other Pauline letters. Our goal in this section will be to engage in a brief comparison of the early Paul with the late Paul and then, in the section that follows, we will present a comparison of the early Paul of 1 Thessalonians with the portrait of the Apostle found in Acts. At the outset it will be important to state a general principle, namely, that the proper starting point for the analysis of Pauline thought must be 1 Thessalonians, especially since it contains the key to the theology of the early Paul, and therefore, we would insist, also the key to understanding the theology of the late Paul. Although a whole range of additional topics needs to be investigated – for example, a further discussion of eschatology, flesh-spirit, sin, pre-existence christology and the related christological developments alluded to earlier on in this study, the theology of the cross, baptism and the church as the body of Christ, the progress and maturation of the Christian in and according to the Spirit, and ethics – we will limit ourselves to some concise remarks with regard to the theme of the law and the theme of justification in view of the fact that these seem to dominate the discussion about the validity of an early Pauline theology different from the later one manifest in Galatians and Romans.

The problem of law in Pauline theology

Why does 1 Thessalonians not contain the same intense discussions of the law as one finds in Galatians and Romans? In order to gain some perspective on this question, the following points need to be considered:

1 The major theological developments in Paul's understanding of the law took place between 1 Thessalonians, written in the early forties, and such later letters as Galatians and Romans, written in the fifties. A relatively tranquil attitude towards the law characterises the Apostle's earliest letter.

2 Although Paul experienced what he was in his later letters to refer to as 'justification' at the time of his conversion, such *terminology*, in its developed form, is probably a result of the Antiochian incident described in Gal. 2:11–17. The specific language used to describe this experience (e.g., justification) and the polemical formulations employed to defend this insight are the result of his unfolding, and often embattled, apostolic ministry.

3 As a result of his call, Paul's liberal view of the law marked by ethical and spiritual reinterpretations of ritual stipulations was similar to that of the Hellenistic Jewish Christians he had persecuted previously.[1] Thus in 1 Thess. 4:7 Paul can take up the distinction between 'uncleanness' (*akatharsia*) and 'holiness' (*en hagiasmo*), which was originally rooted in the ritual of the cult, and use it in a totally non-cultic way. Such an attitude, in and of itself, does not indicate hostility to the law, although it could clearly call forth anger from those, such as the persecutor Paul, who held to a more literal reading of the law.

Part of the strain that is noticeable in the writings of Paul results from the tension between his Antiochian heritage and the necessity to express his thought differently in light of polemical attacks made by conservative Jewish Christians. It is important for the interpreter to recognise that Paul does not necessarily discard his earlier expressions and attitudes despite

---

[1] Heikki Räisänen, 'Paul's Conversion and the Development Today of His View of the Law', *NTS* 33 (1987), 413.

the necessity to shape his thinking differently in new situations. Does the late Paul contradict the early Paul? We would urge that the late Paul, both in general and in relationship to the issue of law, articulates more precisely what was already, at least implicitly, the theological structure of the early Paul. Thus, for example, Paul's christology as expressed already in 1 Thessalonians makes it evident that election is a gift of the Spirit and not a result of the law.

Justification language in Paul

As is well known, 'justification' (*dikaiosynē*) and its cognates do not occur in 1 Thessalonians, except for *dikaios* (righteous) in 2:10, which does not appear to have a direct connection with Paul's later teaching on justification. It is, of course, impossible to take up the whole problem of justification in Paul in a brief paragraph. However, it can be suggested that Paul's teaching on justification is nothing other than his teaching on election, sharpened by his theology of the cross, and applied to a series of polemical situations, as, for example, can be observed already in 1 Cor. 1:18–31. Seen in this way there is an amazing consistency between the emphasis on election and sanctification in 1 Thessalonians and on justification and sanctification in Romans; between learning how to please God and to do his will in 1 Thess. 4:1–3 and the theme of obedience in Rom. 6; between Paul's assertion in 1 Thess. 5:9 that 'God has not destined us for wrath, but to obtain salvation through our Lord Jesus Christ' and his declaration in Rom. 5:9, 'Since, therefore, we are now justified by his blood, much more shall we be saved by him from the wrath of God.' When Paul speaks of the 'activity of faith' in 1 Thess. 1:3 that description of faith is approximated by the formula 'the obedience of faith' in Rom. 1:5 and 16:26.

1 THESSALONIANS AND THE 'PAULINISM' OF ACTS

A study that has dominated much of the discussion with respect to the relationship of Paul and Acts is Philip Vielhauer's 'On the "Paulinism" of Acts'.[2] There is much in Vielhauer's article that is perceptive and accurate; yet there is much that is in need of correction and modification. In his summary he concludes that 'the author of Acts is in his christology pre-Pauline, in his natural theology, concept of the law, and eschatology, post-Pauline. He presents no specifically Pauline idea.'[3] Is that correct?

Following a comparison of Luke's theology of Paul and that offered by the Apostle himself in 1 Thessalonians, one may be permitted to ask whether Luke does not in fact have a reasonable grasp of Paul's *early* theology and whether Vielhauer's failure to differentiate between an early and a late Paul does not lead to results that are skewed. Vielhauer often appears to draw an overly sharp distinction between the 'earliest congregation' and Paul.[4] We need to inquire whether, in fact, a greater coherence exists between the 'earliest congregation', Luke and Paul than Vielhauer allows for.

Let us remind ourselves of some of the specific points shared by 1 Thessalonians and Acts.

1 The theme of joy inspired by the Holy Spirit in the midst of persecution is to be found in both (1 Thess. 1:6, Acts 13:52).

2 In 1 Thess. 1:5 Paul recounts that his proclamation of the gospel was carried out 'in power' (*en dynamei*). This dimension of Paul's apostolic ministry as both proclamatory and performative is well summarised in Acts 19:11, as well as in 14:3,10 and 15:12.

3 The same interchangeability of the terms 'gospel' and 'word' as is found in 1 Thessalonians (1:5 and 2:13) is found also in that part of Acts describing the Pauline mission (14:7, 21; 16:32; 17:11, 13).

4 The term 'apostle' appears only once in 1 Thessalonians (2:7), and as a plural. That Paul is not intending to stress his apostolic authority by use of this title alone is evident. In 1 Thessalonians 2, for example, it is Paul's apostolic activity

---

[2] In *Studies in Luke-Acts*, ed. L. E. Keck and J. L. Martyn (Nashville: Abingdon, 1966), 33–50.

[3] Ibid., 48.

[4] Ibid., 44.

and authority, and not necessarily the designation 'apostle', which conveys his unique role within the foundation and life of the Thessalonian congregation. In fact, there is little in Paul's later concentration on the title 'apostle' that could not be derived from his understanding of this God-given responsibility as outlined in 1 Thess. 2:1–8. Sparse use of the word 'apostle' does not necessarily mean a minimal understanding of Paul's apostolic call, whether the infrequent use of that title be noted in 1 Thessalonians or in Acts.

5 In 1 Thess. 3:2 Paul informs the congregation in Thessalonica that he is sending Timothy to them 'to establish [*stērizai*] you in your faith and to exhort [*parakalesai*] you'. Paul uses the verb 'to establish' only in 1 Thessalonians (3:2, 13) and Romans (1:11, 16:25). This same language is found in Acts 14:22 and 15:32. In fact, Acts 14:22 not only has much in common with the language of 1 Thessalonians (note also the use of the common term 'kingdom' as in 1 Thess. 2:12), but it could well serve as a summary of the purpose of 1 Thessalonians as a *consolatio*: Paul and Barnabas returned to Lystra and to Iconium and to Antioch 'strengthening [*epistarizontes*] the souls of the disciplines, encouraging [*parakalountes*] them to continue in the faith, and saying that through many tribulations [*thlipseōn*] we must enter into the kingdom of God'. With its reference to faith, this verse is again remarkably reminiscent of 1 Thess. 3:2–3: 'to establish [*stērizai*] you in your faith and to encourage [*parakalesai*] you that no one be moved by these afflictions [*thlipsesin*].'

6 It is noteworthy that the theme of the suffering of Christ referred to in 1 Thess. 1:6 and 2:14 is referred to in Acts 17:3, precisely in that section of Acts dealing with Paul's activity in Thessalonica. It is of interest that in this same verse Luke also refers to the resurrection of Christ, using the identical verb that we noted earlier in 1 Thess. 4:14 (*anistēmi*).

7 Paul urges respect for 'those who labour among you and are over you (*proistamenous*) in the Lord and admonish you' in 1 Thess. 5:12–13. This advice is also attested to in Acts 14:23 and 20:28, even if Paul did not specifically refer to these leaders as *presbuteroi* or *episkopoi* in 1 Thessalonians.

8 Given our understanding of 1 Thess. 2:14–16, it is important to assert that Luke not only has a clear perception of Paul's mission to the Gentiles (13:46–7; 22:21) but that he is also essentially accurate that Paul begins his mission to the Gentiles in the synagogue (Acts 13:14; 14:1; 17:1, 2; 19:8; see also 16:13). It is probable that the reference in Gal. 2:7–8, wherein Peter's and Paul's areas of responsibility are divided, is primarily geographical and not religious. Thus Paul is concerned in proclaiming the gospel to Jews and Gentiles, even though his ultimate goal remains the Gentiles. The appropriateness of Paul's beginning his mission in the synagogue is also enhanced when one reflects that the Gentiles most likely to be converted at first are those who were attracted to the synagogue, the 'Godfearers', and who had remained at its periphery. When Paul states in Acts 14:2 that 'the unbelieving Jews stirred up the Gentiles and poisoned their minds against the brethren', a situation also described in Acts 17:5 with reference to Thessalonica, he may well be providing an accurate description.

How is one to understand Paul's negative attitude toward Judaism portrayed in 1 Thess. 2:13–16? As we have already noted, Paul the Jew was called to proclaim to the Gentiles, alongside and through the Jews in the Diaspora, the apocalyptic victory of God through Jesus Christ and its imminent eschatological conclusion. This point is important: Paul does not side-step the Jews to reach the Gentiles but first attempts to gain them as his allies. Precisely for this reason he generates so much opposition from many of his fellow Jews. Through the use of pre-Pauline materials, 1 Thess. 2:13–16 intends both to describe and to reprove the hostility of such Jews against Jesus, the churches in Judea, Paul and the church at Thessalonica.

The key to understanding the controversial phrase 'But God's wrath has come upon them at last' (1 Thess. 2:16b, RSV) is the concept 'wrath of God'. Through the death of Christ, God's judgment and wrath have expressed themselves. In 1 Thess. 2 this is applied particularly to the Jews, a perspective quite parallel to Rom. 1:18–3:20 and 9:22–4. There is little question among contemporary exegetes that *ephthasen* means 'has come, has arrived' and should not be understood as a prophetic aorist. The real issue is whether *eis telos* refers to that same event in the past and is intensifying it – 'finally' – or whether it is referring to the future – 'until the end'. We would argue for the latter meaning for three reasons: the use of 'wrath' in 1 Thessalonians itself, with its present and future references; the use of 'wrath' in Romans and its very similar present and future references; and the use of *eis telos* in an apocalyptic context in the gospel tradition.

There is no need for us in this context to review extensively all the evidence, and so we shall turn immediately to the third point. The critical text is the one found in the Marcan apocalypse, 13:12–13: 'And brother will deliver up brother to death, and the father his child, and children will rise against parents and have them put to death; and you will be hated by all for my name's sake. But he who endures to the end (*eis telos*) will be saved.' In light of this we would translate 1 Thess. 2:16b in this way: 'And now God's wrath has come upon them until the end.' How does this understanding of 1 Thess. 2:16b in particular and 2:13–16 in general relate to the criticism of the inconsistency, if not contradiction, between this passage and what Paul has to say about Israel in Rom. 9–11? We would suggest that the relationship between 1 Thessalonians and Romans is not one of inconsistency. In Romans Paul does not negate what he said in his first letter but augments it; 1 Thessalonians does not contain the last word concerning Israel. 1 Thessalonians reports God's attitude of wrath towards the Jews from the death of Jesus until the last day; Romans adds that at the last day God's mercy will be revealed towards them in an incomprehensible and radically new way.

Not only in this passage of 1 Thessalonians, but elsewhere as well, it is evident that much of the material about Paul in Acts is a reflection of the *early* theology of Paul. Viewed from this perspective there is a good deal of common ground between Acts and 1 Thessalonians. As a result, much of Vielhauer's work on the relationship of Paul to Acts needs revision. Often Luke is not distorting the theology of Paul in his writing of Acts; rather, he is concentrating on the early Paul, the Paul who had not yet engaged in the harsh *theologically reflective polemics* generated, for example, in the Galatian situation. As we know, Luke is interested in presenting a picture of harmony and unity in the early church, and the fact that the late Paul is engaged in such a harsh conflict with various groups of Judaising Christians does not fit the portrait that Luke is developing.

A word does need to be said about the personal relationship between Paul and Luke. Fitzmyer goes against the grain of contemporary New Testament scholarship when he suggests that Luke may at times have been a companion of Paul, although not throughout his entire apostolic career. In fact, Luke would have been absent 'during the major part of his missionary activity, or during the period when Paul's most important letters were being written'.[5] Where Fitzmyer has to be taken seriously is in his support of the earlier positions of Strobel and Glover that Luke was a native of Antioch.[6] This possible congruence of Luke, Paul and the church at Antioch would assist in explaining a common background and allow us to understand how Luke had come to know Paul personally.

We are inclined to think, then, that Luke has a good sense of the total theology of Paul, including his late period. For the purposes of his 'Christian consensus', as C. K. Barrett puts it so nicely,[7] Luke preferred to concentrate on and to shape the teaching and proclamation of the early Paul. Is that any less legitimate than the concentration of many on the late Paul? Is not the whole Paul to be seen precisely in the combination of the early and the late Paul and in the gradual development from the one to the other, as well as in attempting to understand the causes necessitating such further amplification and articulation of his early theology?

[5] Joseph A. Fitzmyer, *The Gospel According to Luke*, I–IX, *AB* 28 (Garden City: Doubleday, 1982), 48.
[6] August Strobel, 'Lukas der Antiochener', *ZNW* 49 (1958), 131–4; R. Glover, 'Luke the Antiochene and Acts', *NTS* 11 (1964–5), 97–106.
[7] C. K. Barrett, 'Acts and Christian Consensus', in *Context*, Fs. P. Borgen (Trondheim: Tapir, 1987), 19–33.

CONCLUSIONS

In light of this study, what conclusions might be reached concerning the relationship of 1 Thessalonians to the wider Pauline corpus and to Acts?

1 Recent study of Pauline chronology has suggested reasons for dating 1 Thessalonians in the early forties of the first century. Although no chronology can claim to be conclusive, the theological development of Pauline thought would suggest more rather than less time and this, in turn, makes plausible certain distinctions between an early and a late Paul.

2 1 Thessalonians contains a fair amount of pre-Pauline material, material that has much in common with the Hellenistic church and the Antiochene tradition. This tradition and its transformation, rather than the late Paul represented in Galatians or Romans, must be the starting point for understanding the evolution of Pauline theology.

3 The phrase *in Christ* may be an especially appropriate place to begin an examination of the development and maturation of Pauline theology since it appears in every Pauline letter.

4 Such Pauline themes as 'law' and 'justification' are *contingent* applications of the basic structure of Pauline thought found already in 1 Thessalonians. Thus Paul's teaching about justification is nothing other than one specific application of his theology of election, sharpened by this theology of the cross and necessitated by a series of polemical confrontations.

5 Although Luke places Paul within his larger theological portrayal of unity and consensus, the portrait of the Apostle he presents is more correct than Vielhauer's study might lead one to believe. Luke does present some accurate accounts of the early Paul as well as some fleeting glances at their common inheritance from the Antiochene tradition.

CHAPTER 4

The significance of 1 Thessalonians for today

The message communicated by Paul to the Thessalonian church some two millennia ago has remarkable relevance for the contemporary church. Increasingly the church in the Western world finds itself in a pagan environment in which the Christian worldview and lifestyle are adhered to with diminishing conviction. 'New age' religions, many with a call to return to goddess worship, atheistic ideologies and deconstructed versions of 'Christianity' abound. To remain authentically Christian, to swim against the popular tides of public opinion, means that often discipleship involves subtle, and in some places overt, harassment, alienation and/or persecution. In this post-Constantinian age, as in the pre-Constantinian, the Christian church often finds itself in a minority position.

But this contemporary situation is paralleled in Pauline Thessalonica. There, too, the church was surrounded by pagan religions and a threatening political environment. It was a tiny minority, bullied, intimidated and persecuted, yet it flourished and had a profound impact upon the development of Christianity not only in Thessalonica but also in provinces of Macedonia and Achaia, and eventually well beyond. Why? What was the source of its power and momentum? How could it so compellingly advance God's cause despite strong opposition?

First, the 'called-out [ekklēsia] of the Thessalonians' were empowered and energised by a trans-human source, the gospel, the transformative and performative word of God which, accompanied by the Holy Spirit, allowed them to abandon idols with their death-bringing capacity and to worship the living and true God. Because Jesus Christ had died and risen there was now the possibility to live 'in Christ', in and through his corporate fellowship, the church, by faith and to live a life pleasing to God. As we observed, faith for Paul is a dynamic term; it is an ongoing activity. When one responds and continues to respond to the gospel in faith, the word can never be viewed as a past event but as an activity 'which is at work in you believers' (1 Thess. 2:13). Faith is the positive response to God's invitation, to his grace, to his calling 'into his own kingdom and glory' (1 Thess. 2:12).

Moreover, 1 Thessalonians reminds the contemporary church that to be a church is to participate in an activity *initiated by God* through the death and resurrection of his Son, the Lord Jesus Christ, and proclaimed and sustained by the energising and joy-bringing word of the Spirit-filled gospel. The church's work and mission has a divine, grace-filled origin, not a human one. The church, as well as the individual believer, is a messenger on behalf of the One who has called her in love. As the church remains imitative of the cruciform existence of its Lord and its apostolic witnesses, it too will be strengthened and sustained – in joy! – when it encounters affliction, suffering and, even, persecution. The gospel as generating power strengthens and sustains those 'in Christ' to be forceful representatives and witnesses for the faith well beyond their local situation.

Second, 1 Thessalonians makes clear that in responding to this performative gospel through faith one is able to 'know' God in contrast to the 'Gentiles who do not know God' (1 Thess. 4:5). This knowledge, enabled only through faith, gives the believer not only hope in general, but hope with specific and concrete substance. Because those 'in Christ' are not ignorant like the Gentiles, who have no genuine hope, they need not grieve like the others (1 Thess. 4:13). This hope, grounded in faith and based on the death and resurrection of Jesus, is fulfilled on the last day, the day of meeting with the Lord, where 'the hope of salvation', that salvation for which the believer is destined (1 Thess. 5:9–10), will be consummated.

Third, this knowledge of God manifesting itself in an escha-

tological hope which is to be fulfilled on the last day gives shape
to the present life of the believer, a life lived in Christ and in his
community through the energising, Spirit-filled gospel. This
life is one always lived in hope, in the context of eschatological
reservation, in the recognition of the already/not yet situation
of God's redemptive purposes. This life lived in hope is a life
lived in the Spirit in anticipation of the final consummation of
the salvific process. Thus Paul can urge the believer both then
and now 'to lead a life worthy of God, who calls you into his
own kingdom and glory' (1 Thess. 2:12). To lead a life that is
pleasing to God (1 Thess. 4:1) is possible to those who have
turned from idols to serve the living and true God, and it must
be pursued at all times; the one in Christ must always 'do so
more and more' (1 Thess. 4:1). Carl Braaten has correctly
observed that the 'modern problem is that the Christian belief
in the future has suffered an eroding rationalisation process, so
that the eschatological idea itself has been eliminated from a
modern view of how God relates to the world of human life and
society. Not only is any expectation of the final advent of Christ
discounted, but no expectation of a future transformation of
God's created world seems to have survived.'[1]

Fourth, for Paul the gospel contains both an indicative as
well as an imperative: 'Gabe und Aufgabe' (gift and responsibility), to use the words of Ernst Käsemann.[2] Ethics are rooted
in the eschatological gift of faith and the resultant new life of
sanctification is made concrete by the articulation of the 'will
of God' given through the 'instructions' from the Lord Jesus.
Now it is not insignificant that Paul emphasises two dimensions
of the Christian lifestyle that are also of great consequence
today: sexuality and love among the believers. In a world at
least as confused with regard to sexuality as first-century pagan
Thessalonica, Paul's declarations are as disturbing and indispensable now as they were then: 'avoid fornication', 'control
your own body in holiness and honour' and do not live 'in the
passion of lust like Gentiles who do not know God'. God has

---

[1] Carl Braaten, *The Apostolic Imperative* (Minneapolis: Augsburg, 1985), 86.
[2] '"The Righteousness of God" in Paul', in *New Testament Questions Today* (Philadelphia: Fortress, 1969), 168–82.

created every dimension of our being, physical and spiritual, as precious and holy. That is why Paul can pray that 'the God of peace himself sanctify you wholly; and may your spirit and soul and body be kept sound and blameless at the coming of our Lord Jesus Christ' (1 Thess. 5:23). Paul's advice on sexuality results not from the most up-to-date religious or psychological theories circulating in Thessalonica about what 'liberates' humans or makes them 'feel good' or 'uninhibited'; rather it is instructions given 'through the Lord Jesus' (4:2). Such a sanctified life, in which especially the body and all of its sexual dimensions are regarded as sacred, is possible not because of human effort or human desire, but because 'He who calls you is faithful, and he will do it' (1 Thess. 5:24). For the Apostle, then, it is the eschatological gift of faith that determines our lifestyle, and not our lifestyle that determines the ethical content of the gospel. One reason the church today is so ineffectual in certain parts of the world is because it no longer offers pagan society an alternative intellectual or ethical option. Not only does the church seldom exist as a contrasting community over against the mores of society, but often it baptises and incorporates into its existence behaviours that are blatantly opposed to the sanctified life in Christ Jesus. It is far from incidental that Paul's exhortations have as one of their goals 'that you may command the respect of the outsiders' (1 Thess. 4:12). One can hardly witness the life-giving power of the gospel if one's behaviour is as scandalous, or even more scandalous, than those who worship the idols.

Paul makes very clear to the Thessalonian Christians, as he must to the modern church, that they are 'children of light and the children of the day' and that they do not belong to the realm of night or to the arena of drunkenness (1 Thess. 5:4–7). If the church and its message are to be credible, then there must be a congruency between assertions and actions. That is why Paul defends so cogently his own behaviour. It is not only radically different from that of the greedy philosophical charlatans who sold their services and message in Thessalonica, but it is also an example that should be imitated by the Thessalonians. Why? Because the credibility of the gospel is affected by the character and integrity of its messengers as well as its adherents.

Fifth, the Apostle unambiguously characterises the community in Christ as an alternative society. Because it has been chosen and 'been taught by God' how to love one another (1 Thess. 4:9), it must do so more and more. To do that includes loving and holding in esteem the leaders of the community. The church is not a free-floating community where all members can do as they please. There are some who labour and who are set over us 'in the Lord' (1 Thess. 5:12), both for proclamation and for exhortation and encouragement. The quality of congregational life is not a matter of indifference, but of grave concern. Care must be manifested towards the idlers, the fainthearted and the weak. Love must be manifested at its profoundest level: do not repay evil for evil 'but always seek to do good to one another and to all' (1 Thess. 5:15). Rather than uncritically relying on or denying the presence of God's Spirit in the midst of the believing community, Paul urges them not to 'quench the Spirit', not to 'despise prophesying', but to 'test everything; hold fast what is good, abstain from every form of evil' (1 Thess. 5:19–22).

By insisting that the church is a discerning community guided by the Spirit, an eschatological perspective is given which places all our efforts in a context of humility and self-restraint that allows for the encouragement and upbuilding of the worldwide community of faith, rather than the further inflation of our own human tendencies towards self-interest and provincialism. For if the church is truly to be a church in a world brought ever closer together through modern travel and communications systems, then it must always be reminded of the gospel Paul preached, viz., that our words and deeds are to be signs and tools of a love *not* our own, 'which neither our blood nor our soil, neither our ethnicity nor our culture, neither our nationality nor our religion, have revealed to us'.[3]

Because the Apostle so fully comprehends this eschatological nature of faith and love, 1 Thessalonians, from beginning to end, is saturated with the theme of prayer. Paul both prays

---

[3] Braaten, *Apostolic Imperative*, 14.

continually on behalf of the Thessalonians, including those who are in tension with him, and exhorts the Thessalonians to 'pray constantly' (1 Thess. 5:7). For Paul, prayer is the openness of the self to the eschatological grace of God as the source of all hope and healing. For this reason, prayer and spiritual formation must play a central role in any community invoking the New Testament as its guide. As a result they are enabled to 'rejoice always' and to 'give thanks in all circumstances' (1 Thess. 5:16–18).

As we move towards the end of our conversation with 1 Thessalonians, it is important that we not be left with the impression that eschatology deals only with praxis. For whenever theology is reduced to praxis, as crucial as praxis is, it moves down a cul-de-sac. Eschatology is precisely that driving force behind Paul's vision of universality and catholicity which is for him nothing other than the mission of the church. The church is universal because of its eschatological character 'reaching temporally and spatially in every direction, crossing all frontiers of culture, class, race, religion, age, sex'[4] and whatever else seems to erect walls of partition. Having stated this as categorically as we have, it is most important that we be careful not to confuse the divine openness of God's mission to the world with a baptism of any and every position found in the world. Here is where 'testing' and 'discernment' are essential. Divine openness, in fact the very catholicity of the church in going beyond the limits of particularity, is intended for the reconciliation of the world so that it may experience God's grace and be sensitive to God's will. Not to be forgotten is that the other side of divine openness is divine demand – being obedient to the will of God. These two sides of the same coin, *divine openness* and *divine demand*, are splendidly portrayed by the Thessalonian church – a mission which seeks out the most diverse and conflicting elements of Macedonian society, yet with an expectation that together they will be obedient to God's will as manifested in Jesus rather than following the ideologies and cultural fads permeating that

---

4 Ibid., 55–6.

society. It is in this sense that the church is called to be ecumenical, viz., by demonstrating the oneness of those called in Christ in doing the will of God. In such a way, then, the call to God's kingdom is the call to the church universal, catholic and ecumenical, to be the sacrament of hope for the world's future as together they move toward God's consummation of history.

Finally, it is necessary to stress once again that the author of 1 Thessalonians is first and foremost an apostle, a missionary, an evangelist. This apostolic, missionary and evangelical dimension must be as central to the being of the contemporary church as it was for the Pauline church, for God has given a unique mandate to the church, viz., to go and preach the gospel of Christ. For if the church is not obedient to this task there is no one else in the world who will do it. Of course, it needs to be emphasised that such a stance in no way seeks to minimise social justice or to divorce it from the gospel. Rather, social justice and liberation are only possible when a meaningful vision of new alternatives invades the conditions of human slavery and idolatry. And for Paul that prospect is only possible when the eschatological word of God, the gospel, enters into the arena of human history. Only when Christ alone is recognised as the Lord of history and the victor of its ruling powers and principalities, is the church enabled and empowered to engage with the demons of our own time and place and to test everything, holding on to what is good and abstaining from every form of evil.

The Apostle's final encouragement is just as timely today as it was when he wrote this first extant Christian document: 'I adjure you by the Lord that this letter be read to all the brothers and sisters. The grace of our Lord Jesus Christ be with you' (1 Thess. 5:27–8).

The theology of 2 Thessalonians

KARL P. DONFRIED

CHAPTER 5

The setting of 2 Thessalonians

THE RHETORICAL STRUCTURE

The introductory comments made about rhetoric in our discussion of 1 Thessalonians are relevant to 2 Thessalonians and we urge the reader to review that material at this time. There is wide consensus that 2 Thessalonians belongs to the deliberative genre of rhetoric. This genre includes honour and advantage as the standard topics. These topics are used in 2 Thessalonians to advise the audience concerning their present actions and the result of those actions in the future.

Frank Witt Hughes provides the following analysis of the rhetorical structure of 2 Thessalonians. It is one that we accept.[1]

I *Exordium* (introduction) (1:1–12)
    A epistolary prescript (1:1–2)
    B thanksgiving prayer (1:3–10)
    C intercessory prayer (1:11–12)
II *Partitio* (statement of the proposition) (2:1–2)
    A subjects to be dealt with in the probatio (2:1–2)
    B point of disagreement (heresy to be refuted) (2:2)
III *Probatio* (proof) (2:3–15)
    A a first proof (refutatio) (2:3–12)
    B second proof (2:13–15)
IV *Peroratio* (epilogue) (stated as an intercessory prayer; 2:16–18)

---

[1] Frank Witt Hughes, *Early Christian Rhetoric*, *JSNT*Sup 30 (Sheffield: JSOT Press, 1989), 68–73.

V Exhortation (3:1–15)
  A command (or request) to pray for Paul (3:1–4)
  B intercessory prayer (3:5)
  C command to work (3:6–15)
VI Epistolary postscript (3:16–17)
  A intercessory prayer (3:16)
  B authentication (3:17)
  C final blessing (3:18)

Knowing that 2 Thessalonians is an example of deliberate rhetoric permits the interpreter to be sensitive to the argumentation of the letter in general, and by examining the various components of this rhetorical structure one can be made sensitive to the central issues at stake in the dialogue between this author and his audience. Thus, the *partitio* (statement of the proposition) immediately indicates that a major point of contention between the writer and his adversaries is related to the claim 'that the day of the Lord has already come' (2:2), and the *probatio* (proof) makes evident that the source of this false teaching is related to the Spirit (2:15). One final example of the importance of examining carefully with smaller rhetorical units can be seen in the exhortation in 2 Thess. 3:1–15 with its rather detailed mandate to work (3:6–15) presented in four different ways. Although these observations about the rhetorical structure of 2 Thessalonians have been cursory, they have nevertheless provided us with some important indications concerning the goal that the author of this document wishes to pursue.

THE PROBLEM OF AUTHORSHIP

One of the most vexing difficulties related to a proper understanding of 2 Thessalonians is the question of authorship. Did Paul write this letter? Contemporary scholarship is not of one mind and the range of opinion is broad. Some scholars hold that the Apostle is indeed the author; others suggest that this is a pseudepigraphical letter written in the late first century to a situation quite different than the one addressed in 1 Thessalonians, even, many would insist, to a church other than Thessalonica itself. In addition to these two widely advocated positions, a variety of other options can be found in the literature.

The factors most frequently discussed in connection with the authenticity of 2 Thessalonians include: the apparent literary dependence of 2 Thessalonians on 1 Thessalonians; the tensions, if not contradictions, that are said to exist between 2 Thess. 2:3–12 and 1 Thess. 4:13–5:11; the paucity of personal references and the formal, solemn tone of 2 Thessalonians; and the references to forgery in 2 Thess. 2:2 and 3:17.

For our present purposes we will limit comments to the first factor, which is certainly the most pivotal topic in the current debate, viz. the claim that *2 Thessalonians reveals an unusual dependence on and imitation of 1 Thessalonians*, in terms not only of ideas but also of terminology and phrases. The best known advocate of this position is William Wrede, who in his 1903 study determined that much of the first letter is repeated in the second, a phenomenon not evidenced elsewhere in the Pauline corpus.[2] Wolfgang Trilling's two subsequent monographs, one a full-scale commentary on 2 Thessalonians, have served both to augment the insights and arguments of Wrede and to keep them in the forefront of the current discussion.[3]

To date there has been no comprehensively compelling refutation of Wrede's analysis. Although we find the most cogent argument for non-Pauline authorship to be that of literary dependence, we are not persuaded that these critics have correctly or convincingly described the circumstances that prompted the writing of this letter, particularly those who place it in the late first or early second century in a location other than Thessalonica. It is difficult to imagine a setting where a letter purportedly addressed to Thessalonica by Paul would be relevant and convincing to a non-Thessalonian church some thirty or more years after the Apostle's death.

[2] Wilhelm Wrede, *Die Echtheit des zweiten Thessalonicherbriefs untersucht*, *T*Un.F. 9/2 (Leipzig: Hinrichs, 1903).
[3] Wolfgang Trilling, *Untersuchungen zum zweiten Thessalonicherbrief*, *EThSt* 27 (Leipzig: St Benno, 1972) and *Der zweite brief an die Thessalonicher*, *EKKNT* 14 (Zürich: Benzinger, 1980).

Compelling evidence simply has not been provided for these conjectures.

We are not persuaded by either of the two major views held by many scholars today, viz., neither the perception that this letter is non-Pauline, written late in the first century and not connected with a specific situation in Thessalonica, nor the more traditional perspective that Paul himself wrote 2 Thessalonians. Our understanding, on the contrary, is that 2 Thessalonians is non-Pauline in the technical sense but that it *is* related to a concrete situation in Thessalonica. We would suggest that the circumstances providing the primary motivation for the writing of 1 Thessalonians continued and escalated. 2 Thessalonians refers to this intensification not only by use of the term *tois diōgmois* (persecutions, 1:4) and by harsh responses to the afflictors (1:5–12), but also by hostile descriptions of the lawless one in 2 Thess. 2:3–12. In terms of authorship, it is possible that one of Paul's co-workers, Timothy or Silvanus, who are listed as joint authors with Paul in both 1 and 2 Thessalonians, wrote the letter.

No matter which option one selects with regard to authorship, 2 Thess. 3:17 ('I, Paul, write this greeting with my own hand. This is the mark in every letter of mine; it is the way I write') remains enigmatic. Those who select option one, i.e., Pauline authorship, have to resolve the problem that, if 1 and 2 Thessalonians are Paul's first letters, there is no evidence of a Pauline letter prior to 2 Thessalonians that contains a greeting in the hand of the Apostle. Those who prefer option two, i.e. 2 Thessalonians as a pseudepigraphical letter, must assume that the writer purposely inserted 2 Thess. 3:17 to beguile the readers into thinking that Paul was the actual author of the letter.

If one of Paul's co-workers, probably Timothy, is the author of 2 Thessalonians, how might we interpret this reference? Removing ourselves from the narrow individualism of the current age and taking more seriously concepts like that of a 'corporate personality' in ancient Israel or what some have described as the 'Pauline school', it may well be that this 'I' is more broad than we might comprehend initially. If 2 Thessalonians is attempting partially to augment and correct a misunderstood 1 Thessalonians, and if Paul and Timothy were co-authors of that letter, could not Timothy refer to Paul in the way he does? After all, Paul, because of his prominence, is the target of misunderstanding even though he and his two co-workers share in this 'geistiges Eigentum'[4] (intellectual property). If Paul is being attacked for something that he and Timothy together are responsible for, and since Timothy knows well what was intended in the original letter (1 Thessalonians), is it not possible that the final rhetorical clincher of 2 Thessalonians is for the author to draw explicitly upon the Pauline apostolic authority, in which he shares, as an important rebuttal to the misunderstandings rampant in Thessalonica? Certainly a letter from Timothy alone would not carry the same weight or be as effective in refuting distortions directed primarily at Paul.

THE SPECIFIC BACKGROUND

Given our understanding that 2 Thessalonians is addressed to the same Christian community as 1 Thessalonians, and written not long after the first letter, the descriptions of the historical settings of Thessalonian Christianity given earlier in this volume need not be repeated and the reader is referred to them. Thus our present task will be to understand the distinctive factors in Thessalonica that necessitated the composition of 2 Thessalonians.

The continuance and intensification of the persecution attested to in 1 Thessalonians is evident. The Thessalonian Christians' proclamation of the kingdom of God (2 Thess. 1:5) generates hostility among non-Christians (2 Thess. 1:8, 2:12). 2 Thess. 1:4 refers not only to *tais thlippsesin* (afflictions), as in 1 Thessalonians, but also to *tois diōgmois* (persecutions). Whereas *thlipsis* (affliction) needs to be specified according to its context, *diōgmos* always refers to persecution. But there is also a noteworthy reference to this later theme in 2 Thess. 2:15: 'So then,

---

[4] Wolfgang Speyer, *Die literarische Fälschung im Altertum, HAW* 1.2 (München: Beck, 1971), 175–6.

brethren, stand firm [*stēkete*] and hold fast to the traditions that you were taught by us, either by word of mouth or by our letter.' As Selwyn has shown, the motif 'stand firm' is part of a well-formed tradition of teaching in the context of persecution.[5]

Set against this environment of protracted and escalated persecution, there are some in the congregation who have proclaimed that 'the day of the Lord is already here [*enestēken*]'. What was meant by this slogan is not altogether clear. It might refer to a spiritualised, almost gnostic-like understanding, viz., that there will not be any future, physical coming of the Lord, much like the problem described in 1 Cor. 15:12–28, or it might suggest that the day of the Lord was at hand, that it would occur before long. The critical question that the student of 2 Thessalonians must ask is how this originally Jewish concept, the day of the Lord, would be interpreted in a congregation composed predominantly of Gentiles in a milieu permeated by Graeco-Roman cults.

It appears that we may be dealing with a misinterpretation of Paul's alleged 'realised eschatology' in 1 Thessalonians. The author of the second letter is concerned not only about this misreading but also with its consequences. For if the day of the Lord is already present and not a future event yet to be consummated, then, of course, the stage is set for the faith of the Thessalonians to be undermined. Our author responds to this problem by portraying an apocalyptic timetable that distances the present situation from the yet future day of the Lord. This shift in eschatological emphasis from the first letter does not mean, however, as we will attempt to explain below, a contradiction between the two. Different situations call for distinct nuances and emphases.

There are two factors, both of which will be described more fully, that suggest that the day of the Lord is being misunderstood in a pseudo-spiritual, gnostic way: the problem of the spirit in 2 Thess. 2:2 and 2:15 and the identification of *to katechon*/*ho katechōn* in 2 Thess. 2:6 and 7 as a seizing or possessing power, some 'pseudocharismatic spirit or agent' that is 'a false imitation of spiritual illumination and inspiration' and that has seized power.[6]

In addition to *correcting this false understanding of the day of the Lord*, the author of 2 Thessalonians is also *urging his readers to stand firm in their afflictions* and not to be shaken or distraught when some proclaim that the day of the Lord has arrived. And, further, in light of this oppressive situation, 2 Thess. 1:5–13, which contains a major expansion of 1 Thessalonians, makes clear that the Lord's vengeance will come against those who are involved in this persecution against the Thessalonian Christians and that they will suffer 'the punishment of eternal destruction' when the Lord appears (2 Thess. 1:9).

[6] Charles H. Giblin, 'The Heartening Apocalyptic of Second Thessalonians', *The Bible Today* 26 (1988), 353.

CHAPTER 6

The theology of 2 Thessalonians

THE GOD OF JUSTICE

The themes of the Thessalonian Christians' election by God
and their suffering, both articulated in 1 Thessalonians, find
resonance in 2 Thessalonians. In 2 Thess. 2:13 the author gives
thanks that 'God chose you as the first fruits for salvation
through sanctification by the Spirit and through belief in the
truth.' If this is a perspective shared by the author and the
Thessalonians, then the critical issue that emerges is why, if
they have been called by God, must they continue to endure
afflictions and intensified persecutions for the sake of the
kingdom of God? Is this not rather a sign that they have been
abandoned by God? The response that is given to this dilemma
is that the ongoing situation and persecution is intended to
make them worthy of the kingdom of God and to signal the
righteous judgment of God against the afflicters on the last day
(2 Thess. 1:5–12). Juridical and apocalyptic concepts are
employed in responding to this crisis of faith: in particular, the
understanding of God as the God of justice and Jesus as his
apocalyptic agent who will vindicate the afflicters and bring
comfort to the afflicted.

The theme of the justice of God is specifically articulated in
2 Thess. 1:6. God, as the chief apocalyptic actor, will repay
with vengeance those who are persecuting the Thessalonians
through the apocalpytic agency of the Lord Jesus at the time of
his future revelation with his mighty angels. The objects of this
vengeance are not only described as those who are aggrieving
the Thessalonians but also as those who 'do not know God' and

who 'do not obey the gospel of our Lord Jesus' (1:8). These two phrases form a synonymous parallelism, implying that those who do not obey the gospel do not, as a result, know God. Whereas the theme of 'not knowing God' is limited to a description of the moral behaviour of the non-Christians in 1 Thessalonians (4:5), here it describes aggressive, anti-Christian persecutorial conduct. A similar subject is taken up in the first proof, 2:10–12. Because the persecutors did not believe in the truth of the gospel God sends to 'them a power delusion, leading them to believe what is false'. As a result of not obeying the truth they 'took pleasure in unrighteousness' and 'will be condemned' (1:12). Those whom God has chosen, however, are those who are characterised by their 'belief in the truth' (1:13).

With keen insight, Edgar Krentz has observed that the 'lens through which all of the language of 2 Thessalonians is refracted is the expectation of apocalyptic vindication through the agent of a just God'.[1] Put simply, the God portrayed in 2 Thessalonians is both the one who repays the persecutors with persecution and the one who gives rest to the persecuted. Yet to limit ourselves only to this dimension of God in 2 Thessalonians would not be wholly correct. Although our author does not specially refer to the 'cross' or 'resurrection' of Jesus in describing the character of God, there are at least two aspects of 2 Thessalonians that must be kept in mind.

The first is *the explicit use of the term 'gospel'* in the prayer of thanksgiving, 1:8, and in the second proof, 2:14. Whether the author of this letter is Paul or not, it is hard to imagine that the term does not have, for the most part, its usual Pauline resonance, viz., the action wrought by God through the life, death, resurrection and future coming of Jesus for the salvation of humanity. If this is the case, then our author is not denying the terms 'cross' and 'resurrection'; he assumes them. Because this aspect of God's revelation, viz., the cross and resurrection of Jesus, is not the primary issue in this exhortation to the Thessalonians, there is no compelling need for elaboration. What does

[1] Edgar Krentz, 'Traditions Held Fast: Theology and Fidelity in 2 Thessalonians', in *The Thessalonian Correspondence*, 515.

need further specification and correction is: a misunderstanding of the implications of the resurrection of Jesus by means of a slogan bandied about urging that the day of the Lord had arrived, and the implications of the gospel already proclaimed by Paul to their specific situation of affliction and persecution. To address this situation with conviction and to uphold the very basis of their faith, it becomes urgent to concentrate on another characteristic of God, i.e., his justice. Therefore 2:14, centrally located in the second proof, is a well-crafted verse: 'For this purpose he called you through our proclamation of the good news, so that you may obtain the glory of our Lord Jesus Christ.' God's calling of the Thessalonians through the gospel as proclaimed by Paul, Silvanus and Timothy, without at all denying the historic basis of that gospel, reveals a gospel that also contains a *promise* for the future despite all the conflicting and contradictory signs current in their social situation, a promise that they will obtain and participate in the future glory of Jesus Christ.

The second aspect we must be mindful of is *the content of 2:13, strategically located in the second proof:* 'But we must always give thanks to God for you, brethren, beloved by the Lord, because God chose you as the first fruits for salvation through sanctification by the Spirit and through belief in the truth.' A close examination of this text will establish that Jesus is not only the future agent of God's apocalyptic plan, but also the demonstration of God's grace (see also 2:16–17) in the past and present. In this verse the believers in Thessalonica are asked to give thanks to God precisely because they have been and are now 'beloved by the Lord'. Because our author always uses the term 'Lord' to refer to Jesus[2] that is the case here as well. This does differ from 1 Thess. 1:4, where it is asserted that the Thessalonians were 'beloved by God'. Nevertheless, Paul himself can speak interchangeably and synonymously of either the love of God or the love of Christ. Thus, Paul can express gratitude to God for the Thessalonian Christians because (a) they have been and still are loved by Jesus and because (b)

---

[2] See the discussion on pp. 94–95.

God chose them from the beginning[3] for salvation through sanctification by the Spirit and (c) through belief in the truth. In the second part (b) of this verse, the theology of election so evident in 1 Thessalonians is also confirmed. Because of God's election, proclaimed in the gospel of Jesus Christ, they, like the other churches (1:4), are a church 'in God our Father and the Lord Jesus Christ'. Therefore the authors of 2 Thessalonians can give thanks for their 'faith and love' (1:3) and the Thessalonians can refer to God as 'Father', a Father who has loved them and will continue to love them, and a Father who through grace gives them an eternal comfort, both in the present and in the future.

The problem of to katechon/ho katechōn

2 Thess. 2:3–12, using strikingly apocalyptic categories and language and marking a major insertion into the framework of 1 Thessalonians, intends to combat the assertion made by some that 'the day of the Lord is already here' (verse 2). It is argued, on the contrary, that the day of the Lord is not yet here, or even close at hand, because certain future events about to be described must first take place. Glenn Holland has shown that we are dealing in this passage with a three-fold apocalyptic schema in which a present phenomenon is portrayed and then personified at a future moment of crisis.[4] This triple repetition of the impending crisis as already partially operative in the present is described as follows in 2 Thessalonians 2:

Present	*Future*
he apostasia (the rebellion)	*ho anthropos tēs anomias* (the lawless one) (2:3–4)
to katechon (the seizing power)	*ho katechōn* (the seizer) (2:6–7)
to mysterion tēs anomias (the mystery of lawlessness)	*ho anomos* (the lawless one) (2:7–8)

---

[3] We understand the textual reading *ap archēs* as preferable to *aparchēn* in 2:13.
[4] Glenn S. Holland, *The Tradition that You Received from Us: 2 Thessalonians in the Pauline Tradition*, HUTh 24 (Tübingen: J. C. B. Mohr, 1988), 112.

In each case it is apparent that what occurs in the future is a personification of those evil forces already operative in the present. Therefore the use of neuter and masculine participles of the verb *katechō* is not determined by that to which these two participles refer but to the apocalyptic pattern itself. In contemporary scholarship the most widespread translation for *to katechon/ho katechōn* is 'what is restraining/the one who restrains'. Giblin has urged an alternative translation: 'the seizing power/the seizer'. In his 1967 study of 2 Thessalonians, Giblin drew some interesting links between the use of *to katechon/ho katechōn* in 1 Thessalonians and the cults of Serapis and Dionysus in Thessalonica and concludes that a 'generic allusion to pagan religious practice, especially to pseudo-prophetic seizure, would seem to account for Paul's choice of this particular term'.[5] It has also been urged that in this *anomos* passage our author is 'hitting out possibly at a Thessalonian cult in which Emperor worship was combined with the cult of Isis and Serapis'.[6]

In short, then, this lawless one, this seizer, whose rebellion and seizing power is exercised in the present, will continue to mislead and confuse all people until the God of justice, through the manifestation of the Lord Jesus, will ultimately dethrone him. Therefore the eschatological day of the Lord has not yet arrived; much wickedness and lawlessness must yet be played out on the world's corrupt stage before God's ultimate show of victory.

CHRISTOLOGY AS ESCHATOLOGICAL JUDGMENT AND FUTURE VINDICATION

The use of christological titles

General observations

It is informative to compare the christological titles used in 2 Thessalonians with those found in 1 Thessalonians. In the first

---

[5] Charles H. Giblin, *The Threat to Faith: An Exegetical and Theological Re-examination of 2 Thessalonians 2*, AnBib 31 (Rome: Pontifical Biblical Institute, 1967), 201.

[6] Rex Witt, 'The Egyptian Cults in Ancient Macedonia', in *Ancient Macedonia* 2 (Thessaloniki: Institute for Balkan Studies, 1977), 331.

letter 'Christ' occurs ten times, 'Lord' twenty-four times and 'Son' once. Of the twenty-four christological references in 2 Thessalonians,[7] every one, with the possible exception of 3:5 ('the steadfastness of Christ'), is either the title 'Lord' or is found in association with that title. There is not, in 2 Thessalonians, any reference to 'Jesus' or 'Christ' aside from this combination with the title 'Lord'. A paradigmatic shift has taken place from 1 to 2 Thessalonians, a modification which includes an altered christological reflection. The prospective, future dimension of christology is emphasised in 2 Thessalonians, whereas 1 Thessalonians is marked by a greater balance between the retrospective and prospective dimensions of christology.

Lord, Lord Jesus and Lord Jesus Christ

In our christological discussion of 1 Thessalonians it was noted that Paul uses the titles 'Lord' and 'Lord Jesus' with regard primarily to five areas of concern: suffering, eschatology, being in the Lord, ethics/exhortation, and the gospel as the word of the Lord. Let us now, within the framework of these five categories, examine the similarities and dissimilarities apparent in the use of the same christological titles in 2 Thessalonians.

Suffering   In 1 Thessalonians suffering was understood to be an imitation of the suffering of Paul, the Lord and the churches in Judea, and, in the midst of these circumstances, the Holy Spirit was proclaimed to be a source of joy despite outward afflictions. All of these examples function as powerful warrants to remain steadfast and they serve as basic sources of encouragement for the Thessalonian Christians as they are being urged to cope with their difficult situation. In 2 Thessalonians all of these emphases have been altered. The persecutions and afflictions that are being endured (1:4) are now understood to be 'evidence of the righteous judgment of God, and [are] intended to make you worthy of the kingdom of God, for which you are

---

[7] 'Christ' (3:5); 'Lord' (1:9; 2:2, 8, 13; 3:1, 3, 4, 5, 16[2]); 'Lord Jesus' (1:7, 12); 'Lord Jesus Christ' (1:1, 2, 8, 12; 2:1, 14, 16; 3:6, 12, 18).

suffering' (1:5). Encouragement is now given on the premise
that those who are faithful to the truth will receive 'the glory of
our Lord Jesus Christ' (2:14). Their present suffering is evidence of both God's election and his justice, a suffering that is
to be vindicated at the future judgment on the day of the Lord.

Eschatology   Although the references to Lord in 1 Thessalonians
are eschatological and refer to the *parousia*, they are specifically
anchored in the death of Jesus, in the Lord Jesus Christ 'who
died for us' (1 Thess. 5:9–10; note also 4:14). Such a specific
soteriological reference is absent in 2 Thessalonians, although
we have suggested that such references may be implied by the
use of the term 'gospel' in 2 Thessalonians (1:8 and 2:14). One
would not be far off the mark to suggest that the primary image
of Jesus in 2 Thessalonians is that of judge, a judge who will be
extolled and celebrated by his saints for his exercise of power
on the last day (1:10). The manner in which that judgment will
be exercised is graphically depicted in all its cosmic ramifi-
cations in 2 Thess. 1:7–10 and 2:3–11, passages intimately
related to one another. The author of this letter is attempting
to deal with a more acute form of persecution by drawing upon
a prior apocalyptic theological tradition (1:7–10 and 2:3–11)
and framing it to meet these new urgencies. It is the consideration of the *parousia* of their benefactor, the Lord Jesus Christ,
that gives these despondent and troubled readers assurance of
their 'being gathered together [*episynagogē*] with him' on that
day (2:1).

Given this thoroughly future-oriented eschatological
response to the problem of persecution in Thessalonica, it is not
surprising that the writer of this letter has no sympathy what-
soever with the position asserted by some in Thessalonica that
'the day of the Lord is already here'. This perspective under-
mines the entire rationale just provided for making sense out of
their suffering and it contradicts the letter's emphasis on 'belief
in the truth' (2:13), an apocalyptically shaped truth that is
fully opposed to the false pronouncements that these persons
are declaring.

Being in the Lord   Since 2 Thessalonians does not make explicit
use of a pre-Pauline baptismal tradition, it is not surprising
that the soteriological-ontological character of Christians
'being in the Lord' as evidenced in 1 Thessalonians is not
prominent. And yet, in 2 Thess. 3:4 the author writes: 'And we
have confidence *in the Lord* concerning you, that you are doing
and will go on doing the things that we command.' Certainly
our author wishes to underscore that Paul's confidence is 'in
the Lord'. But is the meaning of 'in the Lord' in 1 Thess. 3:8
and in 4:1 as well, where it moves beyond a mere instrumental
denotation towards an incorporative one, also to be attributed
to this phrase as it is used in 2 Thess. 3:4? Von Dobschütz
understands this verse in such a manner, viz., that the Apostle
and his readers stand 'in the Lord', paraphrasing the verse as
something like 'since we (including the readers) are in the
Lord'.[8] In 3:6 and 12, however, we do not encounter this same
use of 'in the Lord'. In this explicitly paraenetic section, it is
used in an instrumental sense, viz., that Paul speaks on the
authority of and as a representative of Jesus Christ.

C. F. D. Moule suggested that 'Jesus tends to be spoken of as
"Christ" in the context of verbs and statements in the indicative mood, while he tends to be spoken of as "Lord" when it is
a matter of exhortations or commands, in the subjunctive or
imperative.'[9] Leaving aside the letter openings, if one compares the use of 'in Christ' in 1 Thess. 2:14, 4:16 and 5:18 with
the 'in the Lord' formulae of both 1 Thessalonians (4:1; 5:12)
and 2 Thessalonians (3:4, 6, 12), this general distinction concerning the different contexts in which these two formulae
function is supported in a general, non-rigid manner.[10] Thus it
may well be that the different intentions of the two letters have
a direct bearing on how christological traditions are employed.

---

[8] E. von Dobschütz, *Die Thessalonicher-Briefe*, Meyer*K* 10 (Göttingen: Vandenhoeck
& Ruprecht, 1909, repr. 1974), 307.

[9] C. F. D. Moule, *The Origin of Christology* (Cambridge: Cambridge University Press,
1977), 59.

[10] Yet one must be careful not to make too sharp a distinction between an instrumental
and a locative use of *en* since an instrumental use may in fact presuppose a primary
locative intention.

If this is the case, the differing christological *foci* may offer little assistance in solving the question of the authorship of 2 Thessalonians.

Ethics/Exhortation   The rhetorical genre of the second letter is deliberative and has as its purpose exhortation, i.e., it is primarily a paraenetic letter.[11] These observations are confirmed by the use (or non-use) of three key verbs in the letters. The verb *parakaleō* has a wide range of meanings, but in the context of our letters the translations 'to comfort, to encourage, to urge' are appropriate. The word is used eight times in the first letter (2:12; 3:2, 7; 4:1, 10, 18; 5:11, 14), but only twice in 2 Thessalonians (2:17, 3:12). Just the reverse pattern is observable when we examine the usage of the verb *parangellō*, which has the general meaning of 'to give orders, command or instruct'.[12] This word is used four times in the second letter (3:4, 6, 10, 12) but only once in the first (4:11). But even this reference in 1 Thess. 4:11 is quite different from the context of 2 Thessalonians. In the former *parangellō* is twice preceded by the verb *parakaleō* (4:1, 10), which supports the fact that this *paraenesis* 'was intended to reinforce [the Thessalonians] in their current forms of behaviour rather than direct them to a different pattern of behaviour';[13] while in the latter the primary section of ethical exhortation uses only the verb *parangellō*, which lends support to the view that 2 Thessalonians attempts to alter the future behaviour of the Christians in Thessalonica. To further support our observation that *paraenesis* is found in the context of *paraclesis* in 1 Thessalonians and *paraclesis* in the context of *paraenesis* in 2 Thessalonians is the fact that the verb *paramutheō*, meaning 'to encourage, to cheer up, to console someone concerning someone' is found twice in 1 Thessalonians (2:12; 5:14) and not at all in the second letter.

---

[11] This is not in any way to suggest a rigid demarcation between a 'paracletic' and a 'paraenetic' letter. Each may contain and combine both elements, although their overall emphasis and focus is different.

[12] Walter Bauer, *A Greek-English Lexicon of the New Testament and Other Early Christian Literature*, 613.

[13] Charles A. Wanamaker, *Commentary on 1 & 2 Thessalonians*, *NIGTC* (Grand Rapids: Eerdmans, 1990), 48.

As an example of deliberative rhetoric, 2 Thessalonians is attempting to persuade the Thessalonian Christians both to think and to act differently. The former intention is primarily located in the first proof, 2:1(3)–12, which we have already studied, and the latter in the command to work, 3:6–15. It is now to 2 Thess. 3:6–15 that we turn. In verse 6 the source of Paul's authority is stated, 'in the name of our Lord Jesus Christ', as well as the command to work, expressed negatively, 'to keep away from every brother who is living in idleness [*ataktōs*, used also in 3:11] and not according to the tradition [*paradosis*] that they received from us'. The key issues that confront the interpreter are the meaning of *ataktōs* (also *atakteō* in 3:7) and *paradosis*.

The adjective *ataktos* 'means primarily "out of order," "out of place," and ... is readily employed as a military term to denote a soldier who does not keep the ranks, or an army advancing in disarray'.[14] The verb *atakteō* has much the same meaning and 'is extended to every one who does not perform his proper duty'.[15] Since the interpretation of 2 Thess. 3:6–15 is heavily dependent on the translation of the Greek, it will be useful at this point to offer our own translation of verses 6–12:

[6]Now we command you, brothers, in the name of our Lord Jesus Christ, to keep away from brothers who are not living a well-ordered life and are not in accord with the tradition that you received from us. [7]For you yourselves know how you ought to imitate us; we did not depend on others for our support when we were with you [8]and we did not eat anyone's bread without paying for it; but with toil and labour we worked night and day, so that we might not burden any of you. [9]This was not because we do not have that right, but we waived our right in order to give you an example to imitate. [10]For even when we were with you, we gave you this command: Anyone unwilling to work should not eat. [11]For we hear that some of your number are leading ill-ordered lives, and instead of attending to their own business, are busy with what does not concern them. [12]Now such persons we command and exhort to attend quietly to their own work and to earn their own living.

---

[14] George Milligan, *St Paul's Epistles to the Thessalonians* (London: Macmillan 1908), 152.
[15] Ibid., 153.

This translation varies from several common translations in translating *ataktōs/atakteō* as 'ill-ordered' or 'not well-ordered' rather than 'in idleness' and in translating *periergazomai* as 'not attending to their own business' rather than as 'busybody'. Reading the Greek of 2 Thess. 3:6–12 in this way gives significant support to the thesis of Bengt Holmberg that the author of this letter is critical of a 'charismatic authority' being exercised by some of the congregation who are claiming that because of this self-claimed authority they are to be supported by others in the congregation.[16] This understanding of the problem coheres well not only with the problem of the 'spirit' but also with the 'seizing power' that is already at work in the present. With regard to this latter point, it is indeed fascinating that of only two references (2:6, 3:7) to *oidate* (you know) in this second letter, one appears precisely in the first proof at 2:6a: 'And now you know by experience the seizing power'. The use of the phrase 'you know' suggests that this problem may already have been present in an embryonic fashion as Paul wrote the first letter (1 Thess. 1:9; 4:12–13, 14, 19–22). This circumstance of an economic elitism by a few, based on the claim to charismatic authority, is refuted by 2 Thessalonians on the basis of tradition (*paradosis*), a term that is used in 2 Thess. 3:15 in the plural and in 3:6 in the singular. The plural refers to the larger body of Pauline tradition and the singular to a specific item in that larger tradition.

In 1 Thessalonians we noted the strong emphasis on sanctification and its close linkage with the *parousia*. In 2 Thessalonians the terms *hagiazō* (1 Thess. 5:23) and *hagiōsynē* (1 Thess. 3:13) do not appear at all and the term *hagiasmos* (1 Thess. 4:3, 4, 7) is used only once, in 2 Thess. 2:13. We have already observed the summary nature of this verse. Obviously our author values the concept of sanctification, but because of the different pressures to which he is reacting, 'to be worthy' (1:5, 11) of God's kingdom and call is now presumed to be an

---

[16] Bengt Holmberg, *Paul and Power* (Philadelphia: Fortress, 1980), 159.

adhering to the traditions that Paul and his associates have passed on to the Thessalonian Christians. These include, on the one hand, obedience to Paul's teaching about the day of the Lord and the rejection of the spiritualist idea that it is already here, and, on the other hand, fidelity to Paul's instruction about leading an orderly life.

Word of the Lord This phrase occurs only in 2 Thess. 3:1, 'Finally, brethren, pray for us, so that the word of the Lord may spread rapidly and be glorified everywhere, just as it is among you.' The specific theme of the 'word of the Lord' occurs twice in 1 Thessalonians, in 1:8 and 4:15. The later passage, with its very specific reference, is quite distant from the usage here, while the former provides an almost exact parallel. In both cases the phrase 'word of the Lord' is being used synonymously with the term 'gospel' or 'gospel of our Lord Jesus'.

THE GOSPEL, ECCLESIOLOGY AND THE FUTURE VINDICATION OF THE SAINTS

The truth of the Gospel

What is emphasised in 2 Thessalonians in that one's present attitude toward the gospel will determine God's attitude at the last judgment. Thus the afflicters, and those who do not obey 'the gospel of our Lord Jesus' (1:8), will ultimately experience the divine wrath as opposed to those who have obeyed the gospel and who will be granted relief from their present affliction (1:7). These persecutors are perishing 'because they refused to love the truth and so be saved' (2:10); it is precisely in this context (2:10–12) that the gospel is further described as 'the truth'. The Christians, or as 1:10 refers to them, 'the saints', have been chosen by God 'for salvation through sanctification by the Spirit and through belief in the truth' (2:13), i.e., through the gospel that Paul and his associates had proclaimed (2:14). It is as a result of believing in the truth of this gospel that they will obtain 'the glory of the Lord Jesus Christ'

(2:14). Because of their belief, the word of the Lord is spreading rapidly and is being glorified in their midst; therefore they are encouraged to pray for this same result 'everywhere' (3:1).

The shift from the present-oriented to a future-oriented ecclesiology

2 Thessalonians attempts to correct a misreading of the ecclesiology of 1 Thessalonians. Realised eschatology, carefully delimited by Paul in 1 Thessalonians, has been taken to an extreme and charismatics are attempting to take over the leadership of the congregation, as we have already noted. 'The day' for some at least, is now thoroughly present and realised. They are now fully 'the children of the day' and 'children of the light'. They have been sufficiently 'God-taught' and need no further instruction since they already perfectly participate in the realm of realised exchatology. In order to refute this radical eschatological and ecclesiological distortion of 1 Thessalonians, our author presents an apocalyptic timetable that dramatically de-emphasises any notion of realised eschatology. A graphic distance must be established between their present existence and the future day of the Lord. Only on that future day, which is not yet present, will the suffering of the Thessalonian Christians be vindicated. Such an unrelenting apocalyptic framework, one that gives importance to the future vindication of the church, alone will give hope to these persecuted believers. The locus of faith is shifted from the death and resurrection of Jesus to the fact that God will defend, champion and vindicate his church. Although our author praises the church for its faith and love (2 Thess. 1:3), these rich gifts, described so expressively in 1 Thessalonians, are quickly reduced in 2 Thess. 1:4 to a praise of its 'steadfastness [*hypomonē*] and faithfulness [*pistis*] during all your persecutions and the afflictions that you are enduring'.

Ecclesiology and the Holy Spirit

In 2 Thessalonians there is only one reference to the Holy Spirit, but it is strategically located within the second proof: 'But we must always give thanks to God for you, brethren beloved by the Lord, because God chose you from the beginning for salvation through sanctification by the Spirit [*en hagiasmō pneumatos*] and through belief in the truth' (2:13). The first part of this verse is quite similar to the portrayal of the Spirit in 1 Thessalonians (3:13, 4:7–8, 5:23). It is God-given and is at work in the believers through sanctification for the goal of salvation to be consummated on the last day.

There is, however, another reference to 'spirit' in 2:2, a spirit not from God. Here our author implores his readers 'not to be quickly shaken in mind or alarmed, either by spirit or by word or by letter, as though from us, to the effect that the day of the Lord is already here'. This anti-Spirit, which is manifesting itself in Thessalonica, lies at the cause of the problem – viz., 'the day of the Lord is already here' – that prompts 2 Thessalonians to be written. The significance of this anti-Spirit for 2 Thessalonians as a whole is also made evident by its noticeable *absence* in 2:15: 'So then, brothers, stand firm and hold fast to the traditions that you were taught by us, either by word of mouth or by our letter.'

The second part of 2:13, dealing with 'belief in the truth', does suggest a shift from the first letter. In light of the references to 'truth' in 2:10 and 2:12, the 'belief in the truth' in this verse is not referring primarily to the gospel, but rather to the correct interpretation of the gospel, viz., that the day of the Lord is not yet here and that it is a future phenomenon. At first glance the usage seems distant from Paul, who often refers to the truth of God (Rom. 1:27, 3:7, 15:8) and the truth of the gospel (Gal. 2:5, 14) and closer to the Petrines with their more abstract concept of truth (1 Pet. 1:22; 2 Pet. 1:12, 2:2). And yet Paul can say in Gal. 5:7 that 'you were running well; who prevented you from obeying the truth?' Although this may be implied in Gal. 2:5 and 14, certainly in 2 Thess. 2:13 the phrase 'the truth of the gospel' supposes something about the actualisation, the consequences and even about the logic of the gospel. Is this not really part of the overall intention of 2 Thessalonians? And, although the language is different, is this not what Paul is attempting to do in 1 Thess. 4:13–18, viz., to express the truth of the gospel to the needs of those who are mourning over the loss of loved ones? Here in 2 Thess. 2:13 the author is attempting intentionally to make a linkage between 'sanctification by the Spirit' and 'belief in the truth'. Part of the process of sanctification is to walk the path of the true implications of the gospel, i.e., not to waver when the odds are against the community of believers or to be misled by those who proclaim false gospels, viz., that the day of the Lord is here. It is this knowledge that will allow the Thessalonian Christians not to lose their stability (2:2) and which will give them 'eternal comfort and good hope through grace' (2:16).

CHAPTER 7

2 Thessalonians and the New Testament

It will be beneficial to have a clear understanding of the term 'apocalyptic' before comparing the thought of 2 Thessalonians to other parts of the New Testament. Paul Hanson urges that one must distinguish this concept in three ways: as a distinctive literary genre that can be referred to as an 'apocalypse', as a religious perspective known as 'apocalyptic eschatology', and as a social movement identified as 'apocalypticism' whose identity and interpretation of reality is codified by a symbolic universe of apocalyptic.[1] These distinctions allow for some clarity in comparing 2 Thessalonians with other New Testament writings. *First*, its genre is that of a letter, not an apocalypse. *Second*, within the genre of letter, the eschatology of 2 Thessalonians can be described, as can that of 1 Thessalonians, as apocalyptic eschatology. The second letter is more comprehensively apocalyptic in the sense that it uses more consistently language and descriptive elements drawn from the symbolic universe of apocalyptic, as in the case of the salvation-judgment oracle found in 2 Thess. 2:3–12. *Third*, one may identify the author of 2 Thessalonians with 'apocalypticism' in so far as he 'develops a protest of the apocalyptic community against the dominant society' and is less concerned 'with systematic consistency than with the demands of the immediate crisis, especially those of defining identity within a hostile world, and of sustaining hope for deliverance'.[2]

Using Hanson's categories, one finds several remarkable

---

[1] Paul D. Hanson, 'Apocalypticism', *The Interpreter's Dictionary of the Bible, Supplementary Volume* (Nashville: Abingdon, 1976), 29–31.
[2] Ibid., 30.

similarities between 2 Thessalonians and the book of Revelation. The Apocalypse of John is placed within an overall epistolary framework, for the first three chapters contain letters to seven churches in Asia Minor. Here patient endurance, bearing up and not growing weary are praised (Rev. 2:3); tribulation, faithfulness unto death and martyrdom are held high as examples (Rev. 2:10 and 13); and Satan is portrayed as the enemy (Rev. 2:13; 12:9; 20:2 and 7). In other words, in these seven letters we find exhortations to several congregations whose social situation is not that dissimilar from the congregation represented in 2 Thessalonians: Christians being intimidated by alien powers through persecution and death. The remainder of the book of Revelation, using apocalyptic language and symbolism, is written as a support to just such Christians, who are being oppressed and persecuted by the Roman state because of their adherence to the confession that Jesus Christ is Lord, probably in western Asia Minor at the end of the first century.

Although the 'little apocalypse', as Mark 13 is frequently termed, does not belong to an epistolary genre, it does contain the second and third categories suggested by Hanson and it does disclose similarities with 2 Thessalonians and the congregation to which it is addressed. In Mark, as in Revelation, we find two similar themes: that the end is not yet (13:7) and that terrible things are still to happen, some of which are intended to lead the believers astray (13:21–4). Thus it is hardly surprising to find the summons that 'he who endures to the end will be saved' in Mark 13:13 as well as in Revelation (13:10) and 2 Thessalonians (1:4, 3:5).

Without entering into a detailed analysis of the highly complex redactional composition of Mark 13, it should be noted that there are some other commonalities with 2 Thessalonians, especially with 2 Thess. 2:3–12. Both writings are concerned with correcting an 'over-realised', i.e., spiritualised, eschatological orientation, misunderstandings at least partially occasioned by false prophets (Mark 13:22) present in the respective communities. Both Mark and the author of 2 Thessalonians refute certain *parousia* enthusiasts who look to contemporary events as signs that the end is appearing. Each in his own way takes up and reworks Old Testament, apocalyptic and early Christian traditions, both to disprove blatant mis-interpretations and to render a correct eschatological teaching. Since a paradigmatic shift from explicit to implicit salvific language has taken place in 2 Thessalonians in response to the extraordinary threat confronting this community grounded in the redeeming events of the life and resurrection of Jesus, this New Testament writing has more in common with the apoca-lyptic sections of the synoptic gospels and with the book of Revelation than does 1 Thessalonians.

CHAPTER 8

The significance of 2 Thessalonians for today

PROMISE AND ENCOURAGEMENT DURING PERSECUTION

Persecution and misinterpretation of the faith are the dominant problems present in Thessalonica and they occasioned this second letter. Certainly these problems are not limited to the churches of the first century. Let us reflect on these issues one at a time. Christian communities, in so far as they call into question the values and judgments of persons and societies, can easily become objects of ridicule and derision. This type of negative behaviour can be expressed through such relatively moderate means as marginalisation and isolation of the Christian, or, at the other extreme, through outright floggings, persecution and death. The peripheralisation and persecution of Christians continues to this day and some readers will have encountered or may still be encountering it first-hand.

For those who find themselves in these kinds of situations, an inevitable question arises: is it worth remaining a Christian? Does God know, let alone care, about my predicament? For the author of 2 Thessalonians, the answer is a resounding 'yes'. The fundamental presupposition of his appeal is that the gospel has been proclaimed to the Thessalonians and that they have believed in it (1:8 and 2:14). They have been loved by God and chosen by him. This strong beginning and evident growth and maturation in faith (2:13 – 'sanctification') is a cause for joy for the writer(s) of this letter.

Since this world is corrupted by sin and polluted by the power of Satan, Christian communities can easily be confused by his deceptions. As those in Christ participate in the gift of salvation, so those in Satan 'are perishing, because they refused to love the truth and so be saved' (2:10). These persons are living under 'a powerful delusion' (2:11) and believe what is false. Not trusting in the gospel gives the non-believer a misleading orientation to the totality of life, an illusion that has and will have grave consequences. Such a situation, then, the confrontation of truth with falsehood, will play itself out in the present between believers and unbelievers, and, ultimately, on the last day, between God and Satan. Election by God brings with it as a consequence 'belief in the truth' and this is bound to lead to differing degrees of contemporary conflict. Our writer sees this as the inevitable consequence of the Christian living in a fallen world. To live in light of the truth revealed in Christ results in the illumination of evil as well as in its antagonism. The forces of delusion will lead a vigorous assault upon the community of faith because it threatens their very existence.

The inevitability of conflict as a consequence of faith, although emphasised by our author, is hardly new information to the Thessalonian Christians. Already in 1:4, and again in 2:13, their 'steadfastness and faith during all [their] persecutions and afflictions' is praised. As the situation of conflict is apparently persisting and intensifying, it is important that the need for equilibrium and stability against overwhelming odds be recognised and reinforced by a reminder that the gospel is the only source of genuine hope.

The temptation to think that one has been abandoned by God needs, according to 2 Thessalonians, to be countered by: a reminder of the good news, the gospel – that which established the faith of the Thessalonian Christians is still powerfully effective in their midst; a consciousness that God is fully aware of their present circumstances; and a recognition that God is not only alert to the opposition arrayed against the church, and aware of its origin and activity (2:3–12), but also that he promises the believers that all forms of opposition in the present and the future, even Satan himself, will be destroyed. Thus, Christians facing opposition and encountering the forces of evil, in whatever time and in whatever place, can find certitude in the words that 'the Lord is faithful; he will strengthen you and guard you from the evil one' (3:3) and assurance in the fact that he has promised to the believers 'eternal comfort and good hope' (3:16).

PRESERVING THE FAITH UNDISTORTED

The Thessalonian Christians are urged not only to stand firm with regard to suffering and persecution for the faith but with regard to the content of the faith as well. They are encouraged to 'hold fast to the traditions that you were taught by us, either by word of mouth or by our letter' (2:15). These 'traditions' are the correct actualisations of the gospel over against distortions of it offered in light of current ideologies. The slogan bandied about in Thessalonica, largely because of the influence of the mystery cults and false understandings of 'spirit', is that 'the day of the Lord is already here' (2:2). Then as now there are those who claim to be Christian but who assert that they are able to bypass, through a moment of instant 'redemption', the long and tedious moral maturation required of the believer. Sanctification and hope are often excised as outdated and no longer relevant.

When such deceptions come, when such distortions happen, when such theological confusion reigns, the author of 2 Thessalonians urges those in Christ to 'hold fast to the traditions that you were taught by us, either by word of mouth or by our letter'. In this case the specific reference appears to be the *viva vox* of Paul during his presence in Thessalonica (2:5) and to his subsequent written communication, most likely 1 Thessalonians itself. In other words, we have here a call to consider the apostolic tradition as fundamental and normative. Yet the very composition of 2 Thessalonians also demonstrates that this is not meant in a rigid and legalistic sense. The apostolic witness must always be communicated anew and articulated forcefully to each differing situation. The fundamental eschatological hope of Paul is similar in both letters, yet it must be vastly expanded in 2 Thessalonians to meet the extraordinary challenge of that situation. The author of this second letter, like

Paul in 1 Thessalonians, illustrates how the living tradition of the gospel must ever be applied to new and hitherto unfamiliar circumstances. That is not to say that such a return to the 'tradition' resolves all issues or gives instant solutions; it does, however, bring us back to the basic parameters. With the guidance of the *Holy* Spirit, as opposed to the world's false spirits, the community of faith, through prayer, can begin to discern God's will for them in their current situation.

THE GOSPEL AND THE LIFE OF THE COMMUNITY

There are some in the Thessalonian church who regard themselves as superior to others. They claim a spirit-given charismatic authority that entitles them to be financially supported by other members of the Christian community. The writer of 2 Thessalonians has little sympathy for this claim: 'If anyone will not work, let him not eat' (3:10). This claim to special privilege is rejected by the author of 2 Thessalonians, for when special prerogatives are claimed by some so that they are excused from the customary and established responsibilities of the Christian life, then the community itself becomes disrupted. A falsely claimed influence by some dislocates not only the centrality of the gospel and its implications, but weakens others in the community and leads to disrespect from those outside the church. Baptism and final judgment, the beginning and completion of the Christian life, are forces alien to special privilege. Through the baptismal waters all enter equally into the church and are given unique gifts; but these are gifts of service, not of special status. On the final day the Lord will not ask about one's charismatic gifts, but whether his gospel has been proclaimed and obeyed and whether his will has been done.

We live in a period in history that presents a variety of temptations for the church to lose sight of its centre, i.e., not to live out the gospel in light of the God who will bring the cosmos to its consummation. As a result, such essential biblical thought patterns as 'obedience' or 'disobedience to the gospel' (2 Thess. 1:8) are made to sound antiquated, and considerations such as the priority of 'knowing God' (1:8) are considered to be obsolete. A recent poll in the United States suggests that Americans 'seem intent upon making the God of Israel a generic god. Two out of three adults believe that it doesn't matter what god or higher power you pray to, because that universal force will respond regardless.' Further results of this survey include the observation that we 'are operating in a world in which people's gods are impersonal forces'. As a result there is no such thing 'as absolute truth' and many typically view life as the effort 'to obtain all the satisfaction and pleasure possible during their tenure on this planet', a planet inhabited by people who 'are basically good'.[1] Added to these powerful forces competing with the gospel of Jesus Christ, there are struggles in the church over various political and social agendas. Although there are many compelling issues that need to be addressed with sensitivity and thoughtfulness, when any of them becomes the consuming interest of the church, this diverts attention from the church's central task of proclamation and suppresses that gospel which 2 Thessalonians considers to be the only message having claim to 'truth' and which alone is capable of bringing grace and justice to the dislocations of our common life.

In other words, our contemporary situation may not be so different from that of the Thessalonians. The modern world proclaims a religion that is alien to the gospel of Jesus; and often the church itself substitutes issues of power and privilege in place of obedience to the gospel. Both 1 and 2 Thessalonians make clear that the gospel itself is indeed quite concerned with *all* matters related to our human existence, but that it is the gospel alone which allows these questions to be viewed and addressed in their proper context. To a world that has a vague and confused notion of the divine, the gospel speaks with clarity about the creator God who has revealed himself decisively and finally in Jesus Christ, about the gracious God who has offered forgiveness to a sinful and fallen humanity, about the sanctifying God who has elected his people and who pours out his love and his Spirit in the new community that he has

---

[1] This poll is reported in the Springfield, Mass. *Union-News*, 7 September 1991, 13.

called, and about the righteous God who will lead his obedient people to the glory of the kingdom. For both Thessalonian letters that is a source of comfort in the midst of alienation, affliction and persecution.

The theology of Philippians

I. HOWARD MARSHALL

Author's note

The material in this part of the book contains the substance of the Robinson Lectures for 1989 at Erskine Theological Seminary, Due West, SC; the Gheens Lectures for 1990 at the Southern Baptist Theological Seminary, Louisville; and the J. J. Thiessen Lectures for 1991 at the Canadian Mennonite Bible College, Winnipeg; it has also been presented at the 1990 summer school in New College, Berkeley, and at retreats for ministers of the Methodist Church in Ireland and in the Cumbria District of the Methodist Church in England. I am grateful to these institutions for the invitations to speak and to the audiences whose comments and questions have greatly helped my own understanding of these fascinating Pauline letters.

CHAPTER 9

Exploring the building site

In a well-known passage in 1 Corinthians 3 Paul compares his work as an apostle to that of a builder. The building is the church, and the letters which he writes may fairly be regarded as the tools of his trade. Despite the dangers of over-simplification and of forcing the material into a rigid pattern, it may provide a helpful structure for our consideration of the theology of the letter to the Philippians if we take up this metaphor. We shall therefore consider in successive chapters:

the site on which the building was to be erected,
the foundation on which the building rests,
the materials used to bind the stones together,
the character and structure of the new building,
the relation of this particular task of building a church to Paul's other, similar tasks and
the continuing usefulness of the building for today.

Although there are various other angles from which Paul's work can be considered, we shall confine ourselves to a study of the theology which he develops in order to build the church. The primary aim of Philippians is a theological one, however much personal and social factors may affect its character and presentation, and what we want is to find out the character of the theological points that Paul specifically makes in it and to relate these to his underlying theology.

Paul resembles a person who knows a particular language; what he says on a given occasion does not express all of that language, although from what is said one could produce a tolerable picture of its structure. So there is a general structure to Paul's theology which underlies all that he says but which is not necessarily expressed in detail.

THE ESTABLISHMENT OF THE CHURCH

Philippians was written by Paul to the Christian church that had been founded by his own missionary work in the town of Philippi in Macedonia. It was an ancient town (originally called Crenides) which was renamed by Philip of Macedon, the father of Alexander the Great (ca. 360 BC). Later it became a Roman *colonia*, i.e., a place where veteran soldiers could settle on demobilisation and enjoy the privileges of self-government and freedom from taxation.

Paul and Silas came here from Asia after the former had had his vision summoning him to Macedonia (Acts 16:9f.). The story of their visit – the conversion of Lydia, the encounter with a slave girl who told fortunes, their subsequent arrest and miraculous escape from prison – is well known (Acts 16:11–40). Some scholars detect legendary elements in the story, but there is no good reason to question its essential core.

After moving on to Thessalonica, Paul travelled south through Achaia to Athens and Corinth, where he spent at least eighteen months. He then crossed over to Ephesus, paid a flying visit to Caesarea and Antioch and returned to Ephesus, where he spent at least twenty-seven months in evangelism. Then he journeyed north to Macedonia, and doubtless visited Philippi. His plans to return to Jerusalem via Corinth were changed at the last minute, and so he sailed from Philippi (Acts 20:6).

In between the initial visit and these two visits we know that Timothy and Erastus visited Macedonia (Acts 19:22). It is also probable that Timothy or Silas visited Philippi immediately after Paul first left the town (cf. Acts 19:14).

THE QUESTION OF UNITY

The letter itself raises two problems which cannot be entirely separated from each other. The first concerns the unity of the letter and the second the place of writing.

Many scholars have found it difficult to read the letter as one continuous document. There are two principal reasons for this difficulty. First, there is an abrupt transition from the first part of 3:1 to the strong warning in 3:2 against 'evil workers' and the generally impassioned tone of chapter 3 as a whole. The use of 'finally' in 3:1 suggests that the end of the letter was in sight. And the attack on 'evil workers' who have not been mentioned in the earlier part of the letter suggests that a new and different situation is now in mind. Secondly, in 4:10–20 Paul writes a lengthy 'thank you' for a gift sent to him by the Philippians through Epaphroditus. It has seemed strange to some scholars that Paul waits to the end of the letter to give thanks in this way.

For these reasons it has been proposed that parts of two, or even three, documents have been combined to form one letter. One possible breakdown is as follows:[1]

Letter A		4:10–20	
Letter B	1:1–3:1a	4:4–7	4:21–23
Letter C	3:1b–21; 4:1–3	4:8–9	

In this view the fullest letter (B) was enlarged by the insertion at suitable points of parts of the earlier Letter C and the later Letter A.

This decomposition of the letter has not commended itself to most English-speaking scholars. There are several arguments against it. First, the word translated 'finally' in 3:1 can equally well mean 'furthermore' and is not necessarily a sign of the closing of a letter. The change of subject in 3:1/2 or 3:1a/1b is abrupt but not so abrupt as to be impossible, especially when we bear in mind that letters were not dictated and written in one continuous session. Scholars are in danger of forgetting the tediousness and slowness of ancient letter-writing, the inevitable result of using poor writing materials. Secondly, the existence of opponents of Paul and his readers has already been hinted at earlier in the letter, and there is a remarkable number of common themes, extending to the use of the same (sometimes unusual) vocabulary in chapter 3 and the earlier

---

[1] So J.-F. Collange, *The Epistle of Saint Paul to the Philippians*, 6.

chapters. There is nothing unusual about Paul discussing gifts and money at the end of a letter (cf. 1 Cor. 16), especially when he has already alluded to the topic in passing earlier, and when the letter is primarily concerned with other matters. And, finally, the letter as it stands has a rhetorical structure which would be lost if it were divided up.[2]

THE PLACE OF WRITING

Paul writes about his bonds (1:13, 17) and raises the possibility of his imminent death, although he believes that he will continue to live and serve the Lord (1:19–6). This indicates that he was a prisoner at the time of writing. If the death he feared was by execution, then the imprisonment must have been in Rome – provided we can assume that Paul was a Roman citizen (as Acts 22:25–8 quite explicitly states, and as is implied by the fact that he could appeal to Caesar) and that it was unlikely that a Roman citizen would be illegally executed away from Rome.

Other evidence in the letter fits this assumption. The 'praetorium' (1:13) would be the members of the praetorian regiment stationed in Rome, and 'Caesar's household' (4:22) members of the imperial civil service. The letter would then belong to the period at the end of Paul's life when he was imprisoned in Rome (Acts 28) and was written several years after the foundation of the church.

For various reasons this hypothesis has been called into question in the twentieth century and an earlier dating which might tie up with the story in Acts has been suggested. It can be argued that the letter was composed at Caesarea during Paul's only other lengthy imprisonment recorded in Acts (Acts 25–6). The 'praetorium' can then be understood to be the governor's headquarters in Caesarea, and 'Caesar's household' to be travelling diplomats. This brings the letter nearer in time to the mission to Philippi. But we do not know that Paul

---

[2] Despite their differences in detail and approach see D. E. Garland, 'The Composition and Unity of Philippians. Some Neglected Literary Factors', *NovT* 27 (1985), 141–73, and D. F. Watson, 'A Rhetorical Analysis of Philippians and its Implications for the Unity Question', *NovT* 30 (1988), 57–88.

expected to be set free in Caesarea and able to visit Philippi again. A compelling case for preferring Caesarea to Rome has not yet been offered.[3]

Since it is possible that Paul's frequent imprisonments (2 Cor. 11:23) could have included one at Ephesus, a case for Ephesus being the provenance of Philippians has been strongly and widely defended, not least because of the comparative proximity of the two towns.[4] However, F. F. Bruce has raised an objection to Ephesus which he regards as fatal: 'there is no known instance in imperial times of its use [the word 'praetorium'] for the headquarters of a proconsul, the governor of a senatorial province such as Asia was at this time.'[5] If this linguistic point is correct, the Ephesian hypothesis must be removed from discussion.

THE SITUATION GIVING RISE TO THE LETTER

Paul's own situation

Although Paul wrote his letter primarily to deal with the needs of the church, part of his purpose was to explain his own situation in relation to the readers. They would naturally assume that his detention would hinder his work as a Christian missionary. Paul wanted to assure them that this was not the case, that the reasons for his imprisonment had become known to the people round about and had thus provided an opportunity for witness, and that other Christians in the area had taken fresh courage to proclaim Christ from his example. (He admitted that some were doing so from the wrong motives, but that didn't worry him unduly.) (1:1–18).

At the same time, there was naturally concern about how his imprisonment would end. Imprisonment in the ancient world was used more as a means of keeping people in custody until their trials and less as a form of sentence (except for situations like debt). Paul evidently anticipated the possibility of trial

---

[3] See, however, G. F. Hawthorne, *Philippians*, xxxvi–xliv.
[4] J.-F. Collange, *Epistle*, 15–19.
[5] F. F. Bruce, *Philippians*, 11.

and execution, and had come to terms with it. But he knew that his friends were praying for him, and he expressed his confidence that the answer to their prayers would be his deliverance and consequently the opportunity for him to give them further help (1:19–26).

The Philippians had an especially close relationship with him and regarded themselves as his partners in the work of the gospel. They had entered into an arrangement to provide him with financial help in the early days of the church. When they heard of his imprisonment, they sent another monetary gift to him by the hand of Epaphroditus, who was one of their own company. Epaphroditus fell severely ill and was anxious about the effect that the news of his illness would have on the church. Paul, therefore, decided that it was best for Epaphroditus to return home instead of staying on (as originally intended) to assist him, and the letter was written to accompany him back home (2:25–30).

From the letter we also learn that Timothy was soon to visit Philippi, and that Paul himself hoped to come. He intended to delay sending Timothy until he had a better idea of his own future, and he was confident that this future would include the possibility of his own return to Philippi (2:19–24).

The problems in the church

The letter was motivated principally by concern about the situation in the church at Philippi. Advice and help needed to be given to it immediately, without waiting for Paul's future visit. Paul had a general concern for its spiritual welfare. But there were particular problems that concerned him.

First, there was clear evidence of quarrelling in the church, two women being specifically named in this connection, but it evidently had spread more widely (4:2). This letter is very much the letter of Christian unity, in which the church is urged to live at peace within itself (4:2–9).[6]

---

[6] The significance of the disunity in the church at Philippi for understanding the letter has been helpfully discussed by D. Peterlin in 'Paul's Letter to the Philippians in the

Secondly, the church was under pressure of some kind, so that Paul can speak of its being called to 'suffer' for Christ (1:29f.). It is reasonable to suppose that the reference is to the general hostility which Christians might face at any time in the ancient world. But the problem may include the people who are mentioned in 3:18 as the enemies of the cross (1:27–30).

Thirdly, Paul writes with some vehemence in chapter 3 against some people who constituted a danger to the church. In 3:2 he warns his readers to beware of a group whom he describes variously as dogs, evil-doers and mutilators. He draws a contrast between them and Christians, who are 'the circumcision', i.e., 'the *true* circumcision'. He suggests that the people whom he is opposing trust in the flesh, and cites as examples of such trust reliance on the marks of Jewish piety and zeal. Later on in the chapter he urges his readers to take him as an example to follow, and he warns them against people who are enemies of the cross, whose god is their stomach, who glory in their shame and set their minds on earthly things (3:18f.). Are these the same group of people or a fresh group?[7]

A good starting point is to consider the epithets Paul uses at the beginning of the chapter.

'Dogs' was a term of opprobrium used by Jews for Gentiles.[8] It is commonly held that Paul turns it back on Jews who criticised Gentile Christians. Although it has been argued that Paul would not have done this, it is perfectly possible that he could have been taking the side of his Gentile converts and warning them against Jews who call them '[Gentile] dogs' by sarcastically calling the Jews '[the real] dogs'.

'Evil workers' means that they are missionaries (cf. 2 Cor. 11:13). 'Evil' suggests opponents of Paul, whom he attacks more strongly than the people in his place of imprisonment in chapter 1. 'Workers' suggests that they were not local people but part of a group of travelling missionaries who followed in

---

Light of Disunity in the Church', unpublished Ph.D. thesis, University of Aberdeen, 1992.

[7] There is no suggestion that the two sets of opponents belong to different letters (all reconstructions maintain the unity of this chapter).

[8] K. Grayston, 'The Opponents in Philippians 3', *ExpT* 97:6 (1986), 170–2.

Paul's footsteps. But it is not certain that the group had actually visited Philippi or that any of the members of the church had succumbed to their teaching. They appear to be a potential danger, but nevertheless one that needs to be strongly guarded against.

'The mutilators' is a pun on 'circumcisers'. They practised physical circumcision and were urging it upon Gentile Christians, and Paul was so angry about this inappropriate rite that he labels it 'mutilation'.

It is not difficult to link this up with the description of the opponents in the later part of the chapter. These people trust in the flesh – in the outward signs of religiosity. They reject Christ; they are on the way to destruction; they set their minds on what Paul considers to be earthly things. The important question is whether Judaising can be linked with making a god of their 'appetite' (REB; Greek *koilia*). Although the word often refers to the stomach, it can be a euphemism for the sexual organ.[9] 'Glorying in their shame' is then Paul's sarcastic reference to vaunting their circumcision. The fact that they were the enemies of the cross need not mean that they spoke out against it (though they may have done), but that this was the implication of their attitude. If it was true that, as such people said, salvation was incomplete without the law, then in Paul's view Christ had died in vain (cf. Gal. 2:21). It may seem surprising that Paul would have said that such people were on their way to perdition, but Gal. 1:8f. shows that he regarded such people as accursed and as servants of the devil.

All this makes it likely that the rival missionaries were Judaising Christians who held that the Christian message must be supplemented by circumcision and presumably the Jewish law. They probably held similar views to Paul's Galatian opponents. Paul's language is violent in both Galatians and Philippians.[10]

[9] C. L. Mearns, 'The Identity of Paul's Opponents at Philippi', *NTS* 33 (1987), 194–204.

[10] It is improbable that the rivals were Gnostics or non-Christian Jews. The link between Philippi and Galatia may seem difficult if Galatians belongs (as I believe) to an earlier period, but in fact there is no difficulty about the same Jewish-Christian opposition continuing throughout Paul's mission. We also hear of rival

Why are these people suddenly mentioned at this point?[11] The most likely reason is that Paul deals first of all (in chapters 1 and 2) with the actual problems in the church. Only then does he turn to deal with a possible danger from outside. However, we should also consider seriously the possibility that already in 1:27–30 there is a reference to this potential danger. Although the description there has been taken to refer to persecution from non-Christians, it could also apply to rival missionaries creating trouble and dissension in the church. It could well be that these verses have in view the varied opposition to Pauline Christianity from both outside and inside the church.

The important question which then arises is whether the background we have deduced for chapter 3 is also relevant to the rest of the letter. Is the threat of this false teaching an explanation for the disunity in the church? And is Paul's earlier teaching, especially about Jesus, composed with it in view?

Certainly the disunity appears to arise primarily out of selfishness and unloving attitudes rather than out of doctrinal disagreements. However, the attitude in chapter 2 is partly at least one of looking down on other believers, a lack of humility; it would tie in with the statement that some people considered themselves 'mature' in 3:14 and may have looked down on others. This spiritual self-satisfaction may constitute evidence of an attitude or disposition to which the false teaching might appeal.

It could be also that part of the reason for stressing the exaltation of Jesus Christ as Lord in 2:6–11 is to prepare the way for emphasising that Christians must conform to the pattern of his humility and suffering and set their hopes on resurrection, when they will meet him at his coming as 'the

travelling missionaries in 2 Cor. 10–13, and, while there is nothing in 2 Cor. about circumcision, which is the *main* issue here, it is not unlikely that the opponents of Paul may have included it in their message.

The verses in the centre of the chapter (3:12–16) deal with the danger of some kind of 'perfectionism'. Mearns finds evidence here that these opponents of Paul were confident and 'triumphalist', and that they had a 'predominantly realised' eschatology. This part of his theory is perhaps less convincing.

[11] Advocates of a multiple-letter theory explain that there is no problem if chapter 3 is a separate letter. But the *origin* of the problem is still not explained in this view.

Lord Jesus Christ' and experience the transformation of their fleshly bodies into glorious ones.

The structure of the letter is reasonably straightforward:

1:1–2	salutation
1:3–4:20	body of the letter
1:3–11	opening prayer report
1:12–26	Paul's own situation and prospects
1:27–2:18	appeal for unity in the church and humility
2:19–30	future visits to Philippi by Paul and his colleagues
3:1–4:1	warning against Judaisers
4:2–9	practical instructions for life in the church
4:10–20	thanks for a gift to Paul
4:21–3	closing greetings

In what follows we shall have to unearth Paul's own understanding of the gospel, acceptance of which constituted the community as a church and which was the basis of his attack on other understandings of Christian living. We must explore the nature of Christian living in community in the light of the gospel, and since much of the letter is concerned with Paul's own personal existence, it will be important to see how he saw this in the light of the gospel.

CHAPTER 10

Laying the foundation

We suggested that we could understand Paul's theology of the church in Philippians by examining, first of all, the foundation on which both his theological thinking and the church itself rests. The foundation can be regarded both as the gospel and as Jesus Christ himself.

Paul's central concern in his work is with what he calls 'the gospel' (1:5, 7, 12, 16, 27a and b; 2:22; 4:3, 15). The gospel is also called the 'word' (*logos*, 1:14) which brings 'life' (2:16). There is something called 'the faith of the gospel' (1:27b) which must mean 'the faith prescribed by the gospel', the response which is demanded by it. The Philippians must live in a manner that is worthy of the gospel (1:27a). Thus the gospel controls the life of both Paul and his readers.

When Paul speaks of the gospel he means: the Christian message and its content. But the content of the gospel is 'preaching *Christ*' (1:15, 17f.). Christ is the basis of the individual Christian's life and of the communal life of the church.

It is not surprising, then, that Jesus Christ is central to Paul's thought in this letter. We may demonstrate this, admittedly in a rather superficial way, by noting that Jesus is mentioned by one form of name or another some forty-nine times; by contrast the word 'God' comes only twenty-four times and 'Spirit' five times. More significantly, this is one of the few letters where teaching about Jesus is made thematic in the sense that an extended passage can be said to have Jesus as its direct theme (2:6–11).

This passage stands out by its lofty language from the surrounding material. The questions surrounding it are complicated, and scholarly discussion seems endless. The main problems that arise can be summarised as follows:

1 Was the passage composed earlier, perhaps for a different setting?
2 Did Paul take it over from elsewhere? If so, did he amend it?
3 Has the passage a structure which will enable us to understand it better?
4 How is the passage to be understood in detail?
5 What is the purpose of the passage in its context?[1]

PRE-FORMED MATERIAL?

Was the passage composed, whether by Paul or by somebody else, separately from (and therefore earlier than) the composition of Philippians? This hypothesis seems probable to most scholars. It is supported by the facts that the passage has a much more 'poetic' style than its surroundings and that it may possibly have existed originally in Aramaic.[2] Many would also argue that it does not fit perfectly into its present context and gives the impression of containing teaching for another purpose.[3] Other comparable pieces of christological writing in the NT might suggest that a 'form' of 'hymns' existed.

There is, however, real doubt in many cases as to whether the other so-called 'hymns' in the NT are accurately described thus. We shall also see that this passage fits remarkably well into its immediate context and into the letter as a whole. There are other occasions where Paul adopts poetic-sounding language (1 Corinthians 13) which is eminently appropriate to the context, even if there appears to be something of a break in the flow of thought. We may well conclude that this passage may not have been composed from scratch at the time of the writing of Philippians, but the close relevance of the passage to the

---

[1] We shall consider the question of the background of thought at a later stage. See pp. 162–4.
[2] J. A. Fitzmyer, 'The Aramaic Background of Philippians 2:6–11', *CBQ* 50 (1988), 470–83.
[3] For detailed studies of these and other questions see especially R. P. Martin, *Carmen Christi: Philippians 2:5–11 in Recent Interpretation and in the Setting of Early Christian Worship.* For subsequent study see M. Silva, (*Philippians*, 104–33).

situation suggests that it was carefully moulded for its purpose here.

WHO WAS ITS AUTHOR?

Was the passage composed by Paul himself or by somebody else? The parallel of 1 Corinthians 13 shows that there is no reason why Paul cannot have composed an elevated piece. In order to argue that the passage is not by Paul we would need to demonstrate that it shows a different theology and contains indications of alteration by Paul.

On the first point, the fact that Paul used it here shows that he did not regard it as in any way different from his own views. Again, none of the alterations which scholars suggest he may have made in it materially affect or alter its teaching. The question is then the more subtle one of whether, although the passage contains ideas congenial to him, he is not likely to have put them together or expressed them in this form himself. I can see no reason to adopt this suggestion. The parallel of 2 Corinthians 8:9 points strongly to a Pauline origin.

On the second point, the question reduces to whether the passage betrays signs of a rhetorical shape that has been distorted by Pauline additions. I am not persuaded that we need to subtract any material to recover a hypothetical original 'form' of the material.

On the whole, then, it seems most likely that it is a Pauline composition.

THE STRUCTURE OF THE PASSAGE

Has the passage a 'poetical' or 'hymnic' style? Numerous attempts have been made to recognise a structure in the passage. E. Lohmeyer divided up the passage into six strophes, each of three lines, at the cost of removing the words 'even the death of the cross' as a Pauline addition.[4] J. Jeremias proposed an alternative arrangement of three strophes each of four lines,

---

[4] Silva is attracted to Lohmeyer's structure, but does not finally adopt it (ibid., 106, 112).

at the cost of also removing the phrases 'of beings in heaven and on earth and under the earth' and 'to the glory of God the Father'. Finally, R. P. Martin has proposed an arrangement of six sets of couplets, which turns out to be the same as the proposal of Jeremias without the strophic arrangement:

A   [6]Who, though He bore the stamp of the divine Image,
      Did not use equality with God as a gain to be exploited;
B   [7]But surrendered His rank,
      And took the role of a servant;
C   Accepting a human-like guise,
      And appearing on earth as the Man;
D   [8]He humbled Himself,
      In an obedience which went so far as to die
           [*even death on the cross.*]
E   [9]For this, God raised Him to the highest honour,
      And conferred upon Him the highest rank of all;
F   [10]That, at Jesus' name, every knee should bow,
         [*of things in heaven, on earth and under the earth,*]
      [11]And every tongue should own that 'Jesus Christ is Lord'
         [*to the glory of God the Father.*][5]

An important argument in favour of this scheme is the claim that there is synonymous parallelism in each of the couplets. However, there are a number of difficulties:

1 The lines in the first couplet are not synonymous like the others.
2 The syntactical structure is broken up. Couplet C breaks up a sentence.
3 Various alleged Pauline additions have to be subtracted to make the thing work. It is difficult to know how to evaluate an argument of this kind which may be regarded as circular, but if we can find a structure that does not demand the use of the scissors, this is surely preferable to resorting to hypothetical reconstructions.

---

[5] Martin, *Carmen Christi*, 38.

4 The lines are by no means all the same length, but it is not clear how far this might be expected in a 'hymn'.

When all is said and done, we may wonder how far this arrangement aids the understanding of the passage. I tend to conclude that we are right to see a degree of form in the passage but to emphasise that in no NT 'hymn' is there an absolutely 'regular' form. Commentators have perhaps been misled by looking for a poetic structure when all that is present is a 'rhetorical' prose structure.[6] If so, there is no need to regard any of the additions as true additions.

THE TEACHING OF THE PASSAGE

The original situation of the person

The subject is not stated within the passage itself, but the opening relative pronoun refers to Christ Jesus. The passage is notable because it is introduced as a statement about Christ Jesus who was in the form of God. If, as we shall claim in a moment, the reference is to a pre-existent being, this naming of the person as 'Christ Jesus' is striking. We may contrast the prologue to John's Gospel, which begins by speaking not about Jesus but about the Logos who became incarnate as Jesus. Probably the thought here is to be paraphrased as: 'The person who was later known as Christ Jesus ... '

This person existed 'in the form of God'. The crucial problem is the significance of the word 'form'. In its context it must be understood in the light of v. 7, where the person takes the form of a servant. 'Form' can mean outward appearance, but it may refer to the kind of form that fully expresses the being that underlies it.[7] Somewhat differently the idea of 'mode of existence' has been suggested.[8]

It has also been proposed that the 'form of God' is tanta-

---

[6] C. J. Robbins, 'Rhetorical Structure of Philippians 2:6–11', *CBQ* 42 (1980), 73–82. See further G. D. Fee, 'Philippians 2:5–11: Hymn or Exalted Pauline Prose?', *BBR* 2, 1992, 29–46.

[7] Hawthorne, *Philippians*, 81–4, citing MM s.v.

[8] Silva (*Philippians*, 113–16) argues against adopting too precise a definition of the term.

mount to his 'glory' and to his 'image', in which case we would
have a parallel with Adam, who was created in the divine
image and likeness. This view has been developed especially by
J. D. G. Dunn, who holds that the passage refers to the character of Christ's earthly life in terms of the contrast with Adam:
confronted with the same choice as Adam, who was made in
the image of God and shared his glory, Christ chose not to
grasp equality with God but to empty himself and share
human slavery to corruption and death.[9] However, the argument for this view is tenuous, and we shall do best to think of
the person as possessing the same mode of existence or characteristic qualities as God.[10]

The second phrase refers to being 'equal with God'. If we
regard this equality as something which the person possessed
(see below), then it is clearly closely parallel to the 'form of
God', though not necessarily identical with it. Equality with
God suggests sharing the same rank and hence possessing the
same sovereign status. Thus the thought is of the supremacy
possessed by God and also by this Being.

But the problem is whether or not the person already possessed this. He did not regard equality with God as a '*harpagmos*'. The significance of this word has been endlessly debated.
The recent treatment by N. T. Wright comes out strongly for
the view that the word signifies something that is already
possessed and can be taken advantage of or exploited. Thus the
heir of a wealthy person can take advantage of his wealth to use
it for his own purposes and to make it the basis for increasing
his wealth. The point is then that, although the person possessed this equality with God and could have exploited it to his
own advantage, he did not so use it.[11]

[9] J. D. G. Dunn, *Christology in the Making* (London: SCM Press, 1908), 114–21.

[10] L. D. Hurst, 'Re-Enter the Pre-Existence of Christ in Philippians 2:5–11?' *NTS* 32
(1986), 449–57; C. A. Wanamaker, 'Philippians 2:6–11: Son of God or Adamic
Christology?', *NTS* 33 (1987), 179–93. Dunn has responded to his critics (*Christology*, xviii–xix).

[11] N. T. Wright, '*harpagmos* and the Meaning of Philippians 2:5–11', *JTS* 37 (1986),
321–52. Essentially the same theological result is reached by C. F. D. Moule, who
takes *harpagmos* to mean 'the act of getting': Jesus did not regard equality with
God as 'getting' but as 'giving' ('Further Reflexions on Philippians 2:5–11', in
W. W. Gasque and R. P. Martin, *Apostolic History and the Gospel* (Exeter: Paternoster,
1970), 264–76). Cf. Bruce, (*Philippians*, 76f.).

The self-emptying of the person

Instead, then, of clinging to and using his position, he emptied himself. The various possibilities of interpretation of this phrase include: he said 'no' to his own desires, he retained his position of equality with God but did not use it, he gave up his position of equality with God, or he gave up his divine attributes (but these have not been mentioned in the passage).

The context indicates that the significant thing is that he gave up sovereignty to be a servant. Or, as Wright puts it, he saw that 'self-negation [was] the proper expression of divine character': the true *use* of equality with God lay in a vocation of humiliation and servanthood.[12]

That is to say, it is 'taking the form' of a servant which is the controlling thought and which is then elaborated or expounded. We seem led to the view that the person lays aside the prerogatives of supreme sovereignty in order to take up the position of a servant. It is not a question of giving up divine attributes or nature. These are not in view.

This basic thought is then expounded by stating that he appeared in the likeness of men. As in Rom. 8:3 this means that he took on human form, but without necessarily losing his divine nature. There is no indication that he gave up the 'form of God'. We have then 'incarnation'.

The next phrase appears to gather up what has just been said before passing on to something new. He was 'discovered' to be as a man in outward appearance. The word is perhaps equivalent to 'manifested' but that word has misleading associations in that it implies the appearance of a divine person who is shown or revealed to be such; the point here is that the appearance of the person is simply as a man.

Obedience to the point of death

In this form he then humbled himself by becoming obedient to death. The content of the humbling is the becoming obedient. A sovereign person who gives commands here becomes subject

[12] Wright, '*harpagmos*', 347.

to commands, and that is what is meant by humbling oneself: it is submission to the will of somebody else. He did not of course obey death: his obedience went to the point of willingness to accept death. To whom, then, was he obedient? The text does not say, but presumably it was ultimately to God.

Submitting to being put to death is surely the ultimate in self-humiliation – especially for a supreme sovereign. But not quite – the full depth of the humiliation comes in the last phrase added on dramatically for effect: it was death on the gallows, a fate reserved for slaves and rebels against Rome. The phrase is the climax of the description, and it is either original or else a very apt addition.

Exaltation and homage

From this point on the passage becomes less controversial. There is an important shift in that the subject of the action is no longer Christ Jesus but God the Father. Because of Christ's willingness to submit in this way, God – the supreme ruler – raised him to the loftiest height. Opinions differ whether this means that he was exalted to the position previously held or to an even higher position. It is difficult to see how the absolute position in v. 6 could be exceeded. Therefore we favour the view that the reference is to the 'public' exaltation of the person. Just as he was openly put to death, now he is openly exalted. Whereas previously his position was in a sense implicit and does not appear to have been public or acknowledged, now he is 'greatly exalted' publicly.

Wright suggests that the point is the divine confirmation that the humiliation and death of Jesus was the appropriate manifestation of divine love.[13] This is demonstrated by granting him the name which is superior to all other names – name here signifying the expression of a person's status. The name is generally agreed to be that of 'Lord', especially in view of the confession in v. 11.[14]

[13] Ibid., 351.

[14] The view that 'Jesus' is meant seems most unlikely – he had that name before his death. Nevertheless, see Silva, *Philippians*, 129, for some questioning of the usual interpretation. There is a good summing up in Bruce, *Philippians*, 72f.

The purpose of the exaltation or rather the explication of it is that, when the name of Jesus – just Jesus! – is announced, everybody will do two things. First, they will bow their knees, which is a demonstration of acknowledgment of superior status. It is important to recognise that Isaiah 45:23 is being alluded to, i.e., that the honour normally given to God (see Rom. 14:11!) is now being given to Jesus. This honour is given by the whole universe. Second, they will confess that Jesus Christ is Lord. In other words, they have to echo the divine name-giving, and acknowledge it. To do this is ultimately to glorify not Jesus but God the Father, who retains his supreme sovereignty. There is no question of Jesus being exalted above the Father or of his acting independently of him.

We note in passing that there is not necessarily a reference to universal homage or to the action producing salvation; the theme is that it is Jesus who receives universal exaltation, not that all will be saved or anything of the kind. It is difficult to believe that, if 2:11 refers to universal worship, the attitude of Christians when they confessed 'Jesus is Lord' was anything different. Their attitude was one of worship of Jesus as the Lord. The placing of Jesus on an equality with God is likewise indicated, except that there is a trace of subordination right to the end.

So, in summary, the passage depicts the 'career' of a person who gives up what could have been his as a result of being equal with God, takes on the role of a slave in adopting human form and human destiny and is consequently exalted openly by God, given the name of Lord and made the object of universal worship.

Could early Christians have believed this about Jesus? Perhaps the most serious argument against the view of the passage defended here is that it is unlikely that early Christians with their Jewish monotheistic background could have embraced what looks dangerously like 'binitarianism' – the belief in two deities.[15] However, it is important to remember that from a very early stage Christians were conscious of the

[15] J. D. G. Dunn, 'Was Christianity a Monotheistic Faith from the Beginning?', *SJT* 35 (1982), 303–36.

status of Jesus as the Son of God, and they had to develop an understanding of Jesus – and of God – which took account of this fact. The development of the concept of God as the Father (2:11!) of Jesus enabled them to formulate the matter in a way that did not compromise the supremacy of God or the status of Jesus.[16]

THE PURPOSE OF THE PASSAGE

In its present context the passage serves to put an example before the readers. They are to behave as Christ Jesus behaved, to have the same attitude as he had.[17] We should note, however, that the passage falls into two parts, one with Jesus, the other with God as subject. The readers are therefore called to imitate only what Jesus did. Even more significant is the fact that the hymn culminates in the declaration that Jesus is Lord with the implication that the readers should accept him as Lord – and therefore follow the pattern of life exemplified in him.

The hymn is often misunderstood as teaching that the way to glory and exaltation is through humiliation and suffering. It is true that the readers are promised that they shall be glorified in the same way as Christ (3:20) – provided that they suffer with him (3:10f.). If you want to wear a crown, you must be prepared to carry a cross. But this does not mean that Christians should selfishly seek future glory by present self-sacrifice. Is not the point rather that true greatness, the kind that God recognises, is seen in service and humiliation? The effect of the hymn is to give a redefinition of greatness, to show that service is what really counts and is vindicated by God. It amounts to a glorification of service and the servant.

It follows from what has been said about the present purpose of the hymn that the lack of explicit reference to the saving

---

[16] See in general L. W. Hurtado, *One God, One Lord: Early Christian Devotion and Ancient Jewish Monotheism* (London: SCM Press, 1988).

[17] For the interpretation of 2:5 see below, p. 143. The readers are to consider the career of Jesus who is their Lord, to note his character and in accepting him as Lord to live as he lived.

effects of the death of Jesus is entirely appropriate. They are not mentioned because the hymn is about something else, namely the pattern of service provided by Jesus in his dying. Thus this omission fits in nicely with the view that Paul composed the material with a deliberate ethical intent rather than as a statement of soteriology. It is presented to quarrelling Christians who think too highly of themselves and it calls them to own Christ as Lord – and in so doing to acknowledge that service and humility are the qualities which are honoured by God.

CHAPTER 11

Building the walls

So far we have seen that Jesus Christ is the centre of Paul's thought and message in the letter. Our next task is to explore how the readers are related to him. Pursuing our metaphor of the building, we aim to see how the individual stones relate to the foundation. Paul uses three key phrases in this letter to express the relationship between Christ and Christians: 'in Christ', 'with Christ' and 'knowing Christ'.

'IN CHRIST'

The phrase 'in Christ' (and equivalents) is used about 165 times in the Pauline corpus to express the relationship of believers to Christ. It plays a dominating role in Philippians, occurring twenty-one times (as frequently as in Romans).[1]

Difficulties have sometimes arisen in understanding it because it is assumed that it must have the same force every time it is used.[2] In the most careful study of this phrase in English E. Best has observed that the phrase occurs in nine

---

[1] For discussion of this phrase in English see especially E. Best, *One Body in Christ* (London: SPCK, 1955), 1–33; J. K. S. Reid, *Our Life in Christ* (London: SCM Press, 1963), 1–31; A. J. M. Wedderburn, 'Some Observations on Paul's Use of the Phrases "in Christ" and "with Christ"', *JSNT* 25 (1985), 83–97. In other languages see F. Büchsel, '"In Christus" bei Paulus', *ZNW* 42 (1949), 141–58; M. Bouttier, *En Christ: étude d'exégèse et de théologie pauliniennes* (Paris: Presses universitaires de France, 1962); F. Neugebauer, 'Das paulinische "In Christo"', *NTS* 4 (1957–8), 124–38, and *In Christus: eine Untersuchung zum paulinischen Glaubensverständnis* (Göttingen: Vandenhoeck und Ruprecht, 1961).

[2] J. P. Louw and E. Nida appear to take it to be simply a marker of close personal association (*Greek-English Lexicon of the New Testament Based on Semantic Domains* (New York: United Bible Societies, 1988), vol. 1, 793). It is doubtful whether this does justice to the complex usage.

types of expression.[3] The occurrences in Philippians are allotted by Best to five of his categories. It may be helpful to summarise his analysis and then make some observations starting from it.

a	adjectivally of persons	1:1, 13, 14; 3:9; 4:7, 21
	'A is in Christ'	
b	adverbially of relationships between believers	2:29; 4:2
	'A does/is x to B in Christ'	
c	adverbially of a person's action	1:26; 2:19, 24; 3:1, 3; 4:1, 4, 10
	'A does x in the Lord'	
d	adverbially of God's actions	2:1; 3:14; 4:13
	'God is/does to us x in Christ'	
e	'ordinary', non-technical sense	2:5; 4:19

Some revision of this allocation is needed. In particular, several of the examples allotted to other groups seem to belong to the category Best calls 'ordinary' – cases in which the use of 'in' arises out of normal Greek syntax. Let us attempt a reclassification.

Ordinary usage

First of all, Paul can use a verb that is naturally and normally followed by 'in', and there is no 'technical' use of the phrase.

This applies to the verb 'to trust in'. In 2:24 Paul says that he trusts in the Lord that he will soon be able to visit Philippi. The close parallelism with 3:3–4, where the verb is used in the phrase 'to trust in flesh', indicates that we have this normal usage here.[4] A few lines earlier in 2:19 the thought is similar: 'I hope in the Lord Jesus to send Timothy to you.' Paul's hope, based on the Lord and on his care for him, is that he will make it possible to send Timothy (cf. 1 Cor. 15:19). Likewise, 4:1: 'Stand fast in the Lord' refers to trusting in him and on the basis of him.

In 3:3 Paul says 'We exult in Christ'; i.e., 'The ground of our exulting is Christ and what he has done for us.' The parallelism

---

[3] Best's remaining categories are: A is x in the Lord; The 'gift' of God in Christ; A, B, C ... are one in Christ; 'cosmic' (*One Body in Christ*, 1–33).

[4] Cf. Rom. 14:14, Gal. 5:10, 2 Thess. 3:4; the verb can be used with other prepositions.

with 'to have confidence in' (3:3f.) confirms that this must be the sense. Similarly, when Paul says in 1:26: 'your exulting may increase in Christ in me because of my presence', he means that the readers may exult in Christ on account of him or with reference to him (cf. Rom. 15:17).

We can understand references to rejoicing in the same way. In 3:1 Paul means: 'Let the Lord be the basis/cause of your rejoicing.' Here and in 4:4 and 10 Paul and his readers rejoice because of what the Lord is doing here and now in his care and concern for them.

Finally, we have 4:13: 'I can do everything in the One who strengthens me.' This pretty well means 'in the power of' or possibly 'on account of'.

This gives nine 'ordinary' uses where the 'in' phrase is part of a normal expansion of the verbal idea. It is used to indicate that the basis of Christian confidence and the object of Christian exultation is Christ.

Use with verbs of divine action

In the next group of examples we have actions of God towards Christians, and it seems most likely that Christ is regarded as the channel or instrument through whom these blessings are conveyed. In 3:14 'God's upward call in Christ Jesus' is his call revealed to us in and through Jesus. In 'God's peace will guard your hearts in Christ Jesus' (4:7) Christ is the means or instrument through which the peace comes. We have the same force in 4:19: 'God will fulfil all your needs according to his riches in glory [given] in Christ Jesus.' In 2:1 'If there is any comfort, etc. [sc. given by God] in Christ ...' we want a rendering that will cover all four gifts of God. The verse appears to mean something like 'if there is any comfort ... to be found in Christ and your experience of him as a living person who communicates God's comfort to you'.

In all of these cases the thought of Christ as the channel or means of God's blessings implies that believers must come into a personal relationship with Christ in order to receive them, but it seems to be overtranslation if we take the phrase, as some scholars do, to mean 'in virtue of your union with Christ'.[5]

Use with verbs of human action

In 2:29 – 'Receive him in the Lord' – 'in the Lord' qualifies the verb 'receive' rather than the pronoun 'him'.[6] We may paraphrase the command to mean 'Receive him in a Christian manner.' The fact that the reference is to 'the Lord' rather than to 'Christ' may suggest that it is Jesus as the one who has authority over conduct in the church who is in mind, and that the phrase should be taken to mean something like 'in the manner appropriate to the situation in which Jesus is Lord'. Likewise, in 4:2 – 'I beseech Euodia and Syntyche to agree in the Lord' – the reference is to the kind of conduct appropriate where Jesus is Lord.

Adjectival use

We now come to a usage in which the phrase 'in Christ' functions adjectivally to describe the state of Christians.

In the salutation in 1:1 (cf. Col. 1:2; Eph. 1:1) Paul writes to 'all the saints [who are] in Christ Jesus'. He is characterising his readers as saints by virtue of the fact that they are 'in Christ'.[7] Two types of understanding exist.

First, the phrase could express 'incorporation in Christ' or 'union with Christ'. By way of explanation it is suggested that the phrase is shorthand for 'in the body of Christ' (cf. 1 Cor. 12:18; Col. 3:15); this breaks down on the fact that the latter is not a phrase that Paul uses. Appeal has been made to the idea of corporate personality. The phrase might indicate belonging to a group of people who are united to Christ, and so what is true of him is true of them.

---

[5] E.g. Silva translates: 'by virtue of your union with Christ Jesus, God's peace ... will stand guard ...'.

[6] In Rom. 16:2 the order of words in UBS shows that the phrase goes with the verb.

[7] Similar statements are found in 2 Cor. 5:17 and in Rom. 8:1 and 16:7 and 11. The phrase can be used of individuals or groups.

Second, there is the possibility that the phrase refers to a state of being determined or affected by the fact of Christ – a kind of circumstantial usage.[8] F. Neugebauer has argued strongly that the believer is in a situation which is controlled by the fact of Christ crucified and risen.

These two ideas can be brought together. The idea is one of close union between Christ and the believer. We can see this from the way in which Paul can also speak of Christ being 'in' the believer (Gal. 2:20; cf. 4:19); and in John we have the concept of mutual indwelling, where the language must surely be metaphorical. At the same time, if believers are united with the Christ who died and rose again, then their existence and behaviour must be determined by the pattern of Christ.

The interpretation of 4:21 is uncertain: 'Greet every saint in Christ Jesus.' Does 'in Christ' go with the verb (cf. Rom. 16:22, 1 Cor. 16:19b) or the noun (cf. 1 Cor. 1:2)? Being a saint and extending greetings can both take place 'in Christ', but here the former possibility is more likely.

The usage in 1:14 is also ambiguous. Paul may be saying 'the brothers in the Lord have become confident by my bonds to preach' (cf. Col. 1:2, 4:7 = Eph. 6:21) or 'the brothers have become confident in the Lord by my bonds to preach' (cf. 2:24).

As for 'I want to be found in Christ' (3:9), this example appears to differ from the others in the use of the verb 'to be found', but the difference disappears if we take it to mean 'I want to be found [to be] in Christ'. Paul wants to be closely united to Christ – with the consequence that what is true of him is extended to his people. As he is righteous, so they share in his righteousness. As he experiences the power of God which raised him from the dead, so too do they.

Uncertain uses

'My bonds are manifest in Christ' (1:13) is difficult in that a thing rather than a person is said to be 'in Christ'. Paul appears

---

[8] See especially F. Neugebauer, '"In Christo"'. W. Schenk (*Die Philipperbriefe des Paulus: Kommentar*, 307) suggests that it signifies 'in the area of Christ's rule', local, not 'formal'.

to mean that his 'bonds are seen to have come about because of Christ' and thus they have become a means of testimony to the gospel.

Finally, there is 2:5: 'Let this mind be in you which [was] also in Christ Jesus.' This can mean 'Think in this way which was also thought in the case of Christ Jesus.' However, this may be a case of our fourth type of use. Many scholars take the sentence to mean 'Adopt [then] this frame of mind in your community – which indeed is [proper for those who are] in Christ Jesus.'[9] Either way, the thought is that the readers are to let their conduct be dictated by a consideration of how Christ behaved as described in the following verses.

In summary, the usage is varied and cannot be reduced to one category. The phrase does not necessarily always carry the idea of 'incorporation in Christ', as is often assumed. Rather phrases with 'in' are used in four ways:

> as the appropriate construction with numerous verbs to express the basis of confidence, exultation, rejoicing, etc. *The basis and foundation of Christian experience lies in Jesus.*

> in an instrumental or causal way to express the means by which divine blessings come to people. *Jesus is seen as the channel through which God carries out his work in the lives of believers.*[10]

> in a more circumstantial way to express the parameters affecting their behaviour. *Christian behaviour is determined by 'the Lord'.*

> in a metaphorical way to indicate a close union between Christ and the believer. *Christians are closely linked to Christ both now and at the judgment so that what is true of him becomes true of them.*

Whatever the usage, it is clear that the effect is to show that the Christian life is utterly dominated by Christ. Almost

---

[9] So Silva, *Philippians*, 107.
[10] Wedderburn ('Some Observations') defends an instrumental, causal sense in a number of places, appealing to the analogy with 'in you [sc. Abraham] shall all the nations be blessed' (Gal. 3:8). That is to say, people will be blessed by means of, on account of Abraham. To ask whether the same is true of 'in Adam' (1 Cor. 15:22 only) would take us beyond our present purpose.

everything that Paul says about the Christian life in this letter is conditioned by the phrase 'in Christ'. Further, the Christ is the Christ who humbled himself, died and was exalted, the crucified and risen Christ. God's saving grace comes through this Christ. The behaviour of his people is that patterned and prescribed by this Christ and by no other. Thus cross and resurrection determine the significance of the phrase.

'WITH CHRIST'

So much is it the case that Christ determines the life of Paul that in 1:21 he says that for him living is Christ and dying is gain. He longs to be 'with Christ' (1:23), a state which is better than this earthly life and which must refer to being with him in the next life. The phrase is used in the same way in 1 Thess. 4:17 and 5:10, where it refers to being with the Lord for ever and living with him, and the context is the future life.

The same thought can also be expressed by the use of verbs compounded with the preposition 'with' (*sun*). For example, we have *summorphos* used in 3:21 in reference to receiving a body of glory like Christ's and *summorphizomai* in 3:10 to growing in conformity to the death of Christ.

In 3:10, however, the reference must be to an experience in this life. Some commentators use the word 'sacramental' in this context, thinking especially of the link between baptism and dying with Christ in Rom. 6. But the thought cannot be purely sacramental in the sense that the experience is confined to the moment of baptism. When Paul speaks of being conformed to the death of Jesus he is thinking of an ongoing process which was also the experience of Christ, which is part of being closely associated with him and which thus brings us into closer conformity with him.

There is, then, a state of 'being with Christ' (1:23) that is not realisable in this life. The implication of 3:11 is that those who share in the final glory are those who already in this life know the power of Christ's resurrection and have shared with him in his sufferings.

'KNOWING CHRIST'

In the light of 1:21–3 it is not surprising that in 3:8–10 Paul says that what matters above all else is to know Christ, to gain Christ and to be found in Christ. This language of 'knowing Christ' is rare elsewhere in Paul (2 Cor. 5:16a and b; cf. 2 Cor. 2:14, 'the knowledge of him')[11] and deserves attention. Scholars have suggested various possible keys to understanding it.

For E. Lohmeyer the knowledge of Christ is primarily the completed vision of the Lord in the next world experienced by a martyr who has made his sacrifice: it has not a mystical but an eschatological meaning.[12] The difficulty with this view is that the reference does not appear to be primarily eschatological in the strict sense of that term. Moreover, knowing Christ and sharing his sufferings belong together as simultaneous parts of the Christian's experience.

M. Dibelius held that it was some kind of experience similar to Hellenistic mysticism in which the worshipper enjoys an ecstatic or visionary experience of God and is transformed by it.[13]

A background in Gnosticism is put forward by R. Bultmann.[14] Gnostics are said to have believed in 'a higher salvific knowledge accessible only to themselves and to their initiates'.[15] However, the language is completely unphilosophical, making this background unlikely.[16] Moreover, the Gnostic knowledge appears to have been knowledge of the contents of a myth, and this is not what Paul has in mind here. The ultimate refutation is provided by Bultmann himself who, having mentioned Gnosticism as providing the concepts, then gives a much more plausible existentialist interpretation of the passage which completely ignores the alleged origins.

Over against the suggestion that the language comes from

---

[11] Cf. 2 Tim. 1:12 (God or Christ?) and, especially, 2 Pet. 3:18.
[12] E. Lohmeyer, *Die Briefe an die Philipper, Kolosser und an Philemon*, 134f., 138.
[13] After J. Gnilka, *Der Philipperbrief*, 193 n. 46.
[14] R. Bultmann, *TDNT* 1, 710f.
[15] Hawthorne, *Philippians*, 138.
[16] J. Ernst, *Die Briefe an die Philipper, an Philemon, an die Kolosser, an die Epheser*, 96.

Greek philosophy or Hellenistic mysticism J. Dupont expounds the idea in terms of the Judaistic idea of knowledge of God.[17] In the OT knowing God refers to recognising that the one true God is Yahweh, and this knowledge is then expressed in keeping his commandments. But what Paul expresses here, while it includes these elements, surely goes beyond them.

A mixture of influences is detected by some scholars. For example, F. W. Beare holds that here we have the Hellenistic idea of '*mystical participation* in the accomplished experience of the Saviour'. Yet religious and moral ideas are also carried over from Hebraic usage into a distinctively Christian synthesis. In Paul, as in the OT, knowledge of the divine is 'an impression which masters not only a man's thoughts but his heart and will'.[18]

But here, as so often, it is F. F. Bruce who penetrates most deeply into Paul's thought and expresses it succinctly when he says that it is 'personal knowledge: it includes the experience of being loved by him and loving him in return – and loving, for his sake, all those for whom he died'.[19]

G. F. Hawthorne speaks of a personal appropriation of and communion with Christ himself. It is a personal encounter with Christ which inaugurates a special intimacy with him that is life-changing and ongoing.[20]

J.-F. Collange notes that knowledge is sometimes associated with preaching and baptism and holds that the reference here is to experience in Christian worship. He stresses that Christ is known as Lord.[21]

At this point we may note how in 2 Cor. 4:6 Paul knows the glory of God in the face of Jesus. This suggests that he saw visually the face of Jesus at his conversion and saw it filled with divine glory.[22] The text suggests that this was an ongoing experience, of the sort that fills the recipient with rapture and

---

[17] J. Dupont, *Gnosis* (Paris: J. Gabalda, 1949); cf. W. D. Davies, *Christian Origins and Judaism* (Philadelphia: Fortress, 1962), 141.
[18] G. A. Smith, quoted in F. W. Beare, *The Epistle to the Philippians*, 114.
[19] Bruce, *Philippians*, 113.
[20] Hawthorne, *Philippians*, 138.
[21] Collange, *Epistle*, 129.
[22] See especially S. Kim, *The Origin of Paul's Gospel* (Tübingen: J. C. B. Mohr, 1981).

is thus tending to the so-called 'mystical'. We cannot, therefore, ignore this element.

In summary, Paul is speaking about a knowledge that should be characteristic of Christian experience and is not to be regarded as peculiar to himself or as confined to martyrs. This knowledge is of supreme importance to him. It is of surpassing importance or worth compared with anything else. But, more than this, it is an experience that demands self-sacrifice and abandonment of other aims: it cannot be combined with trusting in worldly things and regarding them as worth having. This knowledge appears to have links with the OT concept of 'knowing God', which is often expounded in terms of knowing God's will. What is important is that Christ is here functioning in the same way as God (this is not surprising in view of 2:6–11). Yet it is more personal than simply knowing Christ's will, for it consists in 'knowing Christ my Lord'. It means a personal relationship with Jesus in which he is apprehended as Lord and is the object of love and devotion. Thus the lordship of Christ in relation to Paul is of the essence of the knowledge.

'Knowing Christ' is further explained in terms of 'gaining Christ'. To know him is worth more than gaining the worldly things of which people boast. There is also a future effect. Since those who are acquitted at the judgment are those who are 'in Christ', Paul wishes that on that day he will be 'discovered' to be 'in Christ'.[23] Those who are 'in Christ' then are so as a result of their already being 'in Christ' now. They have the righteousness that comes from God and is given in response to faith.

The point is then recapitulated in 3:10f. Paul repeats that his aim is to know Christ, but he expands the thought by linking this closely to a further experience:

that I may know:
the power of his resurrection   and the fellowship of his sufferings
being conformed to his death   in order to attain to the resurrection
                                                    from the dead.

---

[23] For this use of 'discovered' see 1 Cor. 4:2 and 2 Cor. 5:3; cf. 1 Pet. 1:7 and 2 Pet. 3:10 and 14.

We note how 'know' here slides over from personal knowledge of a person to personal experience of a power associated with him.[24] This implies that the knowledge is one that changes the person who knows Christ. The 'power of his resurrection' must refer to a present experience since in v. 8 (cf. 1:21) only a present experience of knowing Christ can be meant. It must also be noted that this experience of the power of Christ is inextricably bound up with the experience of sharing in his sufferings. It is Christ crucified and risen who is the object of the believer's experience. Further, since Paul regards justification as a present experience (Rom. 5:1) the language of gaining Christ and having a divine righteousness refers to what he has already experienced as a result of sacrificing his past. So, although the language can point forward to final judgment, the reference is a present one. Nevertheless it must not be forgotten that the experience is an ongoing and incomplete one in this life. 3:12–16 emphasises that Paul has not yet fulfilled his aim completely, and that his aim is to press on until he does so.

We may associate all this with the future hope that is expressed in 3:20f. Christians await as Saviour the Lord Jesus Christ. He will transform their bodies to be like his glorious body. Those who have been conformed to his sufferings will be conformed to his glorious body.

---

24 According to Lightfoot (*Saint Paul's Epistle to the Philippians*, 150): 'The essence of knowing Christ consists in knowing the power of His resurrection.' The verb does not simply mean '"know", but "recognise, feel appropriate"'. The first part of this comment is in danger of reducing the knowledge of Christ to experience of the power of the resurrection. But it is surely a more personal knowledge than that.

CHAPTER 12

The shape of the church

So far we have shown that the foundation of all that Paul has to say in Philippians is Jesus Christ himself. We have seen how believers are related to Jesus Christ in various ways. Now we must examine what Philippians has to tell us about the resulting structure, i.e., about the character of the Christian community.

THE NATURE OF THE CHURCH AS CORPORATE CHRISTIAN EXISTENCE

It goes without saying that Paul views individual believers as constituting communities. In 4:15 the company of people to whom Paul is writing are described as a church and placed alongside other similar groups.

Another name for this group is 'saints'. This name is almost always used in the plural in the NT (in 4:21 'every saint' is in effect plural). This could of course be because Paul is addressing a group rather than an individual, but in fact he is thinking of the group who comprise the people of God.

But the most important indication of the corporate nature of Christian existence is seen in the concept of fellowship (*koinonia*), which is particularly stressed in this letter (1:5; 2:1; 3:10; cf. 1:7; 4:14f.). The basic idea is that two or more people have a common possession, concern or interest in which they participate, and consequently they share together in it. Depending on the situation the elements of participation in the common object or the activity of sharing together may be uppermost.[1]

In 1:5 Paul refers to the sharing of the readers with regard to the gospel. Paul is thinking of how they have helped him in the work of the mission, and the emphasis is thus on their activity, which helped him in their common task. The context indicates that there was a strong bond of love and affection between them as the natural result of this common activity and as the means by which it was promoted.

At the end of the letter (4:15) Paul gives thanks for the gift he had received from them. It reminds him of the fact that at the 'beginning of the gospel', i.e., the mission in Macedonia, no other church had 'shared' in a 'giving and receiving' account except this one at Philippi. Each party gave and received something. The Philippian church gave financial assistance to Paul, and he gave them his spiritual ministry (cf. Gal. 6:6). But the Philippians had continued to send gifts to Paul even when he was no longer with them. Thus fellowship expresses a kind of obligation in which people give to each other as partners in a common task.

In the previous verse (4:14) Paul describes their present action as one of going shares with his affliction. This may mean 'sharing [with him] in his affliction', in the sense that they showed their concern by giving to him, or perhaps that they themselves shared in his affliction by giving themselves although they could ill afford to do so (cf. 2 Cor. 8:1–4).

Paul uses the same idea in 1:7 when he describes how the readers are all of them 'fellow-sharers' in grace, both in his bonds and in the defence and confirmation of the gospel. Here the two elements of sharing and participation both come into play. Paul is saying that in regard to his imprisonment and defence they are his fellow-sharers in grace. This must surely mean that they are his fellows in that 1) they are bound to him

---

[1] H. Seesemann, *Der Begriff KOINONIA im Neuen Testament* (Giessen: Töpelmann, 1933), laid stress on the element of participation to the virtual exclusion of the element of mutuality which results from participation. This latter element has been correctly restored by J. Hainz, *KOINONIA: 'Kirche' als Gemeinschaft bei Paulus* (Regensburg: Friedrich Pustet, 1982).

in affection by their common activity, 2) they are involved in activity like his, for they too are persecuted and having to defend the gospel and 3) they depend upon the same divine grace as the apostles to sustain them in it. The Philippians are thought of as sharing in the grace which inspires apostles and servants of God to do their tasks.[2]

The next passage is 2:1, where Paul's appeal for unity in the church is dependent on the assumed fact that 'in Christ' there is (literally) 'any fellowship of the Spirit'. The problem is whether this fellowship is 'fellowship produced by the Spirit' (subjective genitive). In this case 'fellowship' is much the same as 'unity'. The thought may be that the fellowship produced by the Spirit should lead to expressions of unity in the church (cf. Eph. 4:3). Or is it 'participation in the Spirit' (REB), i.e., in the experience of the Spirit given in conversion or perhaps in his gifts? The thought would then be that common participation in the Spirit should express itself in love between those who so participate. Or is it fellowship with the Spirit, in the sense of communion with, a personal relation with, the Spirit? In this case the thought is possibly that participation in the power and gifts of the Spirit should empower them for unity. But this possibility is unlikely. There is surely no doubt that the sense here should be the same as in 2 Cor. 13:13, but scholars seem to be equally uncertain here.

The key factor is whether there is any evidence whatever for *koinonia* with the genitive case, meaning fellowship arising from or created by somebody or something. In fact, there does not seem to be, and the objective genitive gives a better sense in both passages (cf. 1 Cor. 1:9, 10:16). I am therefore tempted to accept the second possibility, offered above.

Whichever way we take it, however, there exists the idea of a common bond between those who share in the Spirit or which is created by the Spirit. We then have the important thought that part of the nature of the church is that the members each participate in the Spirit and his gifts, and that this brings about a bond between them.

---

[2] See Silva, *Philippians*, 53f.

Finally, we must mention 3:10, where Paul speaks of his personal fellowship with the sufferings of Christ. The nearest parallel is 1 Pet. 4:13 where the thought expressed is that when Christians suffer they are participating in the sufferings of Christ and thus share with him. Fellowship between different Christians is not in mind here.

We can summarise what this means for the church as follows: fellowship is sharing with Paul (and others) in the work of the gospel – specifically by exchange of what each has to offer to the other (1:5; 1:7; 4:14, 15) – and fellowship is sharing together in grace and in the Spirit and is thus being brought together by mutual participation (1:7; 2:1). Such sharing between Christians is inescapable. To be part of the church is to be part of the fellowship and to be involved in the privileges and responsibilities that this entails.

THE CHURCH AS THE NEW PEOPLE OF GOD

Next, we consider the question of the nature of the church in terms of what we may call salvation history. The question is posed for us by what Paul says at the beginning of chapter 3. Here we have a set of warnings and a contrasting description of the church. Basically, it is 'the [true] circumcision', a phrase which refers to the people of God who were marked out in the OT by their submission to this rite. Elsewhere Paul insists that what matters about circumcision is not the physical act but the spiritual reality to which it bears witness: circumcision of the heart is what matters, and it is interpreted as the cutting away of sin from the heart (Dt. 10:16; IQS 5:5). This spiritualised sense is taken up here. The characteristics of such a circumcision are:

'serving [God] by the Spirit of God'. True worship is inward and enabled by the Spirit of God.

'boasting in Jesus Christ'. Believers make him the basis of their confidence and so exult in what he has done.

'not putting one's trust in the flesh'. What this means is spelled out by Paul in a personal manner in the following verses where he claims that he could outdo anybody in such an appeal. The basis of this claim is that he was circumcised as a child (sc. by godly parents); he could trace his Jewish pedigree backwards; he belonged to the most zealous group of observers of the law; he opposed those who were regarded as law-breakers, namely the church; and he was blameless in terms of what the law required. All of these things could have been a basis for confidence in the presence of God. They would have entitled him to a 'righteousness from the law', a righteous standing before God, and therefore he could regard them all as 'gains', as valuable things which he had acquired.

In making these assertions Paul is placing himself over against the physical nation of Israel. He is saying that the things that counted for righteousness in the past no longer count in establishing one's relationship with God.

It is much debated at present whether these things and this standing are to be regarded as 'works of merit' through which people might acquire a righteous standing by their own efforts and in which they might boast. The only questionable point here is 'by their own efforts'. Do we have a works-righteousness which cancels out sins, and do we have a piling up of merit on the basis of which God accepts a person? It is argued that the Jews believed they were God's people by election and grace and not by the works they performed; the works come into the picture only as the means by which one stays in the covenant, or as the signs that one is in the covenant relationship.

Paul certainly believed that a Jew could and did boast on the basis of his works (cf. Rom. 3:27, 4:2; Eph. 2:9). He was also quite clear that boasting is excluded for the Christian (Rom. 3:27). But what is it that is being boasted of? According to the influential work of E. P. Sanders it is a national righteousness, 'the special status of Israel', and thus one can boast of having a righteousness with God based on showing the signs of election – circumcision, and keeping the law in other respects.[3]

---

[3] E. P. Sanders, *Paul, the Law and the Jewish People* (Philadelphia: Fortress, 1983), 43–5; cf. his *Paul and Palestinian Judaism* (London: SCM Press, 1977).

Now this may be correct, but it does not alter the fact that such righteousness does not count with God. Paul now counts as loss what was once a gain to him – i.e., so long as he measured things by the wrong standards. If Paul does not say that 'righteousness is not by law', he nevertheless says that righteousness by the law does not count with God.

What then does 'my righteousness' mean? Sanders labours to show that it does not mean 'self-righteousness' but is 'the peculiar result of being an observant Jew'. However, there is surely a clear contrast between *my* righteousness, which comes *from the law*, and [righteousness] that is *through faith in Christ* and comes *from God*.

The two sets of italicised phrases correspond, and the point is surely the difference between that which I gain or retain by works and that which depends upon trust in what Christ has done. Some of the things Paul claims were his by heredity and some by his own efforts, but they all added up to showing that in terms of the law he was blameless.[4]

Paul rules out this way of attaining righteousness. True righteousness, recognised by God, comes from God and is bestowed on those who have faith. The point in any case is that the claim of *physical* Israel to be the people of God is being disallowed. There is a true circumcision, and it consists of people who exult in Christ and do not trust in the physical signs of belonging to the covenant. Only Paul does not say that Christians are the true circumcision; he says that they are *the* circumcision. He is saying that physical circumcision achieves nothing.

Thus by the time that Paul wrote this letter he had reached the point of identifying the church of God as the true Israel, the real circumcision, and this move would appear to have some implications for the question as to how, or whether, Jews who rejected Christ could any longer be truly part of the Israel of God.

---

[4] For an important corrective to the position of Sanders see S. Westerholm, *Israel's Law and the Church's Faith* (Grand Rapids: Eerdmans, 1988). But see also J. D. G. Dunn, *Jesus, Paul and the Law* (London: SPCK, 1990).

The work of the church is evangelism. Paul thanks his readers
for their fellowship in respect of the gospel (1:5), and he refers
to people who have laboured with him for the gospel, i.e., in
the work of evangelism: Timothy (2:22), Euodia, Syntyche,
Clement and others (4:3). When Paul writes about 'the beginning of the gospel' he means the beginning of the initial period
of evangelism in that part of the world. He reports with
gladness that even his imprisonment has contributed to the
progress of the gospel, i.e., to successful evangelism (1:12).[5]

Paul uses a variety of terms to refer to the people involved in
the work of the gospel. Epaphroditus is described as the messenger (*apostolos*) of the church and as a 'fellow-soldier' (2:25,
Phm. 2) in what is seen as a military campaign. He is also a
'minister' (*leitourgos*; 2:25; Rom. 13:6, 15:16), a word used of a
person who exercised munificence or who served a god in a
temple.[6] Paul and Timothy are 'servants' of Jesus Christ (1:1,
2:22) and the preachers are servants of the churches (2 Cor.
4:5). Two terms in particular are used of Paul's colleagues. The
first is 'brothers', which is used in 4:21 of a group who can be
distinguished from 'all the saints' in 4:22 (cf. 1:14 and 2:25 for
this specialised use).[7] The second term is 'fellow-worker', used
of Epaphroditus (2:25) and of Clement and others (4:3; cf. 3:2
of Paul's rivals).

'Brothers' and 'fellow-workers' between them bring out the
elements of fellowship or partnership in the gospel and the fact
that what they are involved in is a task which requires effort
and which has been entrusted to them by God.

But what about the individual congregation? It is served by
people like Paul who have authority to instruct and command.
It sends out a person like Epaphroditus to share in Paul's
mission. Paul did not ask for personal support from the

---

[5] Schenk (*Die Philipperbriefe*, 134) suggests that in some texts 'in Christ' refers to the
    preaching of the gospel of Christ (e.g. 1:13).
[6] The former sense seems more probable here and in 2:30. However, in 2:17 the
    association with sacrifice suggests the latter sense.
[7] Cf. E. E. Ellis, *Prophecy and Hermeneutic* (Grand Rapids: Eerdmans, 1978), 13–22.

churches, but he did ask for their help in the work by supplying members of his team.[8]

A most unusual feature of this letter is the mention of specific leaders in the church. The local church has leaders called bishops and deacons (1:2). Despite other recent suggestions,[9] two groups of leaders are mentioned, or, shall we say, two groups of people with different functions. Difficulties have been detected in this view, but they are not insurmountable. Indeed, the word used to describe the first group, 'bishop', suggests a supervisory and pastoral role, while the word 'deacon' was on its way to being used of a person who was active in a local church (Rom. 16:1), by contrast with the 'worker' or missionary.

The simplest explanation for Paul's mentioning them may be that by the time this letter was written the leadership was becoming more organised. We may compare this passage to Rom. 16, which also refers to people who were probably leaders in the church (cf. Col. 4:17).

It is noteworthy that even in this letter where the local bishops and deacons are mentioned, Paul writes to the church as a whole, and he does the same thing in all his other letters addressed to churches. What he writes is to be shared with everybody in the church, and he appears to regard the whole church as being involved in making decisions.

Paul regarded the churches that he founded as being involved in his continuing work of mission. But did the local church have an evangelistic responsibility besides that of aiding Paul in his mission? Was 'every member an evangelist'? The following points are relevant.

Paul himself was resident in a place where Christ was being preached by 'the majority of brothers in the Lord' (1:14), admittedly from varied motives. There seems to be some distance between Paul and them. He does not give the impression

---

[8] W.-H. Ollrog, *Paulus und seiner Mitarbeiter*, *WUNT* 50 (Neukirchen: Neukirchener Verlag, 1979).

[9] Schenk (*Die Philipperbriefe*, 78–82) thinks the mention of them is a later interpolation; Collange (*Epistle*, 37–41) argues that there is one group of people characterised in two ways.

that they are members of his 'team' but that they are local people, some of whom show factious tendencies that are inconceivable in the 'team'. Here, then, we seem to have a local church carrying on evangelism.

The Philippians themselves are described as 'holding forth the word of life' (2:16). This could mean to hold fast to the word, and that would cohere with Paul's wish to discover that he had not laboured in vain in the church: they would persevere to the end. Alternatively, they are holding forth the word, or offering it to others, and this fits in with the description of the readers as lights in the world. The point might simply be that they show up the sin and wickedness of the world, but it could have the sense of bringing the revelation of life.

It is most likely that Euodia and Syntyche and others were local people who had been fellow-workers with Paul when he was in Philippi, and it seems unlikely that their activity ceased when he left. Here, then, are people who were active in the gospel, a phrase which must refer primarily to evangelism (4:2f.). And was Epaphroditus chosen to help Paul precisely because he had already demonstrated his gifts to do so?

No hard and fast line can be drawn between those who worked locally and those who worked with Paul. The work of evangelism was not confined to a Pauline travelling team but was carried on locally.

THE GROWTH OF THE CHURCH

Although we have spoken of the church as a building, Paul also uses the metaphor of growth to indicate how it both increases in size by evangelism and develops in maturity. In a sense, the whole of this letter is about growth to Christian maturity. Some people in the church evidently thought that they were already 'perfect' or mature (3:15). While Paul does not pour scorn on such claims (as he does in 1 Cor. 3:1 and 4:8), his letter is nevertheless concerned with deficiencies in the church and the need for growth. It is now time to pull together what Paul says about the growth of the church, which, it may be suggested, is the purpose of this letter.

Let us recapitulate the situation to which Paul was responding. The church was faced by pressure from without, and Paul
feared that its internal disunity could make it incapable of
standing up to such pressure. It faced teaching that emphasised
the need for belonging to the people of God by undergoing
physical circumcision. Nevertheless, it was extremely support-
ive of Paul in his imprisonment and practically concerned for
his welfare.

We have seen that Paul's response to this situation is by
referring the church back to the foundation on which it is built,
the fact of Jesus Christ, who surrendered his privileges as the
Son of God to take on the form of a servant and who has been
now exalted as the Servant-Lord. His crucifixion, resurrection
and future coming are the determining factors in Christian
existence.

1:3–11

In the opening report of what Paul prays for concerning his
friends he gives thanks that God will continue doing a 'good
work' in them right up to the day of Christ. As they share in
Paul's mission, so too they share in God's grace. Specifically,
their love must grow along with knowledge and discernment so
that they may know what is worth doing and be filled with the
fruit of righteousness. We emphasise here the way in which
Paul lays a foundation for subsequent instruction and encouragement by stressing that God is at work in the lives of the
readers. He wants them to have greater love and greater
discernment in understanding God's will for them. All this is
said in a context of deep affection for fellow-workers in
evangelism.

1:12–26

The next section of the letter, which deals with Paul's own
situation, should be taken at its face value of reassuring his
friends about himself. The possibility that he faces of his own
imminent death enables him to reflect on the Christian attitude

to it as a doorway to a closer relationship to the One who already fills and dominates his life. Nevertheless, Paul is confident that he will remain active for the time being. He sees this as partly a result of his friends' intercession for him (1:19). His continued work will enable him to help them to progress and rejoice in their faith (1:24). Thus the most personal and autobiographical part of the letter contains implicit teaching for the readers.

1:27–2:18

The next section deals directly with the danger of disunity (1:27, 2:2–4, 2:14; cf. 4:2). This expresses itself in quarrelling, grumbles and disputes, and these arise out of personal vanity and looking to one's own ends. There is nothing particularly theological about it. But Paul's solution *is* theological.

Basically conduct must be in accordance with the gospel of Christ (1:27). Concretely this means standing fast in one spirit and striving together for the faith. Already at this point readiness for suffering is mentioned (1:27–30). On the basis of the gifts given to Christians by God Paul urges them to avoid arrogance or selfishness (2:1–4). They are to have the same attitude in their relationships with one another – humility and service – as was demonstrated in the case of Christ, whose self-sacrifice was vindicated by God (2:5–11). Acceptance of this Christ as Lord involves obedience to Paul as the messenger of the gospel. Their Christian growth comes about as they work out their salvation. We have here the paradox of the relationship between a divine power working in the lives of Christians and the fact that despite this they can quarrel and sin, and they need to make an effort themselves to achieve what God wants to work in them.

2:19–30

In the remainder of the chapter Paul reverts to personal news about himself and his colleagues, but he does so in such a way that implicitly his friends appear as examples of self-sacrificing attitudes to be emulated (see especially the contrast in 2:20f.), and explicitly they are all described as eager to hear good news of spiritual progress in the church.

3:1–4:1

In chapter 3 the readers are reminded that they are on the way and not yet made perfect. This remark is made in the context of warnings against people who argue that true service of God and grounds for spiritual self-congratulation lie in circumcision and Judaism. Paul insists that Christians should rather exult in Christ, who is the sole source of a righteous standing in God's sight. To know him is a far more satisfying experience than having human grounds for pride. Such knowledge, however, involves readiness to follow the pattern of the cross, and here a further warning is issued against a way of life that makes an idol out of the satisfaction of human, worldly appetites. Rather, Christians pin their hopes on the return of the Lord, who will give them new, glorious bodies.

4:2–9

Next, there is a renewed appeal for unity, linked with a call to rejoicing, prayer and trust in God. There is also a call to think about things that are true and good in every kind of way. This is an unparalleled instruction in Paul. What can have given rise to it? Is there a contrast with the shameful things and the earthly things in 3:19? Is it connected with the spirit of quarrelsomeness and a suggestion that the readers were small-minded?

4:10–20

Finally, there is one theme that runs through the letter and is prominent in chapter 4 and especially in the expression of thanks for the gift brought by Epaphroditus (4:10–20). The theme of joy forms a fitting climax to this survey of spiritual growth. We note that Paul himself rejoices when he thinks of the church and its progress (1:4, 2:2, 4:1) and of their concern for him (4:10); and he rejoices more generally at the progress of the gospel despite the difficulties caused by preachers with mixed motives and by his own imprisonment (1:18). Even if he must pour himself out in sacrifice, it is a cause for joy, and the readers should share in his joy (2:17f.). It is natural for them to rejoice when Epaphroditus returns to them (2:29). But above all he encourages them repeatedly to rejoice in the Lord (3:1; 4:4a, b), for his prayer is for them to progress and have joy through their faith (1:25).

In summary, the basis of the church is the gospel of the crucified and exalted Christ. The essential nature of the church is community expressed in a fellowship constituted by common sharing in the work and the blessings of the gospel. The church is based on faith in Christ, and this constitutes it as 'the circumcision': faith in Christ has replaced circumcision as the mark of God's people. And the church is a body that must grow in faith, love, knowledge and joy. But it can do so only as it conforms to the pattern of Jesus himself, who was prepared to endure humiliation and to follow the path of service.

CHAPTER 13

Philippians and its architect

Having seen something of the theology expressed in Philippians, we must now attempt to 'place' it in relation to other NT documents. Space precludes anything more than a comparison with other Pauline documents. In terms of our 'building' metaphor, we want to compare Philippians with other structures designed by the same builder to see how far they express the same basic design adapted to different situations. According to J. C. Beker, whatever theological differences exist between the various letters of Paul may be explained in terms of the categories of 'coherence' and 'contingency'. Beker sees in the mind of Paul a coherent system of thought which is developed in appropriate ways according to the different contingent circumstances in which he is writing.[1] We shall look at four main areas.

CHRISTOLOGY

What kind of christology is presented in Philippians? Here we have one of the most explicit utterances of Paul on the subject. Can we determine its character? Numerous attempts have been made to categorise it.

Adam christology

A contrast between Adam and Christ is possible. Adam too was made in the image of God, and in Jewish thought was endowed with sovereignty over creation; man is a little lower than the

---

[1] J. C. Beker, *Paul the Apostle: the Triumph of God in Life and Thought* (Edinburgh: T. and T. Clark, 1980).

angels and crowned with glory and honour (Ps. 8). Where Adam fell, Jesus resisted temptation.

This line of thought has been popular with exegetes who have had difficulty in attributing the concept of pre-existence, as traditionally understood, to Paul or to a pre-Pauline source. The contrast between Adam and Christ is familiar elsewhere in Paul (Rom. 5, 1 Cor. 15).[2]

But the difficulties are manifest. This interpretation does not do justice to the stress on becoming a man, nor on the fact that Adam is not said to have been equal to God.[3] Although, therefore, there may well be a sideways look at Adam, it is difficult to believe that this is the major inspiration of the passage.

Wisdom christology

The most plausible alternative suggestion is a background in wisdom speculation. The thought of God sending wisdom, who had been his equal in creation and who now comes to live among human beings, has obvious parallels with the passage and can be traced elsewhere in Paul and the NT (1 Cor. 1:30; cf. Jn 1, Heb. 1). But it does not fully explain the humiliation, suffering and exaltation motifs.[4]

Son christology

We would suggest the possibility of a link with the 'Son' christology developed elsewhere. It is noteworthy that, when the author of Hebrews develops the concept of Jesus as God's Son, he makes use of the concepts of the image of God (Heb. 1:3) and of the lowly position temporarily taken up by him (Heb. 2:9); the vocabulary is different, but the thoughts are

---

[2] J. D. G. Dunn, *Christology*, xviiif., 114–21.

[3] One could, of course, argue that equality with God was what the tempter offered to Adam (cf. Gen. 3:5; Dunn, *Christology*, xix, 116), but this does not really solve the problem of *harpagmos*.

[4] Martin, *Carmen Christi*, 318f., referring to the basic study by D. Georgi, 'Der vorpaulinische Hymnus Phil. 2, 6–11' in *Zeit und Geschichte*, ed. E. Dinkler (Tübingen: J. C. B. Mohr, 1964).

similar. In the same way, John writes of the way in which the Word became flesh but revealed the glory of God precisely in his service of others and his death on the cross.

We thus find evidence of a common pattern of thinking in the early church expressed in varied language. It could well be that a significant role in its development was played by Paul himself. In his earlier letters we have clear evidence that he thinks of Jesus as God's Son sent by him into the world to die in the place of sinners (Rom. 8:32, Gal. 4:4). The important text 2 Corinthians 8:9 admirably sums up in a different idiom what Paul says in Philippians: 'You know the grace of our Lord Jesus Christ, that though he was rich, yet for your sake he became poor, so that you through his poverty might become rich'. Here the mode of expression has been chosen to back up the teaching on the grace of Christian giving which is Paul's immediate theme, but the structure of thought is basically the same: the one possessed of riches lays them aside. The thought of exaltation is not present here explicitly – although it is surely implied in the description of the subject as 'the Lord Jesus Christ', which can only refer to his present position. The stress lies on grace rather than humility, but again this is dictated by the situation.

Given this evidence, and bearing in mind the various background influences in the OT and Judaism which affected him, we have solid ground for claiming that the creative thinking displayed in this passage is Paul's own.

THE CHRISTIAN AND CHRIST

The basic relationship between the Christian and Christ is likewise developed elsewhere in Paul by the same use of the phrase 'in Christ'. We have argued for a variety of usage in Philippians rather than understanding all passages as representative of the same usage, but with different nuances. This same phenomenon could be traced throughout the other letters of Paul where the same varieties of usage are to be found. Similarly, the formula 'with Christ' is not confined to Philippians. Again we are dealing with a specifically Pauline mode of expression.

The thought of union with Christ and specifically with him in his death and resurrection is likewise a basic Pauline concept (see especially Rom. 6, 2 Cor. 4 and Col. 2). And the thought of knowing Christ as being the supreme joy is reflected in 2 Cor. 2:14.

THE NATURE OF THE CHURCH

It is the same with Paul's understanding of the church. We may single out for mention his discussion of the church in relation to Judaism and the Jewish law. What is expressed more polemically and at greater length in Romans and Galatians here comes to incidental expression. The church is composed of Jews and Gentiles, and what once were regarded as the signs of belonging to the people of God – circumcision and obedience to the law – are no longer required of Gentiles and can be counted almost as liabilities by Jews themselves. It is worth observing that in Phil. 3 the concepts of justification by faith and union with Christ in his death and resurrection are very closely tied together: they are not two separate ideas but form a unity in Paul's thought.

THE CHRISTIAN AND THE FUTURE

The connection that Paul makes between the *parousia* and the achievement of salvation (1 Thess. 4:13–18, 5:9) is implicit in the description of the Lord Jesus as Saviour in Phil. 3:20. The presupposition of his thought is that at the end the dead will be raised up (first) to meet with Christ when he comes, and then living believers will be caught up to be with them 'in the air' with Christ, and all will be changed, dead and living alike.

However, in Philippians Paul appears to expect that death will take him straight to a closer union with Christ. In his earlier letters union with Christ might appear to belong to the period after the *parousia* (1 Thess. 4:13–18, 1 Cor. 15). But according to J. Gnilka[5] Paul could have said what he says here

---

[5] Gnilka, *Der Philipperbrief*, 76–93.

at the time of writing 1 Thessalonians or 1 Corinthians. The concept of the imminent *parousia* is common to all the letters. The future transformation of the body which takes place at the *parousia* in 1 Cor. 15 takes place at the same point according to 2 Cor. 5. What is in mind in Phil. 1:23 is a fellowship with Christ in the period between death and the *parousia*. It corresponds to the period of being with (*pros*) the Lord and away from the body, which is mentioned in 2 Cor. 5:8. In Philippians Paul does not raise the question of the state of the Christian after death in terms of bodiless existence or nakedness. He does not fear this state in 2 Cor. 5 and his groaning there is about the tribulations of this life rather than fear of the in-between state.

The effect of what Paul says in Philippians is thus to fill out the rather bald mention of 'being with the Lord' in 2 Cor. 5:8 and to make it clear that this state is one which the believer can anticipate with joy. The scenario from 1 Thess. 4 and 1 Cor. 15 still applies: what is new is Paul's apparent conviction that he will be among the dead rather than the living. It is a change in the personal perspective and not a change in teaching.

From this brief survey of four key areas of Paul's thought we can readily see that the theology of Philippians is an expression of the same thinking that lies behind the other Pauline letters. Special emphasis is given to various topics, in particular the person of Jesus and fellowship in the church, but these fit harmoniously into Paul's theology as a whole. This building is clearly by the same architect as the other Pauline edifices.

CHAPTER 14

A building that still stands

Our final task is to consider the significance of this understanding of Christ and the Christian life for today. There are two aspects to the question.

On the one hand, our aim so far has been to elucidate the thought of the letter to the Philippians as a single document. In the previous chapter we have argued for the coherence of the thinking in Philippians with that expressed in Paul's other letters. But what is the distinctive contribution of Philippians to our understanding of the Christian faith? Suppose that Philippians was missing from the canon: would we be significantly the poorer? If we as Christians regard the Scriptures as being providentially gathered together for our benefit in the church, what is the importance of Philippians within the canon?[1]

On the other hand, we want to know whether we as Christians today can still live in the same theological 'building'. In discussing this question I proceed on the basis that, if we are in the same situation as the original readers, what is said to them will also apply to us, but if our situation is different the message may need reapplication.

We shall attempt to look at both sides of this question simultaneously as we consider a number of areas where the thought of Philippians may be regarded as in some ways distinctive and also applicable to today.

---

[1] This way of putting the question may arouse echoes of B. S. Childs' canonical approach (*The New Testament as Canon: an Introduction* (London: SCM Press, 1984); see pp. 329–37 on Philippians), but is not tied to it.

FAITH IN GOD

We mention, first, two areas where the thought of Philippians is not especially distinctive, but where vital elements of the Christian life are sharply focussed. They are also important in that they demonstrate that in at least some aspects of life there is no essential difference between the Philippian Christians and ourselves.

Consider Epaphroditus, who risked his life on a journey to bring encouragement and help to Paul from the church at Philippi. Is the situation, let us say, of a visitor from a church in Kenya bringing greetings to a church in Scotland any different in principle? Modern travellers, while benefitting from the convenience and accessibility of contemporary methods of transport, yet must accept that risks are involved; they could be caught up in a taxi crash on the way to the airport, subject to delays because of air traffic controllers on strike, suffer severe food poisoning *en route* or the hijacking of the aircraft, and more besides. They may enjoy access to medical care that Epaphroditus never knew, but people still perish as a result of disease and injury while *en route* from one place to another. Those who suggest that the first-century situation is different because people would go first to an exorcist or say their prayers for healing at the shrine of Asclepius underestimate both the fact of ancient medicine and the place of prayer in the Christian life now for 'material things'. It is hard to see any difference in principle between Epaphroditus and his modern counter part.

What this example demonstrates is the need for a confident trust in God to care for all of our life. No doubt Epaphroditus normally took reasonable precautions for his health. On this occasion he 'risked his life' for the sake of Paul – but no more than any person who dives into a swirling torrent to save another person from drowning. The point is that Epaphroditus did all that he did in dependence upon God. The danger in our lives, as in his, is to fail to trust in God, whether as a result of self-confidence or through doubt about the goodness of God and his care for us. Christians who pray 'Give us today our daily bread' are confessing that God is the source of food and whatever else is required for life and that whatever they need comes from him, and therefore they are gratefully owning their dependence upon him. Epaphroditus was doing the same.

PERSONAL RELATIONSHIPS

Consider Euodia and Syntyche. These two women had fallen out with each other. It has been suggested that they may have been the owners of houses (or the wives of owners) in which church groups met; in view of the influence exerted by such people over their dependents a disagreement between them could have damaging effects on the whole church. Paul admonishes them to 'agree in the Lord', and this topic of 'agreement' is emphasised in the letter. We may ask whether the situation is any different today when persons in the same church congregation fall out with one another. It is usually the case that when this happens little groups of supporters back each of the parties concerned. Is the advice to such people today going to be any different?

Again we see how the whole of life is brought under the rubric 'in the Lord'. Clearly Paul could simply have urged them 'to agree' without adding 'in the Lord'. This in itself is good advice for producing harmony in society. But the addition indicates that such agreement is an essential part of life lived under the Lordship of Christ. The issue is not, therefore, whether we judge it expedient to maintain good relations with other people. Harmony is of the essence of the Christian church.

Further, we note that a sharp line cannot be drawn between congregational and secular life. To a great extent the two coincided. A household could well be expected to embrace the religion of the 'master', although not all members necessarily did so (and Paul takes account of that elsewhere – see 1 Cor. 7!). But where the members of the household shared the same faith and became the nucleus of a house church, the standard of behaviour expected between fellow-Christians could not be separated from that between fellow-members of the household.

In any such scrutiny of social duties and their observance the revolutionary factor lay in the person of the Lord. The unique contribution of Philippians to a Christian understanding of relationships is to be found in its presentation of Jesus as the One who renounced all that could have been his as a result of his relationship to God. He gave up all that being equal to God could have bestowed upon him and instead took the form of a servant. The person who does that truly considers other people to be better than himself. Having renounced all claims to self-assertion, such people are freed from the passions that give rise to quarrelling and disunity. There seems to be no reason why this teaching cannot be applied directly to Christians today.

THE PERSON OF JESUS

One of the most difficult issues raised by Philippians, however, is this picture of Jesus. According to the interpretation offered above he is portrayed as the incarnation of a pre-existent person who existed in the image of God and was equal with God. He makes a deliberate choice to empty himself of his privileges and so appears in a human form. After dying on a cross he is exalted by God and is entitled to homage from all beings in heaven, on earth and in the depths. He is expected to return from heaven. What are we to make of such language?

The problem is not peculiar to a consideration of the theology of Philippians. It occurs throughout the New Testament wherever Jesus is depicted as a more than human figure. The status of the language is that of 'myth' where 'myth' is defined as language that refers to the gods or other supernatural actors.

It can be argued that such language is indispensable in the expression of Christian faith. Provided that we remember that the language is symbolic and is not to be taken literally, there would not seem to be any great problem about its usage. Attempts to find fresh ways of expressing the point in contemporary terms are to be welcomed, but it is arguable that a 'demythologisation' which attempts to do away with the concepts of pre-existence and incarnation is not possible without surrendering the essence of Christian belief about Jesus.[2]

THE CHRISTIAN ATTITUDE TO DEATH
AND THE FUTURE LIFE

A tricky problem is presented by Paul's attitude to his own future. Having asserted that for him life means Christ, he goes on to say that death is gain and that, given his choice, he would prefer to depart and to be with Christ, which is far better. The validity of an attitude that apparently regards life in this world as so inferior to the next world that it would be better to uproot one's tent and move on is one that has often been found questionable. It is no doubt one thing to compare life in wretched surroundings and conditions with the life of heaven. It is another thing to state categorically over against the best that life in this world can offer that death is gain.

And of course what Paul is comparing is what he regarded as the best that life can offer – life that consists in knowing and serving Christ. He is really making the point that there will be an even better knowledge of Christ in the next life rather than comparing two spheres of life and dismissing this one outright. If, then, we ask whether Paul's attitude implies a lack of interest in the world as such and a lack of concern for people except insofar as they may be loved and snatched from a hopeless future as brands from the burning, we can reply in several ways. Paul was concerned for a new quality of life in this world in the fellowship of the church. Nothing indicates that he saw this fellowship as purely that of a group of people joined together by a common desire to die. Paul does express concern in this letter that his readers should focus their minds on 'all that is true, all that is noble, all that is just and pure, all that is lovable and attractive' (Phil. 4:8). This important verse indicates quite clearly that his concern was not tied to some kind of world-denying Christ-mysticism which blinded him to all else. For Paul the thought of Christ is linked with a spirit-

---

[2] See the essay 'God Incarnate: Myth or What?', in I. H. Marshall, *Jesus the Saviour* (Downers Grove: InterVarsity Press/London: SPCK, 1990), 181–96.

uality and morality that are concerned with love, humility and purity. It is a renewal of human nature and human society. The love demonstrated within the Christian congregation is something to be enjoyed for its own sake. There is thus already a new world, a new creation, as a result of union with Christ.

It does not appear, therefore, that Paul's religion is other-worldly piety which finds its consummation in life after death. It has in fact something important to say to us in our own context. It reminds us that our existence is not bounded by this world. Paul takes seriously the fact of death and what lies beyond it. A purely this-worldly attitude answers the question posed by death in terms of extinction. One may no doubt have an attitude of 'let us eat, drink and be merry, for tomorrow we die' which is qualified by a genuine love for other people and restricts its own desire for enjoyment in order that enjoyment may be shared by others. But, however valuable this may be, it is not the same thing as Christian faith.

Paul's outlook calls into question an attitude that finds total satisfaction in this world and what it offers. It insists that life is more than food, the body more than clothes, and that even human love and beauty are not the ultimate values.

His emphasis on the 'gain' of the next life indicates that the most important thing in this world is to promote the *anticipation* of that next life here and now. Since the ideal is the new society in which Christ is known and loved, the aim should be to realise such a society within this world, a society governed by love in which the life of heaven becomes a reality. Since Paul believed in the transformation of the body and not in its destruction, the concern will be for all that makes life in the body rich and enjoyable and will not be body-despising.

It thus emerges that Paul's attitude is one that should lead to a balance between the concern to know Christ and the desire to serve him in bringing other people to know him and so to become part of the new society in which all the blessings of the new creation are already beginning to be experienced. Such an attitude is realistic in that it recognises that we still live in a world of corruption which needs to be transformed; it thus avoids a baseless utopianism.

TRUTH AND TOLERATION

To Paul the people who opposed his understanding of the faith were 'enemies of the cross'. This is strong language which may seem inappropriate in days when the trend is towards an ecumenical spirit which welcomes all Christians as brothers and sisters and insists on finding truth in dialogue. Is there an intolerance here which we cannot share?

To put the matter in perspective we remind ourselves that Paul does show two different attitudes in this letter. On the one hand, he alludes to those rivals who preach Christ out of envy in his place of imprisonment and hope that they will cause him some distress by so doing. His attitude to them is one of toleration because, from whatever motives, Christ is being preached. Doubtless there are situations where the motives and the content of preaching cannot be sharply distinguished, and the nature of the motives may prejudice the content of the message. Nevertheless, it is broadly true that the content of the message can be separated from the motives and character of its preachers, otherwise we all of us might hesitate ever to open our mouths as evangelists.

On the other hand, it is a different matter when the actual message is distorted, for example, when preachers in effect rob the cross of significance. It was this above all else which roused Paul's opposition, as we see especially in Galatians. He could not imagine a Christianity in which salvation was not effected by the cross and by faith alone, apart from the works of the Jewish law and human self-confidence based on them. Already in the New Testament we see formulations of this principle where the scope has begun to widen from 'the works of the [Jewish] law' to any kind of human achievement or position that stands in rivalry with the cross.

Paul's example suggests the necessity of clearly perceiving where a so-called Christian message in effect compromises the centrality and significance of the cross. Salvation is through Christ alone. Whatever other kind of experience may be offered in other religions and philosophies, the nature of salvation in the New Testament is that it consists in knowing

Christ and his benefits and cannot be separated from him. It is thus a peculiarly Christian salvation and is not a case of a Christian way to an experience or situation that can, even in theory, be reached by other routes. The route and the destination are alike specifically Christian in that Christ is the way and Christ is the goal.

THE CRUCIFORM LIFE

The effect of Paul's teaching in this letter is accordingly to insist that the life of the Christian must be cruciform. There is a paradox in the Christian life, in that Paul's greatest desire is to know Christ and yet at the same time he has to be willing to undergo humiliation and separation from him for the sake of others. This is not an easy tension to bear, but it is the way that Paul had to go, and in the midst of it he found that he did know and experience Christ. There is thus a kind of 'cross' experience built into the pattern of Christianity. E. C. Hoskyns expressed this finely in his last, posthumous, book on crucifixion and resurrection in which he shows that both crucifixion and resurrection belong inescapably to the pattern of the Christian life.[3] It is in weakness that we are strong, in dying that we live. Dying and living with Christ are two sides of the same experience. That is the message of Philippians about the nature of the Christian life and constitutes its greatest challenge to a 'comfortable' Christianity.

[3] E. C. Hoskyns and F. N. Davey, *Crucifixion – Resurrection*, ed. G. S. Wakefield (London: SPCK, 1981).

The theology of Philemon

I. HOWARD MARSHALL

CHAPTER 15

The Gospel and slavery

THE BACKGROUND AND SITUATION

Philemon is an authentic letter of Paul written to a Christian called Philemon,[1] who lived in Colosse, together with members of the church that met in his house. It is a 'communal' letter addressed to the whole house church, but apart from vs. 1–3 and 24 it is composed throughout as an address to Philemon alone.

The letter was occasioned by the meeting of Philemon's slave, Onesimus, with Paul, who was in prison (whether in Rome or elsewhere is debated); Onesimus was converted by Paul, and the letter is concerned with the ensuing situation.

The situation of Onesimus

It is usually assumed that Onesimus was a runaway slave who had escaped from his master's household, probably with some stolen goods. Somehow he came into touch with Paul, who was in prison, and it was Paul's delicate task to return him to his master. Onesimus could well have been in an unpleasant situation. Although slavery was not always as miserable as it is popularly supposed to have been, the laws were particularly strict against runaway slaves and persons who assisted them, and a master could inflict severe penalties on a slave who was

---

[1] Not to Archippus, *pace* S. C. Winter, 'Paul's Letter to Philemon', *NTS* 33 (1987), 1–15; cf. her 'Methodological Observations on a New Interpretation of Paul's Letter to Philemon', *USQR* 39 (1984), 203–12.

returned to him. A Christian master would not necessarily treat slaves, and especially runaway slaves, any differently.

This theory on its own does not explain adequately how Onesimus came to be in prison with Paul, or how Paul had the authority to *send him back*. Nor does it explain the remarkable coincidence that Onesimus came into contact with – of all people – the one person in prison who knew his master and was in a position to intercede on his behalf. Was it really a chance meeting?

Under some ancient systems of law a slave in danger of his life might seek sanctuary at the altar in a private home; the householder would then have the duty of protecting him while seeking to restore him to his master or sell him to another owner.[2] Similarly, a slave who fell out with his master could go and seek the help of somebody who would intercede for him with his master. In this case the slave was not technically a 'runaway', for he intended to return to service, and the person to whom he would go for protection would be somebody whose word would count with his master. Could it then be that Onesimus was being, as he thought, treated badly by his master, or had he committed some misdemeanour or crime for which he expected to be punished, and did he therefore go to Paul for help?[3] This suggestion entails the fact that Onesimus was not necessarily faced by extreme penalties from his master, and certainly not by the penalty for being a runaway. Nevertheless, he could still have been in an unpleasant situation.

The situation was perhaps eased by the fact that Paul had led Onesimus to become a Christian; when Paul speaks of having 'begotten' or 'become the father of' Onesimus, this metaphor is best understood in this way. It may well have been because of his new faith that Onesimus could be persuaded to return to a master who was himself a Christian as a result of Paul's mission. So the letter is concerned to secure a welcome

[2] E. R. Goodenough, 'Paul and Onesimus', *HTR* 22 (1929), 181–3; cf. F. F. Bruce, 'St Paul in Rome: 2. The Epistle to Philemon', *BJRL* 48 (1965), 81–97.

[3] P. Lampe, 'Keine "Sklavenflucht" des Onesimus', *ZNW* 76 (1985), 135–7. See further B. M. Rapske, 'The Prisoner Paul in the Eyes of Onesimus', *NTS* 37, 1991, 187–203. See also J. G. Nordling, 'Onesimus Fugitivus: A Defense of the Runaway Slave Hypothesis in Philemon', *JSNT* 41 (1991), 97–119.

back home for the runaway slave and reconciliation with the master whom he had offended.

This interpretation assumes that Onesimus had fallen out with his master and it makes reconciliation the main theme. A very different scenario is put forward by W. Schenk,[4] who points out that there is not a word about a fugitive slave in the letter. Rather, Philemon, a former persecutor of Christians (such as Archippus), had been converted and opened up his house to a Christian group in Pergamon. His non-Christian slave Onesimus was sent to tell Paul (who was imprisoned in Ephesus) the news. While he was there, Onesimus accepted the faith of which he had previously heard from his master, and Paul formed a strong desire to have him stay with him as an associate in his mission. He therefore wrote to Philemon asking him to release Onesimus so that he could return to be with Paul; he mentioned that he would repay any debts or losses arising during Onesimus' time with Philemon. The letter is not about forgiveness for a recalcitrant slave, but about welcoming back Onesimus, who is no longer a slave but a Christian brother, into the Christian fellowship as if he were Paul himself. This otherwise rather speculative theory rightly stresses that, whatever else Paul is doing, he is asking quite plainly that Onesimus be his colleague in the work of the gospel.

The purpose of the letter

On any understanding of the matter Paul is sending Onesimus back to his master and asking Philemon to welcome him, to forgive him (if he has done wrong) and to receive him not only as a slave but also as a Christian brother. Paul would have liked to keep Onesimus with himself in order that he might be of service to him in his Christian work. Nevertheless, he fully recognises that Philemon must be free to keep Onesimus, and he does not want to force the issue. But the way in which he promises to repay Philemon for whatever loss he has incurred

---

[4] W. Schenk, 'Der Brief des Paulus an Philemon in der neueren Forschung (1945–1987)', *ANRW* (1987), II.25.4, 3439–95.

from Onesimus probably implies that this would be part of a bargain whereby Onesimus would go and work with Paul. It is not yet clear whether Paul was also hoping that Onesimus might be set free from slavery, whether to be with Paul or to continue to serve Philemon as a 'freedman'. If any such request is made in the letter, it is implicit rather than explicit. Finally, Paul states his hope of visiting Colosse and asks that he may receive hospitality when he comes.

THE ARGUMENT OF THE LETTER

The structure

Like many other ancient letters, Philemon contains the elements of 'friendly attitude', conveying the presence of the absent letter-writer and promoting dialogue or conversation between writer and recipient.[5]

Ancient letters fell into a broad pattern of opening salutation, 'body' and closing greetings. The contents of the 'body' depended on the subject matter and other factors. Here we have a developed 'request'. We offer the following analysis:[6]

1–3   opening greetings
4–7   opening expression of thanks
8–22   body (request)
        8–14   request regarding Onesimus, the new Christian
       15–22   development of request
23–5 closing greetings

The letter is skilfully constructed to achieve its purpose of persuading Philemon to do what the author wants. It illustrates well how an author would envisage his intended audience and frame his rhetoric in the light of his understanding of the person whom he was trying to persuade and how he might

---

[5] J. L. White, *Light from Ancient Letters* (Philadelphia: Fortress, 1986).
[6] This is based on Schenk, 'Brief des Paulus', 3484–6.

most effectively achieve his purpose.[7] Two other factors must
also be borne in mind.

Of principal importance is the fact that Paul employs a
theological argument to persuade Philemon.

Paul pleads in a very moving way for the fugitive; but the outstand-
ing feature of the letter is not so much this personal element, but the
way in which Paul uses it for setting out his message ... The important thing to notice is what Paul makes out of the given situation. The
central idea in his message is the new factor that has come into being
in Christ.[8]

Sociological study of the letter has illuminated the various roles
and relationships of the different participants and how these
are exploited and changed in the course of the letter.[9]

The stages in the appeal

Paul was encouraging Philemon to do something that would
have been highly unlikely (though by no means unprecedented[10]) for a slave-owner at that time – to receive back and
forgive a slave who had done wrong. But Paul was going
further than this in asking Philemon to accept Onesimus as a
fellow-Christian into the bargain. We may wonder whether
this would make the situation more or less difficult. Would
Philemon find it easier to forgive Onesimus now that the latter
had become a Christian? Or had Philemon the fresh problem
of learning to recognise that a slave could be a brother in
Christ?

The relationship between Paul and Philemon

The appeal is based partly on the attitude that Philemon
should have for Paul. Paul does not refer to his authority as an
apostle of Jesus Christ. Instead he bases his appeal initially on

---

7 On 'reader-response criticism' see R. Lundin, A. C. Thiselton and C. Walhout,
   The Responsibility of Hermeneutics (Exeter: Paternoster, 1985), chap. 3 (by Thiselton).
8 W. Marxsen, *Introduction to the New Testament* (Oxford: Blackwell, 1968), 69.
9 N. R. Petersen, *Rediscovering Paul: Philemon and the Sociology of Paul's Narrative World*
   (Philadelphia: Fortress, 1985).
10 See Pliny the Younger, *Epistles* 9.21 and 24, cited in E. Lohse, *Colossians and
    Philemon*, 196f.)

his situation as a servant of Jesus Christ. Paul also refers to himself as an 'old man' (or possibly 'ambassador', v. 9) and now in addition a prisoner of Jesus Christ. Later he implicitly calls himself a 'prisoner of war' of Jesus (v. 23). The picture is one that is meant to encourage some compassion for Paul, or rather respect for one who has had to endure imprisonment for the sake of the gospel. Here he bases his appeal on love rather than apostolic authority. Paul's authority is here more that of a fellow-worker in the service of Christ.

The appeal is strengthened by the fact that the letter mentions Timothy as Paul's 'brother' and co-sender and includes greetings from other Christians who are Paul's fellow-workers and who may be presumed to add their backing to the letter. Further, the letter is not a private communication to Philemon but is sent to a church of which he is part.

All these points show that the appeal depends upon the Christian status of Philemon. He would not respond to Paul's self-description and the references to other Christians would be pointless, were he not himself a Christian and Paul's fellow-worker. The question of Onesimus is not a private or a secular matter: the whole affair is conducted in the church within the context of Christian belief.

The foundation of the appeal

This is laid in vs. 4–7. Paul gives thanks for the love and faith displayed by Philemon towards the Lord Jesus and all the saints. 'Love' and 'faith' sum up the attitudes characteristic of a Christian in relation to other believers and to the Lord Jesus Christ respectively.[11] Love is mentioned first because it is the characteristic which is of supreme importance for the appeal which is to follow. Paul has 'heard' – presumably from Onesimus and possibly from other messengers from Colosse – that Philemon's love has refreshed the hearts of other 'saints'. On this basis Paul can issue his appeal with confidence.

The next part of the sentence (v. 6) is difficult. It is generally taken to be the content of a petition made by Paul to God. The

---

[11] The sentence is arranged chiastically: the love is towards the saints and the faith is in Jesus.

problem centres on the word *koinonia* (fellowship). This word refers to the common sharing of two or more persons in some possession or interest, and the problem is whether the emphasis falls on the *participation* in the common object or on the sense of *partnership* that arises out of this common concern. The former view gives the translation 'May your sharing in the faith become effective in the knowledge of all the good that is in us for the glory of Christ'.[12] The latter view gives 'May the fellowship that has arisen through your share in the faith become effective' or '[May] the mutual participation which is proper to the Christian faith have its full effect in the realisation of every good thing that God wants to accomplish in us to lead us into the fulness of Christian fellowship, i.e., of Christ'.[13] The second of these understandings is the better supported today. The new community that includes Philemon shows itself actively in its recognition of the good things that God has promised for us, or intends to do in us.

The conversion of Onesimus

Paul now comes to the object of his appeal, and he takes it further by describing what has happened to Onesimus. He comments that he has brought Onesimus to 'birth' as a Christian believer (v. 10). He has seen a change in the young man's character from being useless (whether idle, inefficient or dishonest) to becoming a useful person, both to his master – and, in the first hint of Paul's own desire, to himself (v. 11). Paul has developed an affection for the young man, to such an extent that he would have liked to keep Onesimus with him for the service that he could render (v. 13).

The appeal for a welcome for Onesimus

Despite this desire, Paul is sending Onesimus back to his master.[14] If he were to stay with Paul, this could only be by Philemon's consent. But in any case there is prior need for a

---

[12] E. Lohse, *Colossians and Philemon*, 192.
[13] Hainz, *KOINONIA*, 106–8; N. T. Wright, *Colossians and Philemon*, 175–8.
[14] Here *anapempo* is taken in its traditional sense. Schenk's view that it means 'to bring up' is unlikely ('Brief des Paulus', 3448f.). Winter ('Paul's Letter', 7) suggests that it means 'to refer a case' (cf. Acts 25:21).

reconciliation between the two. And Paul pleads primarily for this. Onesimus is to be received back not as a slave but as something more than a slave, as a Christian brother – indeed, not just as a brother (if that were possible) but as a beloved brother. Paul expects Philemon to show the same love for Onesimus as he himself does – and he is to show it both in the flesh and in the Lord. The point is that a master should develop love for the members of his household, including his slaves, but also for those who are joined together in the bond of faith. Onesimus is to be welcomed back in the same way as Philemon would welcome Paul. Let Philemon here and now give Onesimus – the slave! – the same loving welcome that Paul himself hopes to receive later.

This request is based on the *koinonia* which exists between them. Paul is aware that Onesimus has caused loss for his master, but he is determined that Philemon shall not lose out by forgiving Onesimus. He is not asking Philemon to write off his losses. He states, in a formally binding way, that he will repay him whatever is due. Paul states this on the basis that he and Philemon are in effect partners. The term is drawn from the business world, and the language of business persists throughout the verse. At the same time, however, it rouses echoes of the 'fellowship' mentioned in v. 6. Paul, however, goes on to say: 'I won't mention the fact [but he does!] that you owe yourself to me.' Is this a way of saying, 'But of course you won't demand what is owing to you because you are already spiritually in debt to me'?

The request for obedience

Paul expresses his confidence that Philemon will obey his request. The word 'obey' should not be underemphasised. He believes so much in the Christian character of Philemon that he can be confident that Philemon will carry out God's will once he has realised what it is. What he has asked for is that Philemon will demonstrate his faith and love in action. If Philemon is going to obey God, he must consider what obedience in this situation involves.

Paul has expressed the longing that Onesimus stay with him.

He has spoken of the sorrow of parting with him. It is clear that he expresses the wish that Philemon will send Onesimus back to him, but that he wants Philemon to feel quite free to make up his own mind. He does not pre-empt the situation by simply sending a letter; he sends Onesimus back with the letter. He makes the point that Onesimus could serve Paul in his imprisonment for the gospel *on behalf of Philemon* (v. 13!). The implication is that Paul expected the churches which he founded to contribute their share to the continuing work of his mission.[15] The return of Onesimus was *one possible way* in which Philemon could fulfil this obligation.

When, therefore, Paul tells Philemon that he owes himself to Paul, that he hopes that Philemon will do more than he asks, that he longs for a benefit from him and that he is confident that Philemon will be obedient, it seems perfectly clear that Paul is hoping that Philemon will give his support to Paul in precisely this way.

It has been suggested that Paul, so to speak, 'puts Philemon in a corner', so that he has no option but to do what Paul commands – a command reinforced by the pressure of a 'public' letter to the whole house church and of the various colleagues of Paul whose names are appended to the letter. 'Do what I say; remember how much you owe to me'.[16] More likely, Paul knows his man, knows of his Christian faith and love and of the way in which Philemon will want to do God's will, and therefore he writes with great confidence that Philemon will do what God wants him to do.

Whether Paul is envisaging the release of Onesimus from slavery is still not clear. When Paul asks Philemon to do 'more than I ask', is he asking simply that Onesimus be sent back to him or is he also suggesting that he be released from slavery?

PHILEMON IN RELATION TO PAULINE THEOLOGY

We have now seen how the appeal of Paul to Philemon about Onesimus is based on the gospel. Since the letter is about a

---

[15] Ollrog, *Mitarbeiter*. As the leader of the house church, Philemon's willingness to help Paul would be crucial.

[16] A. Suhl, *Der Philemonbrief*, 39.

Christian slave, the question of how he is to be treated is a matter to be discussed within a Christian framework. Yet had the issue been purely the intercession of Paul for a non-Christian slave, it is difficult to imagine that Paul would have treated it in a secular manner (cf. Col. 4:1). The basis is that the acknowledged Christian faith and love of the recipient must be expressed in recognising what the good will of God is and carrying it out. Whatever Philemon does towards Onesimus must be an expression of that will, whether or not it involves letting him remain with Paul. The question, therefore, is how love is to be expressed.

The relationship of one Christian to another is that of brothers. Paul sees a possible divine providence at work in the temporary separation of Onesimus from Philemon, which has as its purpose that they should be permanently joined together on a higher and different level from the master-slave relationship, namely as Christian brothers.

There is also a relationship between Paul and other Christians. He demonstrates great love and affection for them. At the same time he is conscious of a special position as a servant of Jesus Christ, which gives him authority to command what is right, but here, as elsewhere, he prefers to use the language of 'exhortation' and to plead for a benefit. Yet he can in the same letter use the language of obedience.

It should require no demonstration that the theological position of this letter is the same as that of Paul's other letters. The same fundamental understanding of the Christian life as one of faith and love 'in Christ', binding believers together, is to be found in all. The major issue is how the teaching on slaves here is related to that to be found elsewhere.

The basic principle that all believers are one in Christ Jesus, and that this applies regardless of sex, race and status (Gal. 3:28), is clearly upheld. Philemon is to regard Onesimus as a Christian brother, and this relationship in the church overrules the master-slave relationship. Paul can speak of sending Onesimus back as his own representative to Philemon, and he can also speak of Onesimus acting on behalf of his master. In the fellowship of the church the slave is no different from the free man. Onesimus is now 'more than a slave'.

But it is not said that this dissolves the master-slave relationship. On the contrary, the NT understanding is that slaves are to serve their masters the more gladly, knowing that they are faithful and beloved (1 Tim. 6:1f.). Human relationships that involve respect, obedience and mutual duties are not obliterated within the church. Rather, the duties are to be carried out all the more gladly and willingly. The authority of a parent over a child, for example, is not taken away; it is acknowledged that parents must have such authority. Whether the nature of the relationship is fundamentally changed is a matter to which we must return.

Nothing in Philemon stands in contradiction to the principle that Paul enunciates in 1 Cor. 7:20–4, where he comments that if a slave has the opportunity of freedom he should take it. The point here is that if a slave was offered freedom by his master, he could not turn the opportunity down (contrast the OT legislation); at the same time, slaves could explore various ways of gaining freedom.[17]

THE WIDER CONTEXT

What has Philemon to say to Christians in subsequent ages? Or, to put the point otherwise, what is this letter doing in the Christian canon? Surely the absence of so slight a letter on such a limited topic, which is apparently of little contemporary relevance, would be no great loss?

First of all, we should note that the letter is a prime example of the early Christian conviction that faith and love should determine the action of the Christian. Whatever the situation in which decision and action are called for, it is to be seen in the context of this Christian foundation for behaviour. Paul can almost take it for granted that Philemon will think out his response on this basis. This means that we have in the letter a specific example of an approach to Christian behaviour which can be generalised to fit other situations different from that

---

[17] The view that Paul is here telling slaves to refrain from seeking freedom is unlikely; see P. Stuhlmacher, *Der Brief an Philemon*, 43–6) and S. Scott Bartchy, *First-Century Slavery and the Interpretation of 1 Corinthians 7:21* (Missoula, Montana: Scholars' Press, 1973).

envisaged here. A guiding principle that is surely still valid is to ask in what ways a Christian's faith and love should influence action in each and every concrete decision.

Once we have recognised that the basic interpretative question is concerned with the application of this essential principle to our diverse modern situations, we can go on to tackle the question of slavery. In the history of interpretation there have been two types of understanding.[18]

The traditional view was that the letter teaches the duty of slaves to their masters and of masters to their slaves; there is no disturbance of the status quo. This view seriously misunderstands the thrust of the letter. The attempt to see in Philemon teaching on how slaves like *Onesimus* should behave to their masters is quite out of focus; the letter is concerned through and through with how a master like *Philemon* should behave.

A more modern view sees in the letter the beginnings of the move to destroying slavery; the letter contains the kind of teaching that makes slavery ultimately inconsistent with Christian teaching and practice.

In order to take a position on this issue we return to the question: was Onesimus set free, and did Paul envisage this possibility? The following arguments have been offered.

The fact that the letter has been preserved indicates that Philemon responded favourably to it. There was at least reconciliation between Philemon and Onesimus. Ignatius refers to a bishop of Ephesus called Onesimus, and it is a not unreasonable supposition that he is referring to the same person. It is very difficult to read Philemon in any other sense than that Paul says in effect: 'Onesimus has become a Christian. I would have loved to keep him with me as one of my colleagues, but I wouldn't force the point. The essential thing is that there is reconciliation between you and him, and so I am sending him back; receive him, as you would receive me. And I will pay off his debts if you wish. I am sure that you will do what I ask – and more.' If that is not a request for Onesimus to join Paul's circle, I do not know what is.

---

[18] See Stuhlmacher, *Brief.*

But if this reading of Philemon is accepted, then it would surely follow that Onesimus was in all likelihood released from slavery. There would be no point in Philemon retaining him as a slave if he was letting him go and serve Paul – although it must be acknowledged that it would be perfectly possible to do so especially if the period of help was regarded as limited.[19]

Whatever our conclusion on this point, it is clear that there is no question of a general manumission of Philemon's or any other Christian's slaves. That is not the theme of the letter. Paul and other NT writers recognise the existence of the relationship of slave and master, especially in its domestic form. It is part of the structure of society like other relationships. They do nothing to promote a social revolution that would involve the manumission of all slaves. Second, they recognise the need for Christians to show love as the basis of all their relationships. This applies both to those in authority and to those whose duty it is to serve others. Moreover, such love must be shown regardless of the Christian status or otherwise of the other party. Finally, they recognise that in the church all believers are sons and daughters of God and therefore brothers and sisters to one another; this relationship overrides all others in the church, and hence worldly distinctions do not matter in the Christian fellowship. The slave is lifted from being a slave to being 'more than a slave' – a brother who is loved. Is it fair to say that this recognition then calls in question the existence of the relationship of slave and master?

Let us be clear that the existence of relationships involving authority remains. An employee who contracts to work for an employer for a wage contracts to be under the authority of the employer so far as the work is concerned, but the authority must again be exercised in love. Authority remains essential in human society. Nor can the language of divine 'lordship' be erased from Christian theology.

However, the question of the legitimacy of certain types of

[19] On Schenk's interpretation of the letter, the issue is not reconciliation but the sending of Onesimus to Paul to act as his co-worker, and Schenk argues that this implies his release from slavery. Barclay (see n. 20 below) concludes that Paul really did not know what to recommend in the circumstances and therefore refrained from giving clear directions.

relationship remains. The situation where people of one race think that they have authority over members of another race, perhaps in virtue of a military conquest, is regarded as unjust. Racial superiority is unethical. Surely, then, the right to own another person, body and soul as it were, is unethical, even though a 'purchase' has been carried out or a person's freedom is forfeited through military defeat.

The case depends on a recognition of the dignity of humankind in terms of creation. This remains true despite the existence of 'created inequalities' – the greater ability of one person to achieve goals and hence to gain wealth, prestige and so on. Creation is reinforced by redemption, as the sphere in which the 'fall' is undone and the original paradisial intention of the Creator is brought nearer to fulfilment. Creation and redemption must be seen in harmony, with the fall as the disturbance of the Creator's purpose and redemption as the potential situation of each created being. The fact that not all people respond in faith to the Redeemer's will does not affect their dignity as people for whom redemption is in principle possible.

In this way Philemon is to be seen as part of a process in which it becomes inconceivable that a person is treated as less than a person, a brother as less than a brother. To treat people as slaves is to deny their independent personhood. But this insight did not arrive overnight.

The question then is whether this is the correct trajectory along which to see the development of Christian insight. That is to say, once it has been realised that Christian masters must treat their Christian slaves as brothers and sisters in the flesh and in Christ, is it not inevitable that they should treat their other slaves as brothers and sisters in the flesh – with all that this implies?

We thus find ourselves concluding that the fuller implication of Paul's teaching here is that the Christian faith is incompatible with the ownership of slaves. Paul himself may not have come to this realisation, but he had charted a route which leads to this destination.[20]

---

[20] For a somewhat different view see J. M. G. Barclay, 'Paul, Philemon and the Dilemma of Christian Slave-ownership', *NTS* 37 (1991), 161–86.

This is surely the major reason for the presence of the letter in the canon. More clearly than anywhere else in the NT the application of the gospel to the institution of slavery as such is here made a matter for discussion in a way that points to the need to question the whole institution and replace it by something else. For that reason alone Philemon demands its place in the canon.

Select bibliography

THESSALONIANS
Karl P. Donfried

COMMENTARIES

Wanamaker's is the first commentary on 1 and 2 Thessalonians to incorporate a full-scale rhetorical analysis. This, together with its up-to-date bibliography and thorough discussions of the critical issues, makes it the commentary of choice, although the older commentaries by Best, Bruce and Marshall are still most profitable, especially for students who read only English. Anyone who wishes to do serious exegesis must consult the classics by Milligan, von Döbschütz (originally published in 1909) and Rigaux, all presenting a rigorous analysis of the Greek text. The newest German literature is discussed in Holtz, Marxsen and Trilling. Holtz is judicious and comprehensive, Marxsen consistently rich in insight and Trilling argues for the thoroughgoing pseudepigraphic character of 2 Thessalonians.

Best, Ernest *A Commentary on the First and Second Epistles to the Thessalonians*, *BNTC* (London: Black, 1972)

Bruce, F. F. *1 & 2 Thessalonians*, *WBC* 45 (Waco, Texas: Word, 1982)

Döbschütz, Ernst von *Die Thessalonicher-Briefe*, MeyerK 10 (Göttingen: Vandenhoeck & Ruprecht, 1974)

Holtz, Traugott, *Der erste Brief an die Thessalonicher*, *EKKNT* 13 (Zürich: Benzinger, 1986)

Marshall, I. Howard *1 and 2 Thessalonians*, *NCeB* (Grand Rapids: Eerdmans, 1983)

Marxsen, Willi *Der erste Brief an die Thessalonicher*, Züricher Bibelkommentare 11.1 (Zürich: Theologischer Verlag, 1979)

Der zweite Thessalonicherbrief, Züricher Bibelkommentare 11.2 (Zürich: Theologischer Verlag, 1982)

Milligan, George *St Paul's Epistles to the Thessalonians* (London: Macmillan, 1908)

Rigaux, B. *Les Épitres aux Thessaloniciens, EtB* (Paris: Gabalda, 1956)

Trilling, Wolfgang *Der zweite Brief an die Thessalonicher, EKKNT* 14 (Zürich: Benzinger, 1980)

Wanamaker, Charles A. *Commentary on 1 & 2 Thessalonians, NIGTC* (Grand Rapids: Eerdmans, 1990)

STUDIES

A general orientation to both the historical and theological issues facing the interpreter is provided in Krentz's insightful article and in Jewett's comprehensive study. A series of significant individual studies on these and other themes can be found in Collins' own collection of essays as well as in the volume he edited that includes papers delivered at the 1988 *Colloquium Biblicum Lovaniense* on the Thessalonian correspondence. The essays in this publication that have influenced my own reflections on 1 and 2 Thessalonians include the ones by Hughes, Chapa, Marshall, Schnelle, Collins, Giblin, Vander Stichele and Krentz. The articles I have written deal primarily with the social/historical/religious backgrounds of the Thessalonian correspondence and the attempt to see their theology as a response to issues raised by that environment. The provocative and influential studies by Giblin, Hendrix, Holland, Hughes, Malherbe and Wrede are devoted to specific themes and areas of research. Of these, two deserve special mention, one a recent study and the other a classic: Hughes and Wrede. Hughes' monograph is a comprehensive application of classical rhetorical theory to 2 Thessalonians with instructive results; Wrede is the earliest thoroughgoing attempt to demonstrate the imitative and pseudepigraphical nature of 2 Thessalonians and is still widely influential today.

Collins, Raymond F. *Studies on the First Letter to the Thessalonians, BETL* 66 (Leuven: University Press, 1984)

(ed.) *The Thessalonian Correspondence, BETL* 87 (Leuven: University Press, 1990).

Donfried, Karl P. 'The Cults of Thessalonica and the Thessalonian Correspondence', *NTS* 31 (1985), 336–56

'The Theology of 1 Thessalonians as a Reflection of its Purpose', in *To Touch the Text: Biblical and Related Studies in Honor of Joseph A. Fitzmyer, S.J.*, ed. M. P. Horgan and P. J. Kobelski (New York: Crossroad, 1989), 243–60

Giblin, Charles H. *The Threat to Faith: An Exegetical and Theological Re-examination of 2 Thessalonians 2, AnBib* 31 (Rome: Pontifical Biblical Institute, 1967)

Hendrix, Holland L. 'Thessalonicans Honor Romans' (Th.D. thesis, Harvard University, 1984)

Holland, Glenn S. *The Tradition that You Received from Us: 2 Thessalonians in the Pauline Tradition, HUTh* 24 (Tübingen: J. C. B. Mohr, 1988)

Hughes, Frank Witt *Early Christian Rhetoric and 2 Thessalonians, JSNT* Sup 30 (Sheffield: JSOT Press, 1989)

Jewett, Robert *The Thessalonian Correspondence: Pauline Rhetoric and Millenarian Piety* (Philadelphia: Fortress, 1986)

Krentz, Edgar M. 'Thessalonians, First and Second Epistles to the' in *The Anchor Bible Dictionary*, ed. D. N. Freedman (New York: Doubleday, 1992), 6:515–23

Malherbe, Abraham J. *Paul and the Thessalonians: The Philosophical Tradition of Pastoral Care* (Philadelphia: Fortress, 1987)

Wrede, Wilhelm *Die Echtheit des zweiten Thessalonicherbriefs untersucht, TU*n.F. 9/2 (Leipzig: Hinrichs, 1903)

PHILIPPIANS
I. Howard Marshall

Beare, F. W. *The Epistle to the Philippians, BNTC* (London: Black, 1959)
Now beginning to show its age.

Bruce, F. F. *Philippians*, New International Biblical Commentary (Peabody, MA: Hendrickson, 1989)
Excellent short commentary combining clear exposition with scholarly information.

Caird, G. B. *Paul's Letters from Prison*, New Clarendon Bible (Oxford: Oxford University Press, 1976)
Brief and stimulating.

Collange, J.-F. *The Epistle of Saint Paul to the Philippians* (London: Epworth, 1979)
Detailed and scholarly.

Ernst, J. *Die Briefe an die Philipper, an Philemon, an die Kolosser, an die Epheser,* Regensburger Neues Testament (Regensburg: Verlag Friedrich Pustet, 1974
Non-technical, scholarly treatment.

Gnilka, J. *Der Philipperbrief, HTKNT* (Freiburg: Herder, 1987[4])
The standard German work.

Hawthorne, G. F. *Philippians, WBC* (Waco: Word Books, 1983)
Very detailed, occasionally idiosyncratic.

Lightfoot, J. B. *Saint Paul's Epistle to the Philippians* (London: Macmillan, 1890)
   The classic treatment, still worth consulting.
Lohmeyer, E. *Die Briefe an die Philipper, Kolosser und an Philemon*, Meyer*K* (Göttingen: Vandenhoeck und Ruprecht, 1959[11])
   Influential German work.
Marshall, I. H. *The Epistle to the Philippians*, Epworth Commentaries (London: Epworth, 1992)
   Oriented towards preachers.
Martin, R. P. *Philippians*, *NCeB* (London: Marshall, Morgan and Scott, 1980[2])
   Less technical than Collange.
Carmen Christi: Philippians 2:5–11 in Recent Interpretation and in the Setting of Early Christian Worship (Grand Rapids: Eerdmans, 1983[2])
   Detailed history of exegesis.
O'Brien, P. T. *The Epistle to the Philippians*, *NIGTC* (Exeter: Paternoster, 1990)
   Detailed exegesis of Greek text.
Schenk, W. *Die Philipperbriefe des Paulus: Kommentar* (Stuttgart: Kohlhammer, 1984)
   Major work employing modern linguistic methods.
Silva, M. *Philippians*, Wycliffe Exegetical Commentary (Chicago: Moody Press, 1988)
   On the Greek text.

PHILEMON

I. Howard Marshall

In addition to the commentaries by G. B. Caird and E. Lohmeyer above, *see*
Lohse, E. *Colossians and Philemon*, *Hermeneia* (Philadelphia, Fortress Press, 1971)
   Detailed treatment.
O'Brien, P. T. *Colossians, Philemon*, *WBC* (Waco, Texas: Word, 1982)
   Based on the Greek text.
Stuhlmacher, P. *Der Brief an Philemon*, *EKKNT* (Zürich: Benziger Verlag, 1975)
   Useful history of interpretation.
Suhl, A. *Der Philemonbrief*, Züricher Bibelkommentare (Zürich: Theologische Verlag, 1981)
   Less technical than Stuhlmacher.
Wright, N. T. *Colossians and Philemon*, Tyndale NT Commentaries (Leicester: Inter-Varsity Press, 1986)
   Brief but stimulating.

Indices (Thessalonians)

INDEX OF SUBJECTS

Affliction, *see* Persecution

Apocalyptic, 21, 26, 32, 39–40, 46, 69–70, 88, 90–96, 102, 105–107

ataktos/atakteō, 99–100

Authority, 48, 60–62, 67, 87, 97, 99–100, 111

Baptism, 38–39, 41, 46, 55, 57–58, 60, 78, 97, 111

Believe/Believer, 21–22, 29–30, 32–33, 35–36, 42–44, 51–58, 60–61, 63, 74–75, 91–92, 102–104, 106, 108–110

Christological titles, 41–51, 94–101
  'Christ', 21, 26, 31, 33–35, 38–39, 41, 43, 46, 50–51, 54–59, 62–63, 68, 72, 75, 77, 79, 95, 108–110
  'Christ, Jesus', 22, 31, 41, 46, 50, 76
  'Jesus', 16, 21, 29, 31–44, 47–48, 50–51, 55, 57, 59, 62–63, 69–70, 74, 78, 90–92, 95–97, 102, 107, 112
  'Lord', 16–17, 21, 24, 26, 31, 34–36, 39–57, 61, 68, 74, 77, 79, 84, 88–89, 92–97, 101–106, 110–111
  'Lord Jesus', 31, 41–44, 47–48, 57, 75–76, 90–91, 94–95, 101
  'Lord Jesus Christ', 6, 26, 29–31, 35–36, 38, 41–45, 48, 58–59, 66, 74, 76, 79, 92–96, 99, 101
  'Son', 29, 31–33, 36, 38, 41, 50, 59–60, 62, 74, 95

Christology, 31–51, 94–101
  'in Christ', 20–22, 26, 34–35, 38, 40, 43, 46–47, 54–55, 56–60, 62–63, 72, 74–79, 97, 108–110

Chronology, 9–11, 72

Consolation, 5, 9, 24, 26, 28, 40, 45, 60–61, 63, 68, 98

Co-workers, 7–8, 16, 25, 29, 37, 86–87

Cross, 45, 66, 72, 91

Cults of Thessalonica, 12–18, 20, 48–50, 62, 88, 94, 110

Day of the Lord, 84, 88–89, 92–94, 103–104, 110

Death
  of Christians, 5, 21–24, 34–35, 45–46, 51, 62, 70, 106, 108
  of Jesus, 21, 29, 33, 35–36, 43–44, 48, 50, 54–56, 62, 69, 74, 91, 96, 102

Ecclesiology, 41, 46, 101, 102
  Church, 7, 20, 22, 24, 26–27, 30–33, 39, 42, 44, 46, 50–56, 58–63, 69, 71–79, 84–85, 93, 95, 102, 106, 108–112
  Community, 5, 12, 22, 25–26, 30, 36, 42, 48, 53, 56–57, 59–63, 75–78, 87, 104–105, 107, 109, 111–112
  Body of Christ, 42, 56

Election, 16, 28–30, 37, 42, 45–46, 53–56, 59–68, 72–79, 90–93, 96, 100, 109, 112–113

Encouragement, 5, 19, 26–28, 37, 44–45, 53, 61, 63, 68, 77, 79, 95–98, 102, 108, 110

Eschatology, 21–22, 31, 33–37, 40–46, 59–60, 67, 69, 74–79, 88, 94–96, 102, 105–107, 110
  Parousia, 6, 16, 20–21, 26, 32–36, 43–47, 50–51, 62–63, 96, 100, 106

Ethics, 30, 44–45, 47–49, 63, 65, 75–76, 95, 98

Exhortation, 7, 13, 37, 44, 47, 50, 60, 61, 68, 76, 78, 83, 84, 91, 95

Faith, 4, 9, 20–21, 24, 27, 30–31, 37, 43, 51–59, 63, 66, 68, 74–77, 88, 90, 93, 96, 102, 108–111

God, 28–63, 90–104
Gospel, 10, 14, 17, 22–25, 30–32, 37–38, 40, 44, 51–63, 67, 69–70, 73–79, 91–96, 101–104, 108–113
    see also word
Grace, 43, 49, 58, 74, 78–79, 92–93, 104, 112

Holy spirit, 30, 32, 44, 46, 49–53, 56–60, 63, 66–67, 73–77, 84, 90, 92, 95, 101–104, 111–112
Hope, 13–16, 20–21, 24, 27, 30–37, 43–47, 52–58, 60, 62–63, 74–75, 78–79, 102, 104–105, 109–110

Idol, 32–33, 38, 48, 54, 60, 73, 75–76, 79
Imitate/Imitation, 22, 44, 46, 52, 74, 76, 85, 89, 95, 99
    Example, 22, 44, 52, 76, 99, 106
    Model, 52, 55, 61

Judge/Judgment, 45, 69, 90, 94–96, 101, 105, 108, 111
Justice, 79, 90–96, 112
Justification, 45, 58, 64–66, 72

katechon, 88, 93–94
Kingdom/Kingdom of God, 16, 29–30, 34, 36–39, 60, 63, 68, 74–75, 79, 87, 90, 95, 100, 113

Law, 45, 65–67, 72
Leader/Leadership, 56, 61–62, 68, 77, 98–104
Love, 4, 6, 9, 20, 24, 30, 37, 43, 53–63, 74–77, 92–93, 101–103, 108, 112

Martyrdom, 28, 106
Mission/Missionary, 10–11, 31–33, 37, 53, 67, 69, 71, 74, 78–79

Obey/Obedience, 47, 55, 66, 78, 91, 101, 103, 111–113

Persecution, 5, 9, 19–26, 28, 33–34, 44, 46–47, 50–53, 55, 61–62, 67–68, 73–75, 86–92, 95–96, 101–102, 106, 108–110, 113
Praise, 4–5, 19, 23–25, 37, 102, 106, 109
Pray/Prayer, 6, 7, 20, 30, 43, 60, 75, 78, 83, 91, 101–102, 111–112
Promise, 28–31, 43–44, 55–56, 92, 108–110
Prophet/Prophetic, 26, 39–40, 62, 94, 106

Rhetoric, 3–7, 9, 19–21, 24–25, 33, 63, 83–84, 87, 98–99

Salvation, 14, 26–31, 36–38, 43, 45, 50, 54, 57–58, 66, 75
Sanctification, 30, 43, 45, 60–61, 66, 75–76, 90, 93, 100–104, 108, 110, 112
Satan, 19, 106–109
Sin, 45, 108
Suffering, see *Persecution*
Synagogue, 11, 69

Thessalonians, First
    date of writing, 9–12
    place of writing, 7–9
    rhetorical structure, 3–7
    setting, 12–27
Thessalonians, Second
    authorship, 84–87
    relationship to 1 Thess, 85–87
    rhetorical structure, 83–84
    setting, 83–89, 99–101
Thessalonica, 3, 5, 8–27, 37, 42, 45, 47–48, 51–53, 57, 68–69, 73, 75, 84–87, 92–98, 103, 108, 110
Tradition, 31–41, 43, 47, 70, 72, 88, 96–100, 110
Truth, 90–96, 101–104, 109, 112

Vindication, 90–91, 94–104

Will of God, 30, 48, 75, 78–79
Word (*see also Gospel*), 19–26, 34–41, 44, 49–56, 62, 67–68, 70, 73, 74, 79, 88, 95, 101–103, 108
Worship, 73, 76, 94
Wrath, 26, 29, 32, 43, 45, 58, 66, 69, 70, 101

INDEX OF MODERN AUTHORS

Aland, K., xii
Arndt, W. F., 49
Athanassakis, A. N., 13

Bauer, W., 49, 98
Best, E., 17, 192
Borgen, P., 71
Braaten, C., 75, 77, 78
Bromiley, G. W., xii
Bruce, F. F., 20, 21, 22, 28, 192

Chapa, J., 193
Collins, R. F., 5, 193

Dahl, N., 21
Danker, F. W., 49
Deissmann, G. A., 17, 42
Dibelius, M., 16, 17, 51
Donfried, K. P., vii, 1, 21, 22, 57, 193

Eadie, J., 49
Ellis, E. E., 61

Fitzmyer, J. A., 71, 193
Frame, J. E., 51
Freedman, D. N., 194
Friedrich, G., xii

Giblin, C. H., 89, 94, 193
Gingrich, F. W., 49
Glover, R., 71

Haase, W., xi
Hanson, P. D., 105, 106
Heidland, H. W., 14
Hendrix, H. L., 17, 18, 193, 194
Holland, G. S., 93, 193, 194
Holmberg, B., 100
Holtz, T., 192
Horgan, M. P., 193
Horsley, G. H. R., 62
Hughes, F. W., 3, 4, 5, 7, 83, 193, 194

Jewett, R., 193, 194
Judge, E. A., 16, 23

Käsemann, E., 75
Keck, L. E., 67
Kittel, G., xii

Kobelski, P. J., 193
Koester, H., 22
Krentz, E. M., 91, 193, 194

Lehmann, P. W., 14
Lightfoot, R. F., 51
Lüdemann, G., 34

Malherbe, A. J., 193, 194
Marksen, W., 192
Marshall, I. H., vii, viii, 48, 192, 193
Martyn, J. L., 67
Merklein, H., 40, 41
Milligan, G., 16, 99, 192
Milligan, W., xii
Moule, C. F. D., 97
Moulton, J. H., xii

Neirynck, F., 38
Nilsson, M. P., 13

Otto, W. F., 13

Pobee, J. S., 51

Räisänen, H., 65
Rigaux, B., 192

Schnelle, U., 193
Selwyn, E. G., 88
Speyer, W., 87
Spittle, D., 14
Stählin, O., 15
Stowers, S. K., 3
Strobel, A., 71

Temporini, H., xi
Trilling, W., 85, 192, 193

Vander Stichele, C., 193
Vielhauer, P., 66, 67, 70, 72
von Dobschütz, E., 51, 97, 192
von Harnack, A., 61

Walter, N., 38, 39
Wanamaker, C. A., 98, 192, 193
Wengst, K., 3
Witt, R., 94
Wrede, W., 85, 193, 194

INDEX OF TEXTS

OLD TESTAMENT

1 Chronicles

16:13	29

Psalms

89:3	29
105:6	29
105:43	29
106:5	29
106:23	29

Isaiah

40:1	27
42:1	29
43:20	29
45:4	29
59:17	14
65:9	29
65:15	29
65:22	29

NEW TESTAMENT

Mark

13	106
13:7	106
13:12–13	70
13:13	106
13:21–24	106
13:22	106

Acts

7:60	22
11:19 ff	10
13:1	10
13:14	10, 69
13:46–47	69
13:52	67
14:1	69
14:2	69
14:3	67
14:7	67
14:10	67
14:21	67
14:22	68
14:23	68
15:12	67

15:22 ff	10
15:32	68
16:11	14
16:13	69
16:32	67
17	7, 15–16, 21
17:1	69
17:1–9	18
17:2	69
17:3	68
17:5	69
17:6	15
17:7	15
17:8	16
17:11	67
17:13	67
17:27–28	59
18	11–12
18:1	12
18:2	11
18:2–4	12
18:5	7, 9, 12
18:7	11
18:8	11
18:12	11
18:22	10
19:8	69
19:11	67
20:28	68
22:3	10
22:21	69

Romans

1:1	52
1:5	55, 66
1:9	52
1:11	68
1:16	52
1:18–3:20	69
1:27	103
2:16	52
2:17	59
3:7	103
3:25	54
5:1–3	58
5:5	49, 56, 58
5:6	35
5:8	56
5:9	66
5:9–10	58
5:11	59

6	66
6:8	55
8:3	35
8:8	48
8:18	55
8:18–25	56, 58
8:19–21	58
8:23–24	58
9–11	70
9:1	49
9:6	52
9:11	29
9:22–24	69
10:16	52
10:17	54
11:5	29
11:7	29
11:20	55
11:22	57
11:28	29, 52
12:2	49
12:3	55
12:6	55
14:1	55
14:15	35
14:17	37, 49
15:8	103
15:13	49, 55
15:16	49, 52
15:19	49, 52
16:16	55
16:25	52, 68
16:26	66

1 Corinthians

1:2	59
1:18–31	66
1:21	54
2:5	54
3:3	48
4:11–13	39
4:20	37
4:20–21	38
5:1	49
6:9–10	37
6:13	49
6:18	49
7:10	48
7:17	48
8:1	61
9:1–18	39
9:14	39

10:23	61
12:9	55
13:13	55–57
14:3–5	61
14:12	61
14:17	61
14:26	61
15	34, 35
15:2	55, 57
15:3	35
15:6–7	10
15:11	54
15:12–28	88
15:14	55
15:17	55
15:24	37
15:50	34, 37
15:50–58	40
15:51–57	34
16:13	55

2 Corinthians

1:24	55
2:4	56
4:2	48
4:14	55
5:5	57
5:6	57
5:7	48
10:2	48
10:15	54
12:1–10	39
12:18	48
12:21	49
13:14	49

Galatians

1:11–17	39
1:18	10
1:21	10
2:5	103
2:7–8	69
2:11	10
2:11–17	65
2:14	103
2:20	56
2:21	49
3:27–28	55
5:5	55
5:5–6	56–57
5:6	54, 56–57

5:19   49
5:21   37

Ephesians

2:12   57
4:1   38

Philippians

1:25   54
1:27   38, 54
1:29   55
1:30   22
3:7–14   58
4:15   10

Colossians

1:10   38

1 Thessalonians

1:1   6, 9, 28, 29, 30, 41, 42, 43,
                       55, 58, 59
1:1–5   60
1:1–10   5
1:2   30, 60
1:2–3   30
1:2–10   6
1:2–13   60
1:3   5, 20, 29, 37, 41, 43, 53–57, 66
1:4   20, 28, 54, 56, 92, 93
1:4–7   23
1:5   21, 23, 32, 46, 52, 67
1:6   19, 22–23, 44, 46, 52–53,
                       55–56, 67–68
1:6–8   22
1:7   44, 52, 54, 60–61
1:8   23, 30, 50, 52–55, 59, 60, 101
1:9   30, 36, 45, 48, 54, 100
1:9–10   31–33, 35–36, 38, 60
1:10   20, 31, 33, 50
1:23   54

2   26, 67, 69
2:1   6, 21
2:1–8   68
2:1–9   23
2:1–12   4, 5, 31, 39
2:1–16   6
2:1–3:10   6
2:2   21–23, 25, 30, 52–54

2:4   23, 30, 52–53, 61
2:5   21, 25
2:7   14, 67
2:7–8   13
2:8   23, 52
2:8–9   53
2:9   21, 23, 52
2:9–12   25
2:10   21
2:11   21
2:11–12   36–38
2:12   16, 26, 28, 30, 60, 68, 74–75,
                         98–99
2:13   23, 30, 32, 37, 52, 55–56,
                    59–60, 67, 74
2:13–16   18, 69, 70
2:14   19, 30, 42, 46, 59, 60, 68, 97
2:14–15   22, 35
2:14–16   4, 22, 31, 69
2:15   44, 55
2:16   60
2:16b   69, 70
2:17–3:10   4, 6
2:18   19
2:19   20, 45, 57

3:1   8, 60
3:1 ff   8, 10
3:1–3   8
3:1–5   55
3:1–10   57
3:2   23, 52, 55, 68, 98
3:2–3   68
3:3   19
3:3b–4   21
3:4   19
3:5   20
3:6   20, 54
3:6–10   9
3:7   9, 25, 98
3:8   42, 45–47, 59, 97
3:9   30, 60
3:10   20, 55
3:11   6, 29, 47
3:11–13   5–6
3:12   47
3:12–13   6
3:13   6, 20, 29, 45, 68, 100, 1023

4   34
4:1   21, 30, 45–47, 75, 97–98
4:1–3   66
4:1–8   4, 6, 45, 55

4:1–9	48
4:1–12	31
4:1–5:3	6
4:2	21, 47–48, 76
4:3	30, 45, 100
4:3–8	13
4:4	45, 49, 100
4:5	48, 56, 60, 74, 91
4:6	21, 45, 47, 50
4:7	28, 45, 65, 100
4:7–8	103
4:8	30, 46–47, 59
4:9	30, 54, 56, 58, 60, 77
4:9–12	4, 6, 56, 60
4:10	21, 54, 56, 98
4:11	21, 98
4:12	56, 76
4:12–13	100
4:13	21, 33, 43, 56–57, 60, 74
4:13–18	21, 24, 26, 31–32, 34, 40, 55, 57, 103
4:13–5:3	5, 6
4:13–5:11	26
4:14	21, 31, 33–34, 36, 50, 54–55, 68, 96, 100
4:14b	40
4:15	5, 20–21, 23, 34, 36, 39, 45, 50, 101
4:15b	40
4:15–16	39
4:15–17	39–40
4:16	21, 42, 45–47, 59, 97
45:16–17	21, 34, 40
4:17	30, 45
4:18	23, 40, 98
4:19–22	100
5:1	21
5:1–11	55
5:2	45
5:3	16, 54
5:4	6
5:4–7	76
5:4–11	5, 6
5:5	6, 37, 56
5:5–7	50
5:6	6
5:7	6, 78
5:8	14, 20, 37, 53–57
5:8–9	45
5:8–10	7
5:9	26, 29, 38, 41, 43, 48, 54–55, 58, 66
5:9–10	31, 35, 36, 45, 59, 74, 96

5:9–11	26
5:10	33, 35, 42
5:11	7, 61, 98
5:12	7, 42, 45–47, 59, 62, 77, 97
5:12–13	61, 68
5:12–15	58
5:12–22	7
5:14	216, 98–99
5:14–22	7
5:15	77
5:16–18	30, 78
5:18	30, 46, 97
5:19	46–47
5:19–22	50, 77
5:23	20, 42–43, 45, 58, 76, 100, 103
5:23–24	7
5:23–28	7
5:24	28, 76
5:25	7
5:26–27	7
5:27	47, 61
5:27–28	79
5:28	7, 42–43

2 Thessalonians

1:1	95
1:1–2	83
1:1–12	83
1:2	95
1:3	93, 102
1:3–10	83
1:4	86–87, 95, 102, 106, 109
1:5	37, 87, 96, 100
1:5–12	86, 90
1:5–13	89
1:6	90
1:7	95, 101
1:7–10	96
1:8	87, 91, 95–96, 101, 108, 111
1:9	89, 95
1:10	96, 101
1:11	100
1:11–12	83
1:12	91, 95
1:13	91
2	93, 193
2:1	95–96
2:1–2	83
2:1–12	99
2:2	83–85, 88, 95, 103–104, 110
2:3–4	93

2:3–11   96
2:3–12   83, 85–86, 93, 105–106, 109
2:3–15   83
2:5   110
2:6   88, 100
2:6a   100
2:6–7   93
2:7   88
2:7–8   93
2:8   95
2:10   101, 103, 109
2:10–12   91, 101
2:11   109
2:12   87, 103
2:13   90, 92–93, 95–96, 100–101,
                103–104, 108–109
2:14   91–92, 95–96, 101–102, 108
2:15   84, 87–88, 103, 110
2:15–18   83
2:16   95, 104
2:16–17   92
2:17   98

3:1   95, 101–102
3:1–4   84
3:1–15   83–84
3:3   95, 110
3:4   95, 97–98
3:5   84, 95, 106
3:6   95, 97–100
3:6–12   99–100
3:6–15   84, 99
3:7   99–100
3:10   98, 111
3:11   99
3:12   95, 97–98

3:15   100
3:16   84, 95, 110
3:16–17   84
3:17   84–86
3:18   84, 95

4:13–5:11   85

1 Timothy

3:4–5   62

Revelation

2:3   106
2:10   106
2:13   106
12:9   106
13:10   106
20:2   106
20:7   106

Classical and hellenistic texts

Aelianus, *De natura animalium* 17,11   49
Antistius Vetus, *Anthologia graeca*
    16,243,4   49
Cicero, *De inventione* 1,27   6
Clement of Alexandria, *Protrepticus*   15
Dio Chrysostom, *Orationes* 32,11   25
Hesychius   14
Homeric Hymn to Dionysus, 26   13
Quintilian, *Institutio Oratoria*
    4.2.31   6
Rhetorica ad Herennium 1.17   6
Suetonius, *Claudius* 25.4   11

Indices (Philippians, Philemon)

INDEX OF SUBJECTS

Adam, 132, 143, 162f.
Archippus, 177

Bishops, 156
Boasting, 152f.
Brothers, 155–157, 184, 186

Caesarea, 118, 120f.
Caesar's household, 120
Canon, 167, 187, 191
Christ-hymn, 127–137, 162–164
Christian and Christ, 164f.
Christology, 162–164, 170f.
Church, 149–161, 165
Circumcision, 123f., 152–154, 158, 161, 165
Colosse, 177, 180
Creation, 190
Cross/Cruciform life, 136, 142, 144, 147f., 160f., 165, 174

Deacons, 156
Death of Christ, 133f., 136f., 144, 158
Death of Christians, 144, 148, 158f., 165f., 171f.
Disunity in church, 122, 125, 159, 169f.
'Dogs', 123

Epaphroditus, 119, 122, 155, 157, 160f., 168f.
Ephesus, 121, 179
Equality with God, 132f.
Euodia, 155, 157, 169
Evangelism, 155–157
Exaltation, 125, 134–136, 164
Example of Christ, 136f.

Faith, 127, 159, 161, 168f., 182f., 187f.
Fatherhood of God, 134–136
Fellow-workers, 155, 158, 182
Fellowship, 149–152, 155, 161, 166, 171, 183f.
Future life, 165f., 171f.

Glory, 132, 144, 146, 148, 183
Gnosticism/Gnostics, 124, 145
Gospel, 127, 150, 159, 161, 185

Harpagmos, 132
Hellenistic mysticism, 145

Ignatius, 188
Imprisonment, 121
In Christ, 138–144, 151, 164, 186
Incarnation, 131, 170f.

Joy, 160f.
Judaising, 124

Knowing Christ, 145–148, 165, 171–174

Law, 124, 153
Lordship of Christ, 125, 134–137, 140–147, 159, 169f.
Love, 182f., 186–189

Minister, 155
Mission, 155–157
Monotheism, 135f.
'Mutilators', 124

Name, 134f.

Obedience, 133f., 184f.

Onesimus, 177–189
Opponents, 119, 123–125

Parousia, 165f.
People of God, 152–154
Perfect/Perfectionism, 125, 157, 160
Pergamon, 179
Personal relationships, 169f., 186f.
Philemon, 177–191
   structure of, 180f.
Philippi, 118
Philippians
   place of writing, 120f.
   situation, 118, 121–126
   structure of, 120, 126
   unity of, 118–120, 125
Pliny, the younger, 181
Praetorium, 120f.
Prayer, 158f.
Pre-existence, 131f., 163

Quarrelling, 122

Redemption, 190
Righteousness, 153f.

Rome, 120f., 177

Saints, 149, 155
Salvation history, 152–154
Self-emptying, 133
Servanthood, 133, 158, 182
Servants, 151
Service, 136f.
Slavery, 177–179
   Paul's attitude to, 187–191
Son of God, 136, 163f.
Spirit, Holy, 127, 151f.
Suffering of Christ, 152, 163
Suffering of Christians, 123, 136, 152
Syntyche, 155, 157, 169

Timothy, 122, 139, 155, 182
Toleration, 173f.
Truth, 173f.

Wisdom, 163
With Christ, 144, 164, 166
Works, 153f., 173
Worship, 135, 146, 152

INDEX OF MODERN AUTHORS

Barclay, J. M. G., 189f.
Bartchy, S. S., 187
Beare, F. W., 146
Beker, J. C., 162
Best, E., 138f.
Bouttier, M., 138
Bruce, F. F., 121, 132, 134, 146, 178
Büchsel, F., 138
Bultmann, R., 145

Childs, B. S., 167
Collange, J.-F., 119, 121, 146, 156

Davey, F. N., 174
Davies, W. D., 146
Dibelius, M., 145
Dinkler, E., 163
Dunn, J. D. G., 132, 135, 154, 163
Dupont, J., 146

Ellis, E. E., 155
Ernst, J., 145

Fee, G. D., 131
Fitzmyer, J. A., 128

Garland, D. E., 120
Gasque, W. W., 132
Georgi, D., 163
Gnilka, J., 145, 165
Goodenough, E. R., 178
Grayston, K., 123

Hainz, J., 150, 183
Hawthorne, G. F., 121, 131, 145f.
Hoskyns, E. C., 174
Hurst, L. D., 132
Hurtado, L. W., 136

Jeremias, J., 129f.

Kim, S., 146

Lampe, P., 178
Lightfoot, J. B., 148
Lohmeyer, E., 129, 145

Lohse, E., 181, 183
Louw, J. P., 138
Lundin, R., 181

Marshall, I. H., 171
Martin, R. P., 128, 130, 132, 163
Marxsen, W., 181
Mearns, C. L., 124f.
Moule, C. F. D., 132

Neugebauer, F., 138, 142
Nida, E., 138
Nordling, J. G., 178

Ollrog, W.-H., 156, 185

Peterlin, D., 122
Petersen, N. R., 181

Rapske, B. M., 178
Reid, J. K. S., 138

Robbins, C. J., 131

Sanders, E. P., 153f.
Schenk, W., 142, 155f., 179f., 183, 189
Seesemann, H., 150
Silva, M., 128f., 131, 134, 141, 143, 151
Smith, G. A., 146
Stuhlmacher, P., 187f.
Suhl, A., 185

Thiselton, A. C., 181

Wakefield, G. S., 174
Walhout, C., 181
Wanamaker, C. A., 132
Watson, D. F., 120
Wedderburn, A. J. M., 138, 143
Westerholm, S., 154
White, J. L., 180
Winter, S. C., 177, 183
Wright, N. T., 132f., 183

INDEX OF TEXTS

OLD TESTAMENT

Genesis

3:5   163

Deuteronomy

10:16   152

Isaiah

45:23   135

Psalms

8   163

NEW TESTAMENT

John

1   163

Acts

16:9f.   118
16:11–40   118
19:14, 22   118
20:6   118
22:25–8   120

25–26   120
25:21   183
28   120

Romans

3:27   153
4:2   153
5   163
5:1   148
6   144, 165
8:1   141
8:3   133
8:32   164
13:6   155
14:11   135
14:14   139
15:16   155
15:17   140
15:22   143
16:1   156
16:2   141
16:7, 11   141
16:22   142

1 Corinthians

1:2   142
1:9   151

1:30	163
3	117
3:1	157
4:2	147
4:8	157
7	169
7:20–24	187
10:16	151
12:18	141
13	128f.
15	163, 165f.
15:19	139
15:22	143
16	120
16:19	142

2 Corinthians

2:14	145, 165
4	165
4:5	155
4:6	146
5	166
5:3	147
5:8	166
5:16	145
5:17	141
8:1–4	150
8:9	129, 164
10	125
11:13	123
11:23	121
13	125
13:13	151

Galatians

1:8f.	124
2:20	142
2:21	124
3:8	143
3:28	186
4:4	164
4:19	142
5:10	139
6:6	150

Ephesians

1:1	141
2:9	153
4:3	151
6:21	142

Philippians

1:1	139, 141, 155
1:1f.	126
1:1–18	121
1:1–3:1a	119
1:2	156
1:3–11	126, 158
1:3–4:20	126
1:4	160
1:5	127, 149f., 152, 155
1:7	127, 149f., 152
1:12	127, 155
1:12–26	126, 158
1:13	120, 139, 142, 155
1:14	139, 142, 155f.
1:15	127
1:16	127
1:17	120
1:17f.	127
1:18	161
1:19	159
1:19–26	120, 122
1:21	144, 148
1:21–23	145
1:23	144, 166
1:24	159
1:25	161
1:26	139f.
1:27	127, 159
1:27–30	123, 125, 159
1:27–2:18	126, 159
1:29f.	123
2:1	139f., 149, 151f.
2:1–4	159
2:2	160
2:2–4	159
2:5	136, 139, 143
2:5–11	159
2:6	134
2:6–11	125, 127, 147
2:7	131
2:11	134–6
2:14	159
2:16	127, 157
2:17	155
2:17f.	161
2:19	139
2:19–24	122
2:19–30	126, 159
2:20f.	160
2:22	127, 155
2:24	139, 142

2:25	155
2:25–30	122
2:29	139, 141, 161
2:30	155
3:1–4:1	126, 160
3:1	119, 139f., 161
3:1b–21	119
3:2	119, 121, 155
3:3	139
3:3–4	139f.
3:8	148
3:8–10	145
3:9	139, 142
3:10	144, 149, 152
3:10f.	136, 147
3:11	144
3:12–16	125, 148
3:14	125, 139f.
3:15	157
3:18	123
3:18f.	123
3:19	160
3:20	136, 165
3:20f.	148
3:21	144
4:1	139, 160
4:1–3	119
4:2	122, 139, 141, 159
4:2f.	157
4:2–9	122, 126, 160
4:3	127, 155
4:4	139f., 161
4:4–7	119
4:7	139f.
4:8	171
4:8f.	119
4:10	139f., 161
4:10–20	119, 126, 160
4:13	139f.
4:14	150, 152
4:14f.	149
4:15	127, 149f., 152
4:19	139f.
4:21	139, 142, 149, 155
4:21–23	119, 126
4:22	120, 155

Colossians

1:2	141f.
2	165

3:15	141
4:1	186
4:7	142
4:17	156

1 Thessalonians

4	166
4:13–18	165
4:17	144
5:9	165
5:10	144

2 Thessalonians

3:4	139

1 Timothy

6:1f.	187

2 Timothy

1:12	145

Philemon

1–3	177, 180
2	155
4–7	180, 182
6	182f., 184
8–14	180
8–22	180
9	182
10	183
11	183
13	183, 185
15–22	180
23	182
23–5	180
24	177

Hebrews

1	163
1:3	163
2:9	163

1 Peter

1:7	147
4:13	152

2 Peter

3:10, 14	147
3:18	145